On the Right Path:
Walking Through God to Get to the Goddess

By Tara Black

ISBN-13-978-0615606699
MaJiK Publishing

Most of what I have written is true, but I have changed names, dates, places and times, added and exaggerated instances, and largely scrambled things up to protect those involved. Just remember, all resemblances to persons living and dead are merely coincidental, blah blah blah and all that legal jazz.

To my mother who taught me to let go, and my father
who taught me to hold on.

I am just like you, well, mostly. There is the Witch thing, but don't let that word scare you. You can call me Wise Woman instead of Witch, or Goddess Seeker, maybe even Sorceress. Hell, you can call me Bill if you want. I just happen to like the word Witch. I think it perfectly fits how I choose to describe my spiritual path. Barring that, I pretty much am your regular Jane.

I go to work, which some days I am fine with, but most of the time let out a big groan when the alarm goes off. I waste fifteen minutes of needed morning time fantasizing about lying in bed all day while big muscled men in towels feed me grapes.....excuse me while I digress.

I have kids, we do homework, and I stare at the raw chicken breast, and try to figure out something *exciting* to do with it for dinner. I wouldn't really classify the eighth hunt of the day for the elusive missing pacifier, magical. Most of my days consist of the normal working wife-mother cocktail of brain- body overload, and I, like the rest of you, slump down on the sofa at the end of the day with my significant other and flip around the boob tube for something to watch that isn't a crappy reality show.

I break a lot of the Witch/Goddess worshipper stereotypes; I don't wear all black, although it is slimming, and my big Armenian butt needs all the help it can get. I do bathe and I don't grow out my leg hair and hide in a cabin in the woods (although sometimes that sounds nice-the cabin part, not the leg hair part). I don't speak in enigmatic mono-syllables, and I sure as heckfire don't believe in Satan. I am a relatively normal kinda gal.

I said relatively. See, I really am a Witch.

Sorry to disappoint, but this is not a torrid tale of secrecy and mystery. It is not even a semi-torrid tale of

Wiccan initiations or pacts made under the cover of darkness. As a matter of fact this is probably more like a bathwater- warm tale of being stuck in religion and thinking my way out until I stumbled upon what turned out to be the right path for me.

Witchcraft/Walking the path of the Goddess has been the most fulfilling, albeit the hardest, most challenging journey of self- exploration that I have ever been and continue to be on. Ironically enough, that boat set sail in organized religion. Christianity helped me find my path. Through Christianity and a pursuit of God, I found the Goddess.

Yep, I hopped on the Christianity ship at the beginning of my spiritual journey. I spent years swimming through the sometimes deep, sometimes shallow waters of Fundamental, Southern Baptist, and Charismatic Christianity, trying to find something. I met lots of people, most of which I foolishly let myself hate for years after my involvement, till I figured out that they are as human and fallible as I am. I went overboard as a Christian. I doodled Jesus fish on everything. I said hallelujah a lot, I was very obnoxious.

When the *find-what-it-is-I-really-believe* boat finally reached its destination, the flag I flew was a picture of a cauldron, the cross long ago abandoned. I learned religion through Christianity and spirituality through Witchcraft, which for most of us would be a grand kick in the teeth. It was.

So that is what this book is about. Myself, The Higher Power, The Universe, the Grand Poobah, the Supreme Being/Beings, God/ the Goddess, or whatever name you choose to call the Divine in our lives, and all of the people that got in my way. Or that I put in my way. Or that helped me find my way.

This is about the painstakingly and at times, mind-numbingly tedious journey that led me to my spiritual path.

It all started with prayer. For as long as I can remember, my prayers have worked. This was a constant, no matter who I was praying to. Whether it was the fact that every pore in me believed wholeheartedly that whomever I was praying to at the moment would answer, or that I just accepted anything that even remotely looked like an answer as a glorious and shining example of proof of the Higher Power, my prayers have always been answered.

The praying started in earnest when I was 11. For some reason boobs seemed essential. That's right, boobs. I had to have 'em, big ones. So I prayed fervently for them, night and day. One day I woke up and couldn't see my feet. From then on my nickname was Dolly (as in Dolly Parton).

So was it boobs that sold me on the Divine? Well….. let's hope it comes to more than that. I have always felt, for lack of a better word, *connected*. I have always had a deep knowledge that the world was more than I saw with my eyes, that words were the lowest form of human communication; that everything had life, and somehow I was a part of this life. My personal religion was there before I realized it.

I am not trying to sell anything. I am not for or against any religion, even my own beliefs. I truly believe that we have plenty of religion, but spirituality is a neglected part of ourselves, and that means something different for each of us. Hopefully in telling you my story it will help you discard what you have done forever just because you have always done it, and instead you will look for the spirituality within yourself, maybe tinker a bit with your own path.

That is really my only agenda besides trying to be generally entertaining, so before I start sounding too New Agey, let's get on with the story.

Chapter One

"The shoe that fits one person pinches another; there is no recipe for living that suits all cases."
- Carl Jung

I looked down at the royal blue book with the tiny words and silky paper that seemed so important to these people. All I knew about this book is that I had to have it as part of a requirement for the new country Christian school that we had been enrolled in. It wasn't that I didn't know what a Bible was; in my vague childish consciousness small snippets of Vacation Bible School, butter cookies, construction paper crosses, and pictures of a flaxen haired Jesus had given me a brief, broken introduction. If we had owned one as a family, though, I'd never seen it, and it had surely never been cracked open and read 'round the dinner table.

But now I had a problem, we were at a new school with different rules, and the teacher was staring at me expectantly. I was smart enough to realize that her austere look meant that she was one who didn't particularly like her job, or if she did, it was for all the wrong reasons. I knew in the way that you know when you are in third grade that something was expected of me, something I badly wanted to fulfill. Not just to avoid the possibility of punishment from the new frowning teacher, but to impress the students that I hadn't met yet.

My mind was briefly drawn away from the stuffy classroom with its foreign rules to the still warm fall air. I could hear the stillness of the country afternoon, a sound that I wasn't used to. I wanted to explore the new playground, far bigger in my imagination than it was in reality.

Snap. My attention was brought back to Mrs. Smatten's permanent scowl.

"Tara, please read the chapter assigned to you" she said, her patience growing thin. Who knows how long I had been standing there. I looked down sincerely, and cleared my voice.

"Puh-salms chapter 10" I said sheepishly. The room burst into as much laughter as eight third graders can make, the teacher shooting me a *stop clowning around* look. I had no idea what I had done that was so funny, but I was sure that it was nothing to be proud of. As I looked around uncertainly Mrs. Smatten corrected me.

"It is pronounced Psalms, Tara. The *P* is silent." She spoke my name like it had maggots in it. The laughter turned to ashamed silence as the teacher's voice clearly labeled me as a heathen, and someone to be wary of, someone who *didn't know how to pronounce a book of the Bible.* I thought about what would happen if they knew that this was the first time I had read from the Good Book, and I assumed my chances at making friends had been permanently damaged.

Later in the day when I checked on my little sister who had started kindergarten, she looked shell shocked. This new school was light years different from where we had come from, an alien world, and if we didn't learn the ropes and rules soon we were going to drown. I had no idea what I had done that was so wrong, but I felt it. I felt it in the looks, the stares, and the disgust in my teacher's voice, in the tentative way my new friends talked to me, as if I was a foreigner who didn't quite speak the language, or know the ways of the land, I felt it. I felt it all day, and in the years to come. I wasn't like them. I was different. I was BAD.

This was to be my life for the next 13 years; the stiff, unrelenting rainfall of Christian living. Although eventually I learned the ropes. Then busted through them.

From that moment on, I was a target. We were one of the two *bad* families that went to Winter's Pass Baptist school, a very small fundamental Baptist church run school that required the girls to wear skirts or culottes, which is a kind of split skirt and the boys had to have short hair, snipped carefully two inches above the neckline. Among the more religious in the church I often wondered if they were having short hair competitions. The man with the shortest hair, of course, being the most pious. Some of the men looked like a wild monkey had attacked them with a razor.

The church and grounds was located on what used to be a farm. When we moved to this rural area, my parents, excited by the possibility of a safe education far away from the public school world of drugs and guns, enrolled us immediately. The school was on a decent, quiet piece of land, surrounded by forests, and in an area that could be described as rural with random pockets of suburban. The church, sitting in the center point of the land like a cherry on top of a sundae, had a face like its pastor. It wasn't ornate, it wasn't old, and it wasn't awe inspiring; it was simple, strong, and no-nonsense. The main sanctuary had mustard yellow carpet and pews, brass chandeliers, and large windows that looked out into the fields and at the trees. Through the massive windows, you could see rabbits and squirrels playing around the majestic oaks, their antics devilishly averting your attention on a Sunday morning. It was beautiful land, but somehow seemed to be holding its breath for permission to be so.

Life there was like a time warp back to the fifties

where women cooked, cleaned, crocheted, made casseroles, watched the Hallmark channel and most importantly kept *silent*, and submissive. Men worked, preached, and were the definite unquestioning head of the households. Period. Anything else stood out like a sore thumb. It was like being in a weird play where there were only two kinds of characters. There were the Munchkins, the women, who sang merrily, (or un-merrily, as it were), and were supposed to look cute and be afraid of everything, because the world was bigger than they were.

The men were the citizens of the Land of Oz. Deep voiced and other worldly; they had a direct line to God. It was all about work work work, like some Seven Dwarves /Oz hybrid. *Hi Ho Hi Ho, it's off to church we go…* They were untouchable. They were the be all and end all, because after all, God was male.

In this play everyone was acting, everyone was an actor. Most were bad actors, though, and some had been acting for so long, that you got the feeling that if you dug down one or two layers that they didn't even know who they were outside of the play. Like the person that wears a uniform to work every day of his life, and when it is time to get dressed up for a party, can't even remember what it is that they like to wear.

Most of the acting was cliché to the max. (Yes, I am a child of the eighties). Homemaker's class, sewing, knitting, handmade lace collars over eyelet dresses. Carefully coiffed hair. Casseroles. An affinity for *Little House on the Prairie* and Avon Disney knickknacks. Let's get excited over the new Franklin Mint Decorator plates. Demure looks, eyes cast downward.

My God, who did the casting for this play? I often wondered. Sometimes, it had the equivalency of Angelina

Jolie playing something as bland as Old Mother Hubbard, nothing fit.

The men were better actors; I think it was because they were in a position of power. They seemed to eat up the suit wearing, Bible carrying main roles. They didn't have to bother with their wife's opinion, because she was only a woman. The men could have won Oscars for their acting.

All of this deeply affected me because I wasn't your typical Barbie playing, Debbie Gibson loving nine year old. *I thought*….a lot. I was a thinkin' girl. Sitting in church, on the playground, in class, I watched, listened. I watched what people did and listened to what they said. What I came up with were things that to this day I still don't get.

How can a person reconcile an austere lifestyle with no color, zest, or imagination, with abandonment into a religious fairytale? Having no point of reference entering the church, I just could not understand it. The Puritan life with the long skirts, silenced minds, and fear of too much emotion was totally flushed down the toilet with Immaculate Conception, God in the flesh on earth, Heaven and Hell, and people rising from the dead. Like a scruffy, bearded, sunburned, beer- swigging man who operates a jack hammer all day, donning a pink tutu at night. Two opposites supposed to dwell harmoniously together, but which ended up competing with each other. The people in the church seemed to shut out and ignore life around them, while creating a life in their minds.

I don't think the fear of Hell was ever really very strong in me, either. Somehow I knew it didn't exist. I remember the days the pastor would stand up on stage and rile himself up. Normally a calm, self-possessed man who kept amazing control of his emotions as a clean example to us, occasionally he'd lose it. Start sweating. Maybe pace the platform in true altruistic agony. The world was going to Hell…and what were we doing about it? We that made up the audience held our breath. Partly because of his intensity, but also because of the genuine care he showed, part theatrics, part inclusion. The poor poor world, the whole world was going to Hell, and we were worried about getting home in time to watch football. He scolded us like children for this. He knew that his ranting made us uncomfortable, that we just wanted to come to church and feel good, remember God, chat a little afterwards in our nice church clothes. He did this rarely, but often enough to make you wonder when it would happen again.

But I never believed the whole Hell thing. I loved Jesus, and was sure he lived, did the things they said he did. I loved God, even though I thought he went a little overboard telling the Hebrews that they could rush in and take whatever they wanted from the neighboring tribes, kill their women and children, take their lands. Some of the stuff in the Old Testament made me cringe…..but even that I could reconcile later when I learned all of the times that the Bible has been translated. But Hell always seemed like a fantasy, a silly way to understand the real monsters in the world. What else would you do with Hitler, with ruthless leaders, slave traders, child molesters, and evil nasty people? I pictured Hitler screaming and superimposed the compassion I had for even him with the pictures I'd seen of bodies heaped up at Dachau, Buchenwald. He deserved Hell. *But forever?* Surely everyone could get a break at some point, maybe after torment for a century or so.

With the story of Hell I always felt that I was missing a piece of information. A vital spot that would glue together the abstract parts of the picture-they didn't talk about Hitler. They talked about my friends, my neighbors, my then-agnostic dad. The people on the news that wore burkas, saris, turbans, loincloths. Those were people like me....I couldn't see them burning forever in tormented agony. Sorry, just doesn't make sense to me. Never did.

I did a lot of observing those first few years immersed in this new religion, and this new school. I couldn't imagine these church people having sex, I couldn't imagine them accidentally hitting their finger with a hammer and making any face other than the blank stare they wore. In my child's eyes they seemed to have the volume turned down on low, the lamp on the dimmest switch. They wouldn't go to the movies, or let their kids watch TeleTubbies, but they'd embrace a man who was raised from the dead, echoing unicorns and Santa Claus. No wait, they wouldn't even let their kids believe in Santa Claus. This whole lifestyle completely fascinated me. And I watched and watched, looking for inconsistencies. I found plenty.

My parents had their own set of morals, and I found it a bit confusing that they were their own, not the churches. Some part of me thought that they were going to get in trouble for this, that the pastor would march in and catch them wearing pants, or listening to Boz Scaggs (which is a crime), or smoking evil cigarettes. They'd hang their heads in shame, and repent, and the world would make sense to me, but they were unrepentant, and the church as stringent as ever.

My priority list was drastically different from seven am to three pm. During school it was silence, meekness, the Lord. After school it was gratitude for what we had, ambition for what we wanted to be, and knowledge, always knowledge. They didn't make us say yes ma'am and no sir because as my mom put it, "we are your parents not police officers." Pete and Frances Garabedian were basically suburbanites with hippie sensibilities. When I came to the school with my hands hennaed after they took me to the local International Food and Culture Festival, I expected the principal to chop them off in a public execution.

"The accused, Tara, age 10, is guilty of the crime of consorting with SAVAGES (cue angry crowd)."

They didn't say anything, though. I guess they thought I'd drawn swirly designs on my hands in permanent brown ink for a reason.

I was always screwing something up. The rules were so out of my mental framework, I did plenty of things wrong, without trying to. I stood in the corner because my skirts were too short. I washed walls instead of playing at recess for "talking back". In fourth grade I discovered some of the curse word substitutes, like *darn*, and, *what the?*. Using these words got me sent straight to the corner. I really didn't mind, I passed the time memorizing the cobwebs, and making a mental note not to do the particular offence again.

Most places you go rules make sense. If you go on vacation to Niagara Falls, they tell you not to lean on the fence. At a hospital you can't smoke. In our home the rules were simple-do as we were told, try to get good grades, don't hit or bite your sisters or brother. They made sense, and if we offended it was usually on purpose and with full cognitive recognition. But I just could not get the hang of the rules at Winter's Pass, no matter how hard I tried.

"I am giving you a project on health. You must put together a picture presentation of a health issue, and then share it with the class. It is due Tuesday." The teacher wrote the assignment on the board for us to copy.

Hmmm a health issue. This should be easy. My dad was a Chiropractor and we ate pretty healthy as a family. Both my parents exercised and we were the guinea pigs for many health food crazes. The point was, I had no problem doing a health project.

"O.k. girls, homework time" my mom said, as she loaded the dishwasher after dinner. This was a new ritual they'd started, having us all sit down for an hour at the kitchen table after dinner to do homework. I was the only one old enough to have real homework, but that didn't matter. My sister Vanessa played school, using her red pen to grade pretend papers, and my other sister Laura scribbled in her high chair. My baby brother slept in a nearby playpen.

I grabbed a magazine, and thumbed through it loosely for some inspiration. A Coppertone advertisement. *This will work.* It pictured a young woman in a swimmer's one piece bathing suit, her skin so brown and shiny it looked like a champion horse's coat. This was the early eighties, and the dangers of too much sun exposure were starting to get a lot of press, so I decided to focus on that.

"Mooooommmmm …..Do we have any glue?"

"Sure, honey, whatcha makin?" she peered over my shoulder.

"Stop looooking" I whined, "I'll show you when I'm done" I said, jerking the paper out of sight.

I squirted the glue on a piece of notebook paper, and smashed the Coppertone add on top, feeling the cold viscous glue under the thin magazine paper. It looked good (even if it was a little crooked, and even if I just ripped the ad out instead of cutting it) and I was proud of it.

Surely no one will do sunburn; they will probably all be doing the food chart or some such nonsense.

"Ok, mom, I'm done." She walked over and picked it up. A drop of glue fell onto the table. She raised an eyebrow.

"This is nice, Tara……..why don't you show your father?" she said suspiciously.

Dad just happened to step in the room. He saw the wrinkled paper, and crooked add, and cocked one eyebrow.

"Let me help you honey. Let's do one on keeping a healthy spine. We can cut some pictures out of some of my Chiropractic magazines."

I tried not to hide my disappointment. I liked my project. What was wrong with it?

Two hours later and I was packing a very nice cardboard layout with x-ray pictures of a spine on it in my backpack. He even made me give a little practice presentation to my family. They'd applauded, but secretly I snuck my crumpled paper in the backpack, thinking I'd make a decision about which one I'd use tomorrow. I appreciated his effort, but his was boring to me, I liked mine better.

At school the next day I was uncharacteristically aggressive.

"O.k., pull out your presentations. Who'd like to go first?"

"I would!" I said proudly. I had conveniently forgotten my dad's, leaving it in the back of our family van.

"Meee" I raised my hand higher. "I want to go first."

The teacher looked surprised. "Sounds like you have something special for us" she said, feigning interest.

You bet I do.

I stood in front of the class and held my paper up. An audible gasp went up from the class. The teacher got up from her chair to get a look, then snatched the paper from my hands.

"How dare you bring that filth into the class, go to the principal's office."

Filth? What is wrong with it? Does it look that bad? I didn't know what was wrong but I had done something. *What did I do now?*

As I sat in the office I listened as my principal had a long phone conversation with my mother. "I know, just make sure it doesn't happen again."

He hung up and looked at me with exasperation.

"You can go back to class, Tara."

Will someone tell me what I did wrong? Back in class the rest of the students stared in awe. When recess came, Eric, a cute boy that sat next to me, approached. He walked over to me carefully as if he wasn't sure what I'd do. I stared at him.

"Why did you bring pornography to school?"

Huh? "What's pornography?"

"The picture of the naked lady." He leaned in. "Did they give it back to you? Can I have it when you are done?"

A sort of dull understanding was pieced together in my brain from fragments of information. My religious aunt who wouldn't wear a bathing suit, she swam only with other women, and wearing culottes down to her calves. The girl next door who asked me if I wanted to see naked pictures she had swiped from her dad- somehow in this new school, these were one and the same. I sort of understood.

Great, now I'll never have any friends here.

There were many faux pas at Winter's Pass, and they were definitely categorized into *o.k. bad, really bad,* and *wicked.* Being any branch of Christianity other than fundamental Baptist was *o.k. bad.* I guess they figured you were still going to heaven. It was kinda like someone from Brooklyn, meeting someone from Alabama. Two different worlds, really...but they were still both Americans.

Going to the movies, however, was *really bad*, as was listening to secular music. The church world moved in slow motion, and every pinched, righteous face in the joint knew the rules. There were very specific rules. Drinkin', playing the lottery, and women wearing pants was *WICKED,* and if spotted was talked about for months.

"Did you see the woman so and so brought to Sunday service?" said in disbelief. "Yeah, she was wearing PANTS." A self-righteous silence followed.

There was also a record breaking amount of gossip going on.

The second of the *bad* families were the Wildes. They were Methodist, and fell into the *o.k. bad* bordering on *really bad* category. That rogue John Wesley. Lisa Wilde was my best friend in the school, a bond quickly formed out of necessity. The Wilde's were definitely the baddest of the two families, both of her parents were divorced, and there was the Methodist thing, but as far as badness goes, my family was considered pretty bad.

My dad smoked, and cursed occasionally. Something that caused me to giggle to myself, and made my mom say, HONEEYYY in a, come- on- now- not- in- front –of- the- children voice. We all wore pants, and we didn't go to church on Sunday nights, or Wednesday nights, only Sunday mornings. None of my family sang in the choir, or worked in the bus ministry, or did anything but show up on Sunday morning, which I thought was a pretty big deal considering how much time it took to get a family of six fed, dressed, and in the car on time, but apparently it was not enough for an *in* with the super-religious. All that nine am frantic yelling, breakfast gulping, and scurrying around looking for white tights without holes in them had to be worth something in God's eyes, right?

Sunday mornings were an event, and by the time we were all piled in the car and headed for Sunday service, we were cross and uptight. We needed to relax for an hour in the cushy pews. I daydreamed about boys during service, and doodled on the tithe envelopes; when that wore thin, I watched the breeze sway the oaks, and imagined what sound the leaves made as the wind harassed them. My dad would catch me not paying attention, or worse, nodding off, and gently tug at my hair. Looking over at him he would smile, and make a silly face.

He doesn't buy all this, either, I used to think. When the service was over, and the last amen was said along with the last hand shaken, we were more than ready to happily pour back into the car and head out for General Tso's and fortune cookies, followed by an afternoon nap and some TV. Those itchy tights and shoes that hurt my feet were piled in a corner and lost again until we searched for them the next week.

I always thought of going to church like this: it was putting on your best face to go visit Aunt Gladys in the nursing home. Something you didn't *have* to do, per say, but something that was good to do in some unnamable, and not immediately returned way. I was in charge of getting my two younger sisters and baby brother dressed, and as I sat, slumped in the corner Sunday after Sunday, wondering where my sister's wretched other patent leather shoe was, or where my baby brother's clip- on tie was hiding, I knew that the end of the day were rewards in the form of *He-Man* on the TV, and two hours of unattended fun while my parents napped, following the bliss of good Chinese food.

We also took full advantage of the one- free- Sunday – off- a- month -without –looking- bad pass that most church-going people get. It can be two Sundays' if someone is sick. Any more than that and you'll be getting a phone call from the pastor wondering where you've been.

But even with all that, my parents were definitely not church people. I always felt like they were sorta playing at it. Like they were humoring someone.

"Stop it, stop it, honey, please!" my mom was gripping the seat and turning an interesting shade of green.

Her terror wasn't enough to encourage us from having a ball, though. This was Wild Armenian Ride, and my favorite part of a Sunday morning. It didn't happen every Sunday; it really depended on my dad's mood. Now I understand that it hinged on what kind of week he'd had, or whether or not he'd stayed up till two am writing reports. Maybe it had a direct correlation to how uptight the sermon was that day; my dad did and to this day dislikes being told what to think or even worse, do. Maybe he had to shake things up a bit. In my magical child world it seemed as random as the wind.

Wild Armenian Ride first happened on our back country roads one morning after church. It almost seemed to loosen the threads that were woven tightly around us by the sermon.

We shook them off, literally.

Mom drove to church, dad drove home, don't know why. On the way to our favorite Chinese restaurant we'd be predictably coasting along in our blue Dodge conversion van.

All of the sudden dad would shout, "wild Armenian

ride, wild Armenian ride!!!" and weave dramatically back and forth across the road causing all six of us to lean heavily out of our seats and my mother to plead with him to stop. Roller coasters made her sick. Escalators made her sick. Lava lamps even made her sick. She is just a queasy person.

Wild Armenian Ride never lasted long, it was dangerous of course. But it lasted long enough to get our adrenaline pumping, and get us good and wound up. Dad hated being predictable, still does. If we asked him to do it, he wouldn't. If we forgot to ask, he'd do it. If we tried to do reverse psychology and not ask, he wouldn't do it, or he'd do the Wild Armenian Ride hybrid, Mild Armenian Ride.

Mild Armenian Ride was just as fun, it felt like a mockery of restraint. He'd loosely jiggle the steering wheel, sitting ramrod straight in the driver's seat, a parody of constraint.

"Mild Armenian ride, mild Armenian ride" he'd say in a silly robotic voice, as the van jerked in small zig zags across the road.

"More more more" we'd chant in unison.

"No. no." he'd pause.

"O.k…….. Mild Armenian ride! "

"Yay!" all four of us would shout. My poor mom tried to keep from throwing up.

Sometimes Mild Armenian Ride turned into Wild Armenian Ride.

A friend of mine recently told me "you are a born anarchist."

Guess I got that from my dad.

But mom was pretty wild in her own way, too. She danced around the house, and sang to Bob Seger, Willie

Nelson, and Neil Sadaka. All labeled secular music, and surely straight from the devil himself. Of course, I figured out all this out on accident. Once, when I had Nancy Aims, the daughter of a couple very involved in the church over to spend the night, the gig was up. She walked in and saw my dad smoking a cigarette, and heard Anne Murray on the kitchen radio, and from that moment on, I was a bonafied Heretic.

"Does your dad smoke?" she said in hushed, awed tones.

"Yeah" I said, thinking for a moment why a sight I was so used to would garner such a response...... "um, we do lots of bad things." She stared at me with a mixture of disbelief, and admiration. There was an awkward silence punctuated by the radio ...*spread your tiny wings and fly away*.... Mrs. Murray sang in the background. I timidly looked into my new friends eyes, and hoped she wouldn't want to leave. This new reality was like walking on thin ice, and I needed all the allies I could get. She pondered it for a moment, then chose not to address it further, tucking it away for Sunday school gossip later on. We went back to our Malibu Barbies. Of course my parents had heard *that* conversation. They pulled me aside and I vaguely remember a talk about how we weren't bad, and that people look at things differently. Of course it didn't matter, in my new world with all my friends and three-fourths of my daily experience, we *were* bad, and now it was worse than ever.

Much to the unknown chagrin of the church my cigarette smoking, wicked dad not only managed to be an amazing father, but was very much a part of my early experience with spirituality. He was a learned man, always questioning reality, authority... he never spoke of religion, only of possibility. Once I woke up to the silverware drawer dumped out on the kitchen table, him fixedly staring at a spoon.

"Um, what are you doing" I said, sleepily. It was 11pm.

"Shhhhh" he said. "I'm trying to bend it with my mind." Lying on the table next to the forks was a book on the amazing power of the mind.

Neato, I thought and watched it for a while, hoping to see this phenomenon. I *believed* in my dad. I stood there a while in my Holly Hobby polyester nightgown, then eventually went to bed, wondering how he was going to use this new power, thoughts of Superman drifting through my head. *Where would I hide my diary now?* I wondered.

He taught us to meditate once, idly lying around on the sofa after a big meal.

"Imagine a white room with nothing in it. Now picture a big red ball bouncing." His voice was low and deep. "Just focus on the ball bouncing up and down."

I loved these lessons, I felt like they were brief, magical entrances into his world. I was only able to focus on the image for a short time, my child mind like the Yogic wild monkey, but I did notice the calm I felt afterwards.

His bookcases were filled with Carlos Castaneda, and *Pyramid Power*. He read these books with excitement, then apathy, then forgetfulness; several copies of each lay dusty on his many tall bookshelves. He was hungry for knowledge, something that I inherited. His thirst for anything his brain could gobble up was unmatched, the stack of books on his nightstand attested to his ever growing quest for more. When he wasn't tired from his career as a successful Chiropractor, or planning some new idea, he challenged our ideas of reality. A simple quizzing of spelling homework became an exercise in self-confidence.

"Learn this" he would say, "and don't ask me to quiz you until you KNOW it."

He handed me back the spelling workbook. I would return to the kitchen table, and go over it once more. Spelling has always made sense to me, so it wasn't long before I'd return. Looking up from whatever book he was reading, he would take the book from my hands, and start drilling.

"Spell thermometer" he'd say in a disinterested voice.

"T-H-E-R-M-O-M-E-T-E-R. There, no problem, dad."

"Are you sure?" he'd ask, a bit of a glint in his eye.

"Yeah" I'd say defiantly.

"Are you really sure?" he'd say, glancing down at the book for effect.

"Um, yeah." Now I was starting to doubt. *Why is he doing this?* I thought I knew it. *Why is he looking at the book like that?*

"Tara, you have to be sure of what you know" he'd say, handing the book back to me.

I came away from those experiences with confusion, peppered with the seeds of something new in my soul. No matter what, no matter who challenged me, I had to stand on what I was sure of. The problem was, I wasn't sure of much. I couldn't figure out who God was between the rigidity of Winter's Pass, the indefinable thing that was his religion, and my own unshakable connection, that I had always known, but couldn't quite put a finger on.

This would continue to drive me crazy for years.

In hindsight I realized that I was always confused. My life was drastically unbalanced. The ride to school in dad's tiny CRX smelled like cigarettes and cologne. On those chilly mornings we listened to NPR, and I counted the change in his console to improve my ever-poor math skills. I loved the way my dad babied the clutch at the stop signs on the hilly country roads. With an honest kiss, I got out of the car and into a different world. A solemn, rigid, joyless world.

When we got into the classroom, and put away our things, we prayed. We pledged to the American flag, to the Christian flag, then to the Bible. Then came the songs. No one wanted to sing really loud in the schoolroom located in a drafty, sound -proof basement, with no musical accompaniment. With only five of us, I dreaded the days when someone was out sick, because it only made the raspy singing sound worse. We timidly sang out the Star Spangled Banner, followed by *Onward Christian Soldier*, followed by the *B-I-B-L-E*.

"Oh the Bible, yes that's the book for me. I stand alone on the word of God, the Bible. BIBLE!" (You yelled the last part.)

The blank –faced teacher stood by the human sized flags at the front of the room, monotonely singing along. We ended the 20 minute morning fiasco with more prayer. By the time we sat down to the actual first class, I was exhausted with thinking. How can you go from talking about God to checking Math homework with the exact same tone of voice? It was like God was another thing we did, like science studies or recess. Was God a blanket that you draped over yourself to cover up life, the life you had, or the life you left? Did the blanket work?

I needed to know if it worked for these people. They acted like it, everything on the outside said that the God-Blanket was worth surrendering all identity, but I wanted to know……..did it go to the core? Was this who they were when they were alone, their real selves? Anyone could put on an identity; I wanted to know if there was something real.

I kept thinking *if God is so important that we spend this much time on all this, then why isn't anyone happy about it?* And that question was to reverberate over and over in my mind for years. *WHY ARE THESE PEOPLE SO UNHAPPY?*

Children are remarkably adaptable. My life at Winter's Pass flopped from talk of Hell and salvation to kick ball in the back field (a very badly cleared piece of land, full of potholes). As I started to accept this bizarre world, I started to have fun. Even though there were only five in my class, we were a colorful bunch.

Eric Smart was my crush, and once I had set my sights on him, it was all over. With a father that was my hero, I was one of those girls who was naturally boy crazy and I was smitten with Eric. Of course, he was not interested in girls. I was convinced we were going to get married, and passed the time in class writing, and re-writing Tara Smart over and over in big scrolled script. The fact that he barely knew I existed didn't stop me from milking every bit of childish hope I could from a mistaken glance my way, or an accidental brush against my hand in chapel. One of only two boys in my class, all of the girls liked Eric. He was quiet, studious, imaginative, and very grown up for his age. He wore his chestnut brown hair slicked to the side in a very grownup way, matching his grownup eyes. The reason Eric was grownup was because his family lived in poverty. He wore shoes and clothes that were given to him by the old deacons in the church, and we all knew he struggled. I knew this bothered him to the core, and I could almost hear his silent resolve to get out of it as soon as he could. (For what it is worth, he has made a very nice life for himself, and is very happy now).

The one conversation we had about it haunts me to this day.

It was fifth grade, springtime. We were waiting for class to start, and for some reason I had the floor, my classmates were busy with other things. Tori was fiddling with her hair sprayed bangs, Jennifer was finishing up her science homework, and Nancy was in another room, no doubt talking up the teacher. Lisa was out sick.

So that left everyone in the room half listening, and Eric looking at me. I tried to think of something cool to say.

Even though I have never been materialistic, I was at that age when I was a total slave to my peers. I chose the superiority of Reeboks to coolly comment on, I had heard Lisa raving about them earlier.

"Reeboks are so rad. Why would anyone wear anything else?" I said offhandedly. The second it left my mouth three things happened simultaneously. Eric's expression turned to a deep frown, I looked at his orthopedic off-white old man shoes, and regret like a tidal wave rushed over me.

His reaction was sharp as a knife.

"Not everyone can afford Reeboks, Tara" he said as he shuffled his too big shoes under his desk.

If I could have smacked myself, I would have. Twice. It took a week before he would talk to me again, and when he did, it wasn't at all pleasant.

The way to win a man is laugh at all his jokes. I employed this theory to infinity. Funny or not, when Eric even so much as came up with a knock knock joke, I burst out in doubled over faux belly laughs.

This happened one day while the teacher was scribbling sums on the chalkboard. We used this time to make fun of her, or whisper to each other. Eric was on the other side of the room, and I could barely hear him. I was stuck with Tori who wasn't interested in goofing off.

This stinks. He is obviously having a good time over there with Nancy and Jennifer. I could see them laughing and scribbling notes. I looked over at my scrooge of a classmate. Tori was engrossed in whatever she was reading, and didn't even notice me. I crumpled up a piece of paper and threw it at her leg, hoping to start a paper fight. She ignored it. Sighing, I slumped down in my desk in my little forgotten corner of the classroom.

"I need to step out a minute, read chapter four while I'm gone" said Mrs. Peels. We held our breath till the door shut behind her, and then turned up the volume by a decibel or two.

My attention was drawn to Eric's corner of the room, where he had obviously said something hilarious.

Quick, Tara, laugh!

"Hahahahahaha!" I mustered as loudly as I could.

"What are you laughing at?" he asked. It was the first thing he said to me since the fateful Reebok conversation. I didn't care if there was scorn in his voice, he was TALKING TO ME!

"Um….I" I stuttered.

"You didn't hear what I said" he said, a little cocky. Jennifer and Nancy were looking at me now, as in fact was the whole classroom. Tori had even looked up from her book.

"Well, what did you say then?" I said in a voice that I hoped sounded playful and confident, but actually came out kinda pathetic.

The room was quiet now, and all eyes were on us.

"I said your face looks like an elephant's butt!" laughter roared all around me.

I guess I deserved that. He was pretty nice to me from then on out, he'd had his revenge.

Eric was way out of my league, though, his family were definitely church people. As far as degrees of churchyness, they were a good ninety-eight percent. Not as deep in as the pastor, who turned the TV when a beer commercial came on, but they were close. I needed to face it, there was no way Eric would want *me*. In all my marriage fantasies, I never wore skirts twenty-four hours a day, or listened to bland, droning hymns. Nah, not my idea of a good time.

The only other male crush option was John Dodman, we called him Johnny. He was always tugging at his oversized dirt stained pants and his hair was unkempt. Not out of neglect, but out of sheer enjoyment for the outdoors. John played hard. He also spit when he talked, not a good thing in the world of image-obsessed prepubescents. John was a last option. He was always in trouble for not walking in a straight line, for being sloppy, for talking out of turn. Basically, for anything our power-hungry sadistic principal, Mr. Clemson decided he wanted to be upset with Johnny for. Maybe just for being himself. He lived in the principal's office, usually getting spanked for some imaginary treachery.

The thing was, John was not bad. He didn't talk back, or do anything wrong. He was just a real rough and tumble boy and in a world where this was the closest thing the teachers could find to disobedience, Johnny became a scapegoat.

I suppose when you are on a lifelong self-professed manhunt for sin, then you gotta find some sin, by gum.

John's parents didn't care if the principal spanked him constantly. There were a lot of kids in his family, and a healthy rowdy boy was nothing more than something else to worry about. Not that they didn't love him, they did, they just thought that this was an expression of love.

I felt sick every time John went to the principal to get spanked. I felt sorry for him, and the rebel spirit in me just wanted to fly in there like a Valkrie, and snatch him out of the hands of the oppressor, screeching as my heavy wings flapped at the polished oak doors. I could just see the look of relief on his face, and the astonished visage of the Principal. I also felt guilty; our parents wouldn't let them spank us. We were the only kids in school with this privilege, something else that made us stand out.

My dad, when they were signing us up for school, scared the be-jeses out of the principal on the first day making sure, in no uncertain terms that no one was to lay a hand on any of his children. I heard the whole story second hand, my mom on the phone with my grandma. I got most of my adult information this way, casting my eyes downward, and pretending I was not listening.

"And then he told him if they need a spanking that bad, call me, and I'll come give it to them, but you had better not touch any of my girls, and if I find out that you have there will be a (and he leans forward) *A BIG PROBLEM.*" My mom said the whole thing like she was reciting the lines of a play, slowly with lots of inflection, and drama at the right points. I'm sure the principal, said "whatever you wish Dr. Garabedian" and then snuck to the bathroom to clean the urine off of his leg.

My dad had a thousand looks. But he saved the *big*

three for certain situations. The If -I –ever- catch -you – smoking- again stare, the, I'm -gonna –kill- him,- if -I –go- to- jail, -then- you -will -know -why stare, and the famous yeah-they-can-go-to-your-kooky-school-but-don't-lay-a-finger-on-them-or-I'm-gonna-mop-up-the-floor-with-your-guts stare. Mustachioed Armenian Chiropractors from the streets can be very intimidating.

Poor Johnny, he was frustrated, picked on, singled out and miserable...... but I couldn't focus on that. Like most people, when faced with true tragedy, a few heartfelt glances are thrown, but it is one's own problems that take first place. I had to deal with all the female rivalry in the class, because other than Eric and Johnny, the rest of us were girls. Nancy, Jennifer, Tori, my best friend Lisa, and me. As women do when they are bored, we were catty, snotty. We broke into factions, argued, and then formed new ones.

The only alliance that stayed true was Lisa and I; she was my pre-teen partner in crime. We spent our time listening to Madonna and putting on her mom's Avon castoff makeup, slicking on the baby blue eye shadow with the expertise of a blind man. Our favorite thing was to deck ourselves out in whatever our moms' and dads' would never allow us out of the house in, like spiked double belts and fingerless gloves, run down to her basement and dance to Janet Jackson's *Nasty Boys*, or the brand new Madonna's *Like A Virgin*. I didn't know what a *Like a Virgin* meant, but I was sure by the way it sounded that it was very cool.

School days with the five of us was like being shut up in a cabin in the middle of the wilderness, with some really harsh rules to follow. To sum it up, we were under a dictatorship, we were sick of looking at each other, and we were all stir crazy. As far as the rules went, they were pretty normal, walk in a straight line, respect to your elders, and so on- until Mr. Clemson came into power.

Mr. Clemson was our new principal. He was fresh out of Baptist Bible College, one of the severely religious colleges where they make the girls and guys swim in different swimming pools, and walk on different sidewalks colored blue and pink for each sex. He was green, and as is often the case with someone that doesn't know what they are doing, he came down on us hard.

His first rule was *no talking in the lunchroom*. He did not have kids, and didn't want any (much to the displeasure of his poor wife), and it was obvious that kids got on his nerves. So the rule was implemented almost immediately.

I remember the day I choked on a piece of candy my mom had packed in my lunch.

Alright, candy!, I thought as I opened up my Rainbow Brite lunchbox, and pulled out the turkey sandwich on mashed up looking wheat bread. I ignored the apple, and devoured the potato chips. After a few half-hearted bites of the lukewarm sandwich, it was time for the grand finale. I could smell the buttery sweet smell of the banana taffy, wrapped in bright yellow paper. I immediately popped it in my mouth.

Which was a mistake. It went in too far, and like someone shooting a basketball, it got lodged in the net, my throat. I was gasping for air. I looked up at Jennifer idly chewing her bologna on white bread, and alternating it with sips of milk from a thermos. She chewed with her mouth open, like a cow chewed its cud. I caught a glimpse of the white and grey mess in her mouth churning like a cement mixer, and tried to wave her down so she could see I needed help. But we weren't allowed to talk. At all.

Most of us coped with this imposition in an almost Zen-like manner. We stared into space and methodically chewed. We weren't allowed to do what it is that kids do which is play, throw food, and chat about so and so has a crush on so and so, and we didn't trust ourselves to not do it. So we zoned out-we all did. From the first graders to the eighth, there was only the sound of chewing and sipping quietly through straws, so as not to be heard.

No one was even looking at me.

I couldn't breathe..........I was panicking.

After a second or two, my survival instincts kicked in and I went over to the teachers table. Making what sounded like burps, and low deep gasps I pointed to the bathroom, and to my throat. Mr. Clemson looked up lazily from his carefully organized salad, where each tomato dared not step out of line. He gave an irritated nod, and then went back to eating.

I ran downstairs, stopping a couple of times, because I was losing air. I remember feeling very dizzy. Making my way to the tiny kid's bathroom, I gave myself the Heimlich by hurling myself onto the edge of the sink, coughing up the banana disaster in one big spit covered chunk. I stared at it for a moment and tried not to cry. Not wanting to get in trouble for being gone too long, I made my way back to the silent lunchroom.

Do you know what was running through my scared and relieved nine year old brain?

I hope I don't get in trouble for making noise.

Luckily, Mr. Clemson didn't punish me; I guess choking is an acceptable noise to make in the lunchroom. Apparently though, having lunch in silence wasn't enough for him. The next week he decided that we wouldn't be allowed to talk ON THE PLAYGROUND. This lasted for one long, very depressing week, when even the conservative parents decided that enough was enough. But very well do I remember that week….. imagine playing with no talking. We did most of our communication by hand gestures. Playing G.I. Joes is no fun if you can't talk. How would anyone know that I was Scarlett, and NOT Jennifer, even though SHE had red hair, and mine was dark brown, like the Baroness? I didn't want to be the Baroness, because she was bad. I didn't want to be bad. But I was bad anyway.

***

Why has always been one of my main questions. Relentless questioning when I was a child drove my mom crazy. She was often met with the remark "because that's the way it is" when she was growing up, so she tried her best to answer us with honest explanations. I think she gave up after a few years. The conversations went a little something like this…..

"Mom, why is do escalators go up and down?"

She would think about it for a minute, and then give an answer. Fifteen related questions later and she would start to tire. Then came the defeated sigh of exasperation.

"That's just the way things are, Tara" she would say before cutting me off.

This questioning was, and still is a vital part of my makeup. I figured people who wouldn't ask or answer why had something to hide. Even if it was simply to say "I don't know". I quickly learned that asking why was seriously looked down upon at Winter's Pass, even ignored.

Why meant you had to think.

This meant you had to have some responsibility for

your actions. This meant that the super-pious who sat on the front row, and nodded, and amen'd at the pastors every word, couldn't be the worst gossips in the church. Or the church Sunday school teacher, whose children could do no wrong, and looked at us like we were beneath him, had to notice when his angel of a daughter lied to them about everything, and methodically acted out the opposite of the strict doctrine they professed.... they didn't want to think. The world was an easier place to deal with when it was broken into absolutes. Right and wrong. Heaven and hell. Bad and good. Everything easily fit into a category, and the things that didn't fit, the pastor would tell them what category they belonged to. With this kind of segregation, once someone was labeled *bad* it was easy to keep away from them.

Now, there were a few exceptions. People who made it work, people who glowed with some kind of heavenly light. People who really carried what I perceived as the love of Jesus around: Ruth Linden, Chuck Best, and Mrs. Wingfield. Three of the kindest, most gentle people I've ever met. Yes, they followed the so called rules at Winter's Pass, wearing skirts, keeping silent, not playing the lottery, but there was something else there. It was as if their existence wasn't based on those things. They did them as an afterthought and there was something real about them.

Ruth Linden was the meek, skirt wearin' prototype for Winter's Pass. She had sixties throwback, fashionless, straight light brown hair. She made her own A-line skirts out of a sort of rough blue fabric- store -clearance material. If you looked at her, playing the pipe organ on Sunday mornings, you would think that she was as dry as toast.

But she was a joy to be around. She seemed to uncannily address whatever was in your heart at the moment, and then provide a remedy for the malady, whatever it was. She would pull some M & M's out of her magic bottomless purse, or give a hug, or say the right words. She had a smile that came from her heart. I was always happy whenever I was sent on an errand for the teacher to run into her on the school grounds. You always walked away from her feeling better than when you arrived. She *noticed* you. She had a gift.

Chuck Best was the church groundskeeper. He was the only man that did not embrace the penis waving male dominant role that pervaded every breath we took at Winter's Pass. He was gentle, kind, and humble. He always waved at you, whoever you were, and then smiled a genuine apologetic smile, as if he didn't want to disturb you with his presence. He never boasted, or even seemed to want to be noticed. He worked like a dog, and never complained. His smile was always ready to be brought out even on the sweltering hottest of days when he was out hoeing the flower beds dripping with sweat while we were sitting in air conditioned luxury. It was always the same smile, it made you want to smile too.

Mrs.Wingfield was one of a kind, I don't think they make people like her anymore. She was a teacher at the school, and happened to teach my sister, Laura, who at the time was painfully shy. Mrs. Wingfield was just what she needed. She loved, genuinely loved each and every child in her class. She was jolly, and looked like a female version of Santa Claus (without the beard). She had rosy cheeks, a never-ending smile, and she was round and just, well, jolly. For a woman who had many terrible things happen to her in her life, like her husband of 25 years leaving her for a younger woman, she seemed to channel all that would-be hate and bitterness into pure Jesus-like unconditional love.

She was dirt poor, and spent all her money on trinkets for the kids. She could say "I'm really disappointed in you", and it would sound the same as "you are my sunshine". She emulated the love of Mother Teresa.

They all three had this beautiful humility, and I swear to just so much as look at them was to think that they had indeed been in the presence of Jesus himself. I think that confused me more than anything. If the whole lot had been two faced, then I could have dismissed all of Christianity with not so much as a thought, but somehow these three made it work. They really did IT. Whatever IT was.

Saved. Salvation. Get saved. Soul winning. They must be saved. If life at Winter's Pass centered on anything it was on that one phrase…. GET SAVED. At every event. Every Bar-B-Q, church service, chapel service, knitting club, trip to the bathroom. There was always a salvation message, or prayer at the end, mumbled like a mantra.

"Lord, and if there be anyone here that isn't for sure that they know where they are going when they die, let them come forward and recite the sinners prayer." Sometimes they even led you in it from your seat, if it was a large crowd, or if they were short on time.

"Lord please forgive me of my sins, and I acknowledge that you sent your son to save me of my sins, please keep me from Hell, and let me go to heaven."

Bada-bing-bada- bang. Done. Bye-bye Hell.

I must have gotten saved a thousand times. Some for real, some because I just wanted to get up from the uncomfortable church seat, some because I was scared to go to Hell, and some because I wanted to be in the spotlight. Getting saved meant going up in front of the church, to kneel at the altar. Throw in a few tears…instant attention.

The first time I got "saved" was at Vacation Bible School. Kneeling down, and repeating the prayer in the musty old room, I remember staring at the green and brown shag carpet, and knowing that after I said the words that this lady wanted me to say then I wouldn't go to Hell. All I knew about Hell was that it was hot and horrible, and from the way they made it sound, I wanted no part of it. I was kinda mad that my parents had never mentioned something as important as this. *I was going to Hell*, and they had never told me. How could have they neglected something so important?

After saying the prayer, I checked myself. Did I feel different? I cautiously went outside and looked around..... things looked the same. I could hear the din of the other kid's parents arriving to pick them up. Were things supposed to glow? Was I supposed to have magical powers? Would Jesus show himself to me? If I was "a new man, reborn in Christ", shouldn't I feel different? They said I should. I didn't really feel any different, so I filed that question away in my mind to ask later, but constant thoughts of Hell haunted me.

I decided it was time for my family to get saved. Maybe the reason that my mom and dad never mentioned it was because they didn't know! I certainly didn't want them to face eternal damnation. If it was simple as this, then they would all repeat the prayer, I had made up my mind. My mom was first.

"Mom are you saved?" We were barely out of the church parking lot, when I started with the question. She reacted like I had asked her about her menstrual cycle.

In a shy, quiet voice, so that my siblings wouldn't hear she said "Tara, yes, I am, but this is not something you ask people. What people believe is personal."

She turned up the radio louder. WFEZ easy listening tried to drown out my thoughts…. I didn't get it. They had said that we were all going to Hell if we didn't say this prayer, so just to be safe I had to make sure that my family said it. I couldn't see why there was any question about it. My sister Vanessa had gotten saved, so I didn't have to worry about her, I rationalized. The vision of her light brown crimped hair, head bowed low, I was sure she'd done it. My other sister, Laura was only three, and barely talking. I calculated that in another year, I'd make her recite it, pulling her away from whatever toy she was playing with. I was confident in my position as a big sister just how persuasive I could be. As long as she could get the words out, I figured it would work….. I'd make her say it again when she was older, just to be safe. My brother Jonathan was just a baby; I'd have plenty of time to make him say it. But dad. There was a problem. I was scared to ask dad. I didn't know why, but something in me told me that things like this weren't his cup of tea.

"Is dad saved?" I broke my silent thoughts and asked my mom. I was like a machine, determined. She turned the radio back down, annoyed.

"I don't want to talk about this anymore, Tara." She turned the radio back up.

But I was on a mission, and when we got home, I confidently made a beeline for dad.

"Dad" I said in my most adult of tones. I took a deep breath. "Dad, are you saved?" I asked timidly. Holding my breath, I waited. He looked up from the book he was reading, his eyes briefly adjusting to the world around him, and my question, from the book world he had just left. He paused for a moment, then let out a hearty laugh, and walked away. I stood there in front of the kitchen door, feeling confused. This baffled me, either he was saved, and the very thought of me asking was funny, or he was laughing *at* me for some reason. Either way, it took years before he would even discuss religion with me. And even longer to figure out what the heck was so funny.

Chapter Two

"The important thing is to not stop questioning."
-Albert Einstein

Today was different. For starters, the pastor's wife was preening in the women's bathroom, straightening her hoopskirt. The navy sateen civil-war dress she was wearing went well with her suntanned skin and dimpled smile- she looked the part. The pastor seemed to be hurrying through the sermon. You could smell the spicy baked beans, and the charcoal on the grill even inside the white washed walls of the sanctuary.

It was Old Fashioned Day. In the church, there seemed to be a general consensus that life was better back in the good old days before the world became really evil. So, one of the fun days we celebrated after Sunday service was Old Fashioned Day.

I loved it, the place was transformed. The pastor was decked out in a Colonel Saunders- looking suit complete with black velvet string tie. Most of the women in the church were accomplished seamstresses, so stepping out of the service, and onto the picnic area was like stepping into a civil war re-enactment. Large hoop skirts, parasols, and bonnets abounded.

Of course my parents didn't dress up, because they are way too cool for that, but they let us. I was reading a lot of Anne of Green Gables books at the time, so I got out my long skirt, and yard-sale cameo brooch. I stepped into the pale green georgette, and carefully pinned the brooch to my high lace collar. Then, one by one, tried to put each of my sisters' hair up into a Civil war meets Victorian era poufy bun.

I walked the grounds with a nostalgic feeling. At 13 years old, this was my last year at Winter's Pass Baptist School. I waved at Ruth, and smiled at Chuck, who was quietly putting up a tarp over the food. I found the spot under a tree that I had grown up climbing, sat on the cool earth, and watched the scene.

I saw the Beeton's talking with the Radcliffe's, the adults bent ear to ear in sacred whispering. Heard shouts of "over there" and "batter batter batter" as an impromptu softball game started between some of the men. The pastor had even gotten involved, and I watched as the long tails of his suit flapped when he ran from base to base.

The sunshine and cool breeze were kind, and despite having not figured out the puzzle of religion, the world felt right. I had been there long enough to kinda fit. It was like the last day at an unsatisfying job, you couldn't wait to get out of there, but small things like the beep of the cashier, or the boss's annoying laugh made you sentimental.

Just a little bit.

I could see most of my classmates, and each was fulfilling obvious roles. Nancy was aggressively playing ball with the guys, and probably winning, I speculated. Jennifer was helping with the food, and Tori was probably off looking in a mirror somewhere. I watched Eric as he was helping his mother with his sisters and brothers, his tired face triggering a small ache in my heart.

Feelings became thoughts as I sat there for what seemed like an eternity. The sensation of walking on eggshells was there when I was in any authority figure's presence. The fifties /Nazi values of total control of authority had made me all but salute every time I saw a teacher, pastor, or local Indian chief...... I thought what I wanted, but I did what they asked.

Christianity offered me nothing that seemed worth taking, yet. The immersion in fanaticism had made me skittish enough to not explore other beliefs for fear of Hell, but unsatisfied enough to leave me hungry. *I knew* that for most of the people I'd met in the church, Christianity was just this thing they did, like sugar added to their coffee. It was an adornment, a robe, a well applied lipstick, or blush. Underneath, and every time I looked into their eyes, I knew-they didn't mean it. If something was really that powerful, then shouldn't it have the power to change people? Really change people?

Deep inside my heart, there was always something louder for me. Something that I heard, or felt, rather, that far out rang the rehearsed words of the pastor and the practiced lifestyle of the church people. I heard the force that was in the wind, the earth. I heard Spirit that cannot be put into words, like a ray of sunshine I detected the pulse of life over the brick shell of the church and the words that for a moment became nothing but sounds upon the air. This force, this wisdom was around me, and it was around them, too, but they could not see it.

My connection was primarily this nameless force that was outside the mind, and could not, absolutely could not be put into words. It could not be confined and since it did not dwell in the realm of the mind, and neither did I at that age; I had no desire to confine it. No desire to describe it. In hindsight this was my religion up to this point. I never looked at the church as the same thing as it. The church was what I was trying to figure out, the namelessness of the Divine was what I lived, enjoyed. Being outside, breathing the air, marking the change of seasons fed something in my soul, and even as a child filled me with an indescribable joy. I knew that I was the same thing as it, it was me, we were one and the same.

Previous to this first experience with Winter's Pass and organized religion, I had made my own spiritual contact. One spring day while playing, I sat down on the new grass to rest. My legs stretched out on the sloped hill in our back yard and as I leaned back I felt what can only be described as *waves*. The earth seemed to be moving in rhythmic energetic patterns underneath me. I accepted this without question, as all kids do, but the memory has stuck with me to this day. I had tuned into something, and it felt wonderful. For years I tried to go back to that same spot and make it happen again, to no avail. This was my religion.

Unfortunately the older I got, and the more I was taught to use my mind as a starting place for knowledge, I forwent the unkempt freedom that was namelessness, and I got more and more frustrated. I thought too much. And that was what I was doing sitting there, under that tree, saying goodbye to the world that surrounded me, which at first seemed hostile, now familiar. As I nibbled from the plate I had made for myself from the plethora of Southern-style potluck dishes, and bathed in the languid sunshine, my long skirt swishing at my legs I wondered two things.

Would Christianity make more sense to me in the future and was Andrea Beeton's potato salad always this bad?

Our eighth grade graduation was a lot like any normal young adults. Over cupcakes with little diploma's on them we excitedly talked of our new schools. We were in the middle of puberty with our minds trying desperately to keep up with our bodies. Sad to be leaving each other, but excited about "getting out of here" we put on our best clothes, and graduated to the big world of high school. The church school only went up to eighth grade, so we all had to go to another high school, and my parents chose Baptist Christian School. It was big (compared to what we were used to), and liberal (compared to what we were used to).

Baptist Christian was a lot like a very watered down version of Winter's Pass. On a one to ten scale, ten being the highest religious fervor, and the more devout, then Winter's Pass was about a nine. Baptist Christian was about a four. A lot of the difference was sheer size; I went from a class of five to two classes of 25. The school had a little bit of everything; really religious students, their families very active in the church-they made up about thirty percent of the school. Then there were the regular kids who had families like mine, not too religious, but wanted a private school education, and the assurance of a safe environment-we were fifty percent of the school. The last twenty percent were kids that had been kicked out of public schools for such things as dealing cocaine, marijuana, and toting guns; they were the ones who were major influences in the school. I learned a lot at BCS.

It smelled like a normal high school, a mix between sweat socks, pre-packaged cafeteria food, and cheap teenaged perfume like Love's Baby Soft. We tried to act like we were going to a normal high school, I guess it was as normal as it could get and still be religious.

Going to High School meant giving up my search for religious clarity. What I didn't find at Winter's Pass I knew in an instant I certainly wasn't going to find at BCS, they didn't even TRY. The church face was so pathetic there, even I didn't believe it. So I went in the other direction. The bad kids were easy to find, and very accepting of new members; within my first year, I smoked pot, and messed around with guys. The keeping your virginity thing had been drilled into me too hard to let go of, but I tiptoed that line very closely. I listened to Metal. I listened to The Cure and pretended to be depressed. I finally bought all the Tarot cards, and silver jewelry bearing snakes, faeries, dragons, and various other symbols I had always enjoyed without feeling guilty. I had always had an uncanny draw to Tarot, or anything I could get my hands on about Witches. My parents would catch my playing with my grandma's crystal pendulum (a divination tool) and tell me to leave it alone, like I had just touched poison, or I would acquire these things, then throw them away, in repentance.

I started a "Witch Box", the fear of Hell becoming less and less threatening to me. In there I placed shells, candles, and anything that even remotely hinted at Witchcraft.

Within the first three months at the new school my best friend Lisa approached me in the hallway after science class.

"Tara, I don't like who you've become and I don't want to be your friend anymore." She said haughtily. I pretended not to care. Secretly hurt, but also pleased at the fact that how *bad* I was had gotten around the school, I shrugged my shoulders and walked away.

I hooked up with the worst kinds of people you can find in a Christian school, namely Dustin, who had been kicked out of all the county public schools for dealing drugs. We got high, listened to Pink Floyd, and messed around. I wasn't happy, but I wasn't tired from thinking, either. The pale substitute for Christianity at BCS could easily be ignored, these people were Christians in name only. There were no Ruth's or Chuck's here.

The religious kids were made fun of. Nobody paid

attention in the requisite Bible class, which was a ridiculous excuse for the teacher to rant about her college years for an hour. Aside from the normal high school stuff, hanging out with friends, trying to be cool, various crushes and so-on, I was steadily on a road that would lead me to self destruction. It wouldn't stop at the normal teenage exploration of messing around and experimenting with drugs and alcohol. I was trying to find something, and if I couldn't find it outside of myself then I'd just turn off the switch. They had said I was bad, so I would try to show them what bad really was.

I, like most people of the human persuasion, hated high school. I didn't wear *Guess?*, I wasn't tiny. I wasn't content with doing homework, and toeing the line. I wanted to discover, I wanted to learn- I really didn't fit in. (I can hear the heads nodding in painful understanding.) Most of the girls were cute, small and quiet. I had huge boobs (thanks to God) and huge hips (thanks to my Armenian genes), and a huge butt (thanks to ice cream sandwiches for breakfast). I lumbered, while the other girls glided. If a boy gave me attention I tripped over myself, instead of coolly brushing him off. Were these High School girls another breed? Did they grow upon a girl-producing farm? Did they take classes in non-chalance? I couldn't have faked non-chalance if I'd tried. I was all rough material, all raw matter; anything that came from me was totally organic, baby. These girls came to school every day looking as if they had sprung from a factory, plastic packaging and all.

Oh, I tried to mainstream, believe me. I joined the cheerleading squad, and talked of boys and clothes. I bought some *Benetton* perfume, and wore the one skirt from *The Limited* clothing store I had out. Finally I gave up; the girls were shallow, and boring. I was never mainstream, why should I try to be? The bad crowd was way more fun. They were mostly dudes and I was comfortable around guys, they were real even if they were jerks, they didn't pretend that they weren't jerks. I knew who they were, and I knew where I stood with them. Some of the girls I went to high school with were so plastic, so wholly practiced, I wondered if they lead double lives. Did Tammy Swain come home from school, and transform into Cat Woman at night? I envisioned her in a shiny black costume. Hey, it made sense. All the "I'm so bored and perfect" had to end sometime. Right?

Also like most people on two legs at that age, had no idea who I was. Identity was something you dealt with at the DMV. At sixteen you really are just getting out of the doofy stage where your head and teeth are way out of proportion with your body. The religious groups, white supremacists, gangs, and various other vile organizations that prey on teenagers have got it right. At that point in your life, and I'm not telling you something you don't already know, you are ready to assume a mantle of anything that will help you make sense of yourself. Most kids choose lighter identities, like Jock, or Preppy, or Goth, or whatever it is these days. They choose something that can be easily discarded for a new vegan, bi-sexual, Birkenstock wearing identity at college, then traded in again when you are out in the real world, and the real soul searching starts. I was way too extreme for all that- for me it was all or nothing. When I arrived in high school, I knew it wouldn't be religion, so I hung out with the bad kids. I had been bad my whole life anyway, why not give it a try for real?

Doing bad things fed me. I did things just because they were *bad*, conducted like some sort of sick science experiment, I was going to uncover the mechanics of bad. I was the kid in the group who was ready to take it to the next level, with seeming fearlessness. This was actually the truth of it, I had done the other thing, been to the so-called good side, it was nothing like what people said it was. I was going to find out about the bad side. *How bad can it be?* I naively thought.

I'll admit my start was a little slow, making out, smoking pot. All things which in my previous world would have gotten open mouthed stares, but in the grand scheme of things really just part of normal teenage exploration. But I wasn't doing these things for themselves. Yeah, I was curious about pot, but had never really given it much thought until a bong hit was offered to me. I took it, coughed a lot, and instead of thinking, man this makes me feel….fill in the blank, I just had this feeling of exhilaration. I've gotten away with something. *Done something bad*, I thought. I had allowed the flimsy church definition of bad to become a sort of Holy Grail for me.

In High School, I felt Lost and Liberated. I was traveling between two completely opposite states, Hawaii and Wyoming. Wyoming was Lost. The watered down Christianity that I was now offered confused me even more. At Winter's Pass at least they *believed* that they believed it. Here at my new school, if they spoke of God, you got the feeling that they were reciting a poem, while thinking about what's for dinner, like having a conversation with someone who isn't listening. The teachers were sickening. They deified the students who spouted the Christian rhetoric, despite their actions or who they were inside, and they methodically demonized the kids who weren't from Christian homes, or who had no Christian upbringing. These were often the kids who needed love, support, and understanding the most of all, but instead they felt worse about themselves.

In this vast expanse of unknown territory I was hapless, hopeless, wandering. The things I tried to do to occupy time, only seemed to steal it. Lost can be a beautiful place, but it can also swallow you up.

My Liberated was Hawaii. I enjoyed the freedom to breathe. There was no one keeping a tight watch on me. I didn't hear about Hell as much, and I rarely heard about Salvation any more. It felt good, as if finally I was a horse drawing a carriage, and had accidentally become unhitched. The bit was gone, so I was free to speak. The reins were gone, so I could go where I wanted, there was no one telling me what to think, or even what to believe. I was free, and it was beautiful. But I'd usually only spend a day or two in this amazing landscape, the waves of freedom lapping at my feet before I'd wander back to no-man's land. My guilt always brought me back to Lost. So I continued to wander, nothing satisfied me.

***

Harrison Ford. Barring the uncanny name, and zero resemblance to the superstar, he was one of my good friends. Blond, cute, and with an odd sense of humor, Harrison was a Christian. I didn't care, though, because he never pushed anything on me, or made me feel like he was better than me. In the back of my mind I knew that the church he went to was different than the subdued Baptist church that ran the school, but it was never any of my concern until he invited me to go to church with him.

"Church? You want me to go to church? Man, I have had enough of that. I'm churched out" I said over my turkey sandwich in the lunchroom.

"I promise you'll like it, it is cool" he said, casually trying to convince me. He had the sweetest smile.

"How can church be cool?" I thought of the deacons dressing up like whatever pop culture icon they thought would give them an instant *in* with the kids, and how unbelievably stupid they looked. I wanted no part of that.

"No. They have awesome music, a real band. My youth pastor is really cool. I promise that if you hate it, I'll never ask you again."

A band, I thought. My interest was piqued. *A band at church. How does THAT work?* I tried to keep my face emotionless. I certainly didn't want him to think I was curious or even mildly interested.

"Let me think about it" I said.

Finally I agreed to go, mostly because I really liked Harrison, and respected him a lot. And any place with a real band can't suck too bad, I rationalized.

We set out for New Glory Christian center on a Wednesday night in April. I said I'd go with him to their Wednesday night youth group, expecting a bunch of middle aged youth leaders trying halfheartedly to be hip. Lots of talk about drugs, alcohol, and keeping your virginity, with a nightcap of chips, dip and soda. But I'd rather do a Wednesday night, than a Sunday morning getting dressed up (*did I even own a dress anymore?*) and listening to some egomaniac rant.

Boy, was I wrong.

From the second we walked into the youth center and the smell of new wood hit me, I knew that THESE people were different. First of all, it was a real band. Guitars, drums, bass, amps, the real deal. They sounded very rock n roll, but they were singing about Jesus. It was a little

53

strange, hearing that music, coupled with religious lyrics, but I had to admit, I kind of enjoyed it. As far as I was concerned I was exploring a hitherto unknown planet.

Everyone was standing. Everyone had their hands swaying in the air, their eyes closed, fervently praying. Even the kids my age! The standard teenage rule was that it wasn't cool to be a Christian. I looked around. There were no rebellious kids sulking in the back, I couldn't believe it! I quickly turned around not wanting to miss any of the spectacle.

The girl next to me was speaking some strange tongue, it sounded like someone stuttering a foreign language. *Da-dada-muh-kit-kit- whar-duh-duh-duh.* I knew from all the Bible teaching I'd had that this was called "praying in tongues". I studied her. She seemed caught up in another world, eyes closed tight, lost in spiritual ecstasy. It was very bizarre, but fascinating, kind of like watching a National Geographic show. I checked myself, and was surprised that I didn't feel even the least bit uncomfortable. It was odd, yeah, but it was like Winter's Pass had mutated into an entirely different creature, a brand new being. Something interesting, something with heart.

After all the singing, I knew what was next. *The famous salvation message*, I thought sarcastically. *Oh well, shows over. This is the part where all of this Jesus lovin' charade will fall apart and the hypocrisy underneath will be uncovered.* I knew that this was when they would come down on us hard, and was a little mad at myself for getting so into it. I slumped back in my chair, folded my arms and waited for the inevitable.

As the youth pastor took the stage, I looked in my purse for a scrap of paper, and prepared to doodle my way through the remainder of the message, thinking that watching paint dry would be more interesting. As the message unfolded I realized that I was wrong, he was interesting. Real. He gave intimate details of his life. He admitted to his faults, and saw them as a gateway to being closer to God. There was no falseness here. And it wasn't all about salvation, like it was at Winter's Pass. He seemed to talk about life. Living. He wasn't waiting for the day God would rescue him from this wicked world. He wanted to experience God now.......here. He was serious, funny, and passionately believed all of it. Instead of the normal, boring, self-righteous message, this was one of humility and love, with a good splash of humor thrown in. I found myself listening to his message intently, forgetting I was even holding a piece of paper until he was done. I ashamedly put it back in my purse.

Afterwards when we were all munching on chips and talking, or "fellowshipping" as they called it, the youth pastor, Tom, approached me. He was a little intimidating as I was used to people trying to convert me, or condescendingly telling me that I'd better repent. Tom was different. His appearance wasn't particularly striking. He was tall and had an ordinary looking face, but he had so much personality and passion it seemed to be on the edge of bursting out of him. For some reason it wasn't the least bit hokey, or it didn't seem to be.

"Hi" he said brightly. "What did you think of the service?"

"It was alright" I said casually, veiling my eyes, so he couldn't read them. I don't think that I wanted to admit to myself how much I'd actually enjoyed it.

"Well, we'd love to have you back" he said with a genuine smile, and then walked away.

That was it. No preaching. No acting superior. He

talked to me like I was his equal, I was stunned. Several minutes later his very pretty, very sweet wife, Lindsay came up to me, and we had basically the same conversation. I was blown away......this was user-friendly Christianity.

All the way home I tried to pretend that the whole thing hadn't gotten to me. I kept thinking over and over, *these people mean it! All of them. Not just one or two. They all mean it!* I couldn't figure it out. It was the complete opposite of what I'd been exposed to, I had no idea that such a thing even existed.

A week later, when I was invited to a Home Bible study group at one of the kid's houses, I accepted. The house was dimly lit and packed with kids my age, and it was alive with excitement. There were one or two adults casually chatting, and drinking Cokes, everyone else was talking and laughing. It looked like fun. I went outside to smoke a cigarette, figuring I'd check out the "bad" kids. There were only two, and THEY were the odd ones out. After sucking down a cig in the cold, I decided to go inside and see what these people were all about. I recognized a girl from my study hall, Elizabeth.

"Hey, I didn't know you went to this church." I said, half-surprised. Liz and I raided the vending machines at the school, and she was one of the only really cool girls I knew.

"Yeah" she said with a half-grin, "this is my house." My mouth dropped open. She was cool, AND a Christian.

Maybe there was such a thing as a cool Christian? Obviously there was something to this. Maybe they could help me figure it all out.

Unfortunately, I have never been one for subtlety. I don't eat just one chocolate, I eat the whole box. I only show restraint when I am forced into it.

Obsessive perfectionist extremism is my middle name.

The smart thing would have been to start slow with this new church. Be objective. Look at what the people in the church did and not what they said they did. Read. Take breaks. Think about what level of commitment I wanted, if any. Instead, I was so overwhelmed by the apparent zeal for God I had severely lacked all my life that I jumped right in the New Glory swimming pool, clothes and all.

***

"But dad" I whined. "I want to do this." I had a garbage bag full of all my worldly things. Iron Maiden tapes, silk wall hangings of the Doors, even a Guns-n-Roses license plate that said *Axl Rows*. It had hung over my bed for two years. A good $350.00 worth of tapes, and music paphernalia. What was I going to do with it? I was going to burn it all at a church meeting.

"Tara, listen to me," my dad said from his ever present place on his brown recliner. "You are rolling down a hill so fast that you can't see where you are going. Why don't you sell those things? Why burn them?" From him, this was more of a statement than a question.

I recited back Tom's words, proud of myself. "Because they aren't good for my spiritual development." *Rolling down a hill*, I thought. *Humph. I'm the one that is doing the right thing. He is just blinded by his own sin and pride. I'll pray for him.*

I had only been at the church for two months, but I had been a sponge. Soaking up anything, and everything I could learn. I was half crazed with the joy of my re-connection to the Higher Power, and drunk with the reality of my new friends and spiritual family. I was gone, far gone.

I remember that fire, as one remembers color and light. It was a red fire, and not particularly brash. I expected the flames to consume the evil in my belongings, but instead it just slowly melted them. Axl Rose's face became a hot pile of black goo. As we went in for some hamburgers afterwards, I had that stab of an old feeling. *This is it? Sin and hamburgers? Where is GOD in all this?* I shook it off.

Quickly, my parents' uninvolvement in the church became an issue for me, a rallying point. A common occurrence was for a random adult to pity my poor lonesome self on Sunday mornings.

"You poor thing, your parents aren't saved, are they?" the church secretary patted me on the back and walked away.

Huh? While I was trying to figure this out, the cute guitarist in the church band spoke for me.

"No, her mom is definitely saved, I don't think her dad is. Her parents go to this boring Baptist church." He seemed confident that this was the truth.

I had never looked at it like this. *Poor old me.* My parents thought I was a going a little overboard for joining the church, and they continued to go to Winter's Pass despite my numerous protests. The handsome guitarist for the youth group, Mike, seemed to gather from the one time he'd met them that I was indeed a poor old me. I had no support at home (of course, I didn't mention the fact that even though it wasn't their thing, they supported, and put up with my zealous and supremely annoying fanaticism). But that patronizing pat on the back put the whole thing in motion, it was poison that entered my veins. There was now a clear divide, *us* and *them*. We were the righteous.

God's Army. The truth bearers. I had really stumbled on the truth, and I was a part of something everlasting. The church encouraged and pushed this kind of thinking. I failed to see that this was the same message that Winter's Pass served, wrapped up in a more palatable package, nevertheless I believed it. Here was my young unseasoned brain:

In this corner: Tara, the sixteen year old phenomenon, and her posse the New Glory Crew! They have the Truth! They know God! Aaaannnnnddd they are kind and Jesus-like enough to share this truth!

In the opposing corner: (cue *Jaws* music) the world! They are going to Hell and don't know it. They are ALL blinded by Satan. They cannot win! They are everybody but Tara and her exclusive crew!

New Glory Christian Center was located on what used to be a pecan plantation. It was huge, and picturesque, with rolling open fields, a large sanctuary, and clusters of buildings. There were tennis courts and a swimming pool, even apartments and a movie theatre to show Christian movies located on the premises. It was like a large compound, and the sanctuary could seat over a thousand people.

I liked everyone I met there. All the adults had this accessible thing about them, which for a teenager used to adults trying to control them, was a big deal. They seemed to be real, and they all seemed to love God with all their hearts. They insisted I call them by their first names, something that took me forever to get used to.

"Mr. White!" I'd say shouting for the junior pastor to help me with a question.

"Tara, I've told you so many times, it's Bill!" He'd

say, firmly, but smiling.

"Ok, Bill" I said, wincing. I wasn't used to an adult treating me like an equal, even enjoying my company. It was hard to swallow.

I remember the first time I saw the church, on a balmy Sunday morning. The outside looked like a creepy Waco/warehouse crossbreed. I was a little scared to go in.

Walking in the main sanctuary I was instantly swallowed up by the expanse of it. Gave the impression of holiness it did, it was as big as God himself. You could have probably landed an airplane comfortably in there. It smelled the holy smell of fresh paint and newness. Newness was definitely holy. It was a car that had never been driven, argued in, rear ended, it had never had coffee spilled in it, there were no Mc Donald's french fries petrified under the car seats. The sanctuary always gave off the impression that this was the first time you had ever stepped through its pearly gates.

The carpet was a Gibson Girl mauve, the seats were periwinkle. There was no hiding under safe sturdy browns, reds and boring yellows. The color scheme screamed life! Glamour! And passion! The platform where Pastor Sam preached, and the musicians played was the perfect accessible height. It was satiny polished wood, and usually clogged with amps, speakers and the red and silver of musical instruments. Guitars, drum sets, keyboards and podium all tangled in wires coming from every which way. It looked like a plate of silver outer-space spaghetti.

Enormous handmade tapestries hung on the wall, each one depicting a part of Jesus' life. Like the pop-up touch me books for kids with fuzzy chicks, and horse's manes to touch and feel, each detail had been made with a different fabric, and different materials. Each detail shouted "notice me!" from the enormous walls.

Jesus' scratchy burlap coat showed his humble roots as a carpenter from Nazareth.

The royal deep purple satin that hung over the empty cross made you know that indeed a King had walked among us.

The real thorns on the crown of his agony had the same effect on everyone. They brought up goose bumps.

The sanctuary was 11,000 square feet of posh, polished magnificence.

If the church was a great book, then Pastor Sam was the index. Helpful, yes, but most of the time mind numbingly boring. He really was a nice guy, spacey, maybe a little flaky, but nice as he could be. He didn't seem to have a bit of an ego. He knew everyone by name. He really cared, or seemed to. The most important part of pastoring (in my opinion), he excelled at. When it came to the hands-on part: helping people, visiting nursing homes, etc, he blew the haughty distance that you get from most pastors out of the water. But all in all you got the impression that he would have been a better accountant, or farmer, or stock broker- his verbal and oratory skills were lacking.

On a Sunday morning the church swallowed him up, it overtook him. With the music that grabbed you and shook you till you *had* to feel something, to the squadron of men in little neon jackets with flashlights to direct parking, you got the feeling that this was a major operation. It all seemed so much bigger than his occasional surprisingly inspirational, but most of the time bland, meandering sermons. You expected someone with the charisma of Winston Churchill, instead you got Where's Waldo? Nice yes, but not exactly riveting reading.

I stayed for the music. I think most people stayed for

the same reason.

It was like God was a lover/partner, and the music and beautiful surroundings were a romantic candlelit dinner for two. You made your connection during a time they called "praise and worship". Where Winter's Pass relied on fear, guilt, and Hell to keep people on track, New Glory dazzled you with riches, and courted you with joy and emotional stimulation…..and kick ass music. You came back for your weekly fix.

It was a Sunday morning pick- me- up. No matter what else was going on in your life at the time, no matter what crappy job you had, or what state your marriage was in, you could get dressed up and go to another place. You could go to a palace with marbled halls, and YOU belonged, you belonged as much as the person seated next to you. You became something important.

The church services were intense, with singing, shouting, and music that played for hours. Sometimes the musicians would just jam, letting the music flow. They were all accomplished musicians, having played with some big names in "the world". The music constantly touched me, and I felt like God himself was speaking through the huge black speakers.

See, as a kid, Vacation Bible School was fun. Everyone was happy, and the songs, crafts, games, and snacks carefully hid the message….the message that was drilled into you all day, but that you didn't notice because you were having so much fun. The songs that you shouted and rowdily marched to (I'm in the Lord's Army) The songs with the elaborate hand gestures, that the boys always took too far and had to be told to take it down a notch, (This Little Light of Mine), and the sand art, finger paints, and paper windsocks that we made all proudly displayed the Jesus fish, or the Cross. We were kids. We were having fun. We were being indoctrinated, and didn't know it.

Somewhere, though, I guess when they figure you are old enough to think for yourself (ironic, isn't it) the fun goes away, and at Winter's Pass was replaced with a sour expression, and a binding, suffocating lifestyle. All of the sudden fun wasn't needed to mask what you should be doing, you were expected to do it. Fearful imaginings of Hell kept you on the right track.

This was where New Glory got it right; they cleverly kept the fun in. The music would rival that of any modern band, and that kept us interested. The church outings were mostly to those massive adult play centers with arcade games, bumper cars, and bungee jumps. They didn't wear outdated sack dresses or shun society, they were very fashionable people. They looked normal.

We were wild, radical, and it was all for Jesus. Those *smart smart* charismatics. I liked to live life too much to adopt the rigors of pinchy-face religion. I could be myself at my new church, for the most part. As long as I added a "praise Jesus", or wore a radical to the point of disturbing T-shirt, I could have as much fun as I wanted without looking over my shoulder thinking the devil was following me. New Glory said that God *wanted* us to have fun, not quiet fun, like sewing, but loud fun, like riding the Scorpion rollercoaster 10 times in a row, yelling your head off. At the end of the day when you sat down for the message, you were ready for some quiet. New Glory had the right formula.

I loved my new "family". This church fulfilled the need for definition in me. I finally had a purpose; I finally had a reason to exist. The wandering and exploration of youth was bypassed, and replaced with instant canned understanding. The church was my extended family and the youth group was my close family, I spent most of my time with them. The Youth Leaders were fun people, most of them being only a few years older than the oldest kid in the youth group.

Delia Beaken was one of the first to "welcome me into the flock". Like most of the women there, she had strayed from the church during her teens with disastrous results. She was an artist, and something about her was very strong, very New –York-Poetry- Room- Goddess-like. She was beautiful, with high cheekbones, and a straightforward way of talking that made her get rebukes from some of the elders. She wore interesting velvet patchwork clothes, and had long pale fingers that seemed to bring the best out of a paint and paintbrush. I wanted to be like her. She would have fit in just as well in a N.O.W. parade as in a Sunday school service.

As we sat in my stuffy Prelude on a sticky hot Wednesday night, she told me her story, it was the standard one I was to hear over and over again. But this was the first time I was to hear it, and I was appalled and enthralled. Winter's Pass never talked about stuff like that.

"At one point, after having my sixth abortion, I tried to kill myself by smashing my head on the bathtub. I was smacked out on coke." She said this, and her high cheekbones shone like an ivory carving. I sat there still as night, and listened to the rest of her story. I was a sheltered sixteen and couldn't imagine anyone that wasn't on a TV show ever having to live through anything like that, and better yet sitting here in front of me. I suppressed an urge to reach out and touch her to see if she was an apparition.

"What happened next?"

"Somehow I managed to survive. But the Lord was still trying to get my attention."

She told her story and the night drew darker. When she was done and I said all my ooh' s and ahh's, I was convinced that either this God they worshipped was the real deal, or she was some sort of carved out Goddess herself. I'll never forget what she said when we finally got out of the car to go home.

"I like you, Tara" she said as she smiled a rare smile at me.

I didn't know how to answer that so I said awkwardly "thanks."

The women in this church were equal with the men, or appeared to be at first. There was still that whole *women must submit* thing, but even the pastor insisted that he AND his wife were the pastors of the church. Occasionally there was a woman pastor that would come through, and the women I liked best, the Youth Leaders were my role models. They were all strong, admirable women, some of which I will never forget.

As I write about Lindsay, Geena, Delia, and my favorite, Kore, my heart opens and swells with love. These women were the Goddess before I was conscious of Her. They were strong, proud, flawed, beautiful, Mothers, Maidens and Crones. They took me under their rainbow wings, and I believed they loved me. They didn't judge, and equally opened up to me as I showed my bare emotions to them. We gathered on those church outings, crying together, praying together, hugging, and feeling completely o.k. with our feminity and our power as women.

I've told you about Delia with her Scandinavian skin,

African cheekbones, and dry speech. Next up was Lindsay. She happened to be Tom's wife, and while she wasn't the kind of woman I was used to, she was sweet. Fun, and supportive, but quiet. She had a tranquil way, and a peaceful aura. I usually hung out with loud, bold women, so I learned from her that you can be quiet, and just as strong as the loud women around you.

I met Geena at a picnic. Geena was very tall, with a mess of blond curls, and an anything goes attitude. She was a total goofball, and a whole lot of fun. Geena was the kind of fun that you have when you are a kid, the unhindered, unburdened kind- the laughing, dirty, messy, free kind. She carried this around inside her, and looked for every opportunity to work it. Her Ex-Navy background made me extra comfortable with her. I knew this woman had probably heard everything, so when I had a particularly shocking problem, or thought, I went to her. Without so much as a flicker of disdain in her face, she listened, and always helped.

Her best friend and partner in crime was Kore, the one I remember most fondly of all.

Kore had been through a world of hurt. Abused by her stepfather until the time she was eighteen, she went through a string of abusive relationships, and drugs. After rehab she came to the church, and married a nice man. She had made it through hell, and had created a nice life for herself and her family. I was over their house a lot. Something about her was very reachable, accessible.

I noticed a phenomenon at around this time. When I had a problem, question, or issue, I started going exclusively to these four women. Was it because they were the be all and end all? No. It was because sometimes they *didn't* have answers. I noticed that when I went to most of the pastors (who happened to be men) they always had an answer. Tom was the exception. But the others had an answer to anything and everything I said. Sometimes I really felt them listen, more often, I felt them tune out, and their admonitions seemed like pat answers. But when I went to one of these four women, they kept it real. If they didn't have an answer they would pause, then say, "Well, Tara, I don't know, you should pray about it." They were humans, not robots.

Kore was the most real of these women. I watched her struggle with her nature, and I watched her ride highs and lows. She spoke in a soft voice, and made little cooing sounds when she talked and listened. Coming from anyone else this would have been off-putting, but it fit her. She was broken and strong. Sad, and full of love. Tall (our church had a lot of really tall women), pretty, and with the gait of a model. She cried a lot, and I never knew if this was for the present, past or future, her tears flowed from all women and out of her. She felt every pain that has ever been felt by every woman that has ever felt it, and she bore it all with willingness and dignity. It was her *humanity* that touched me and changed me. Outside of the God cloak we all wore, and all the God-talk, she had running through her the true current of the Divine. It was in every tear, every coo, every day in which I thought, *this woman can't handle life*, and every day in which I thought *this woman could rule the world if she wanted to*. She was so much bigger and smaller than the church, and I am happy to have known her.

Seeing these women and all of my new friends was a treat. I was at church whenever their doors were open. Sunday mornings, and nights. Wednesday nights. I often lamented that we should have church more often. I was starving, and couldn't get enough. I became a walking "hallelujah".

This brand of Christianity had room for my emotional nature. At Winter's Pass emotions were something to be suppressed, hidden. Emotions led to sin. At New Glory, they were encouraged. Excitement about God. Passion about God. Love for God. Tears for God. Jumping, shouting, hand-waving, kneeling, dancing, anything short of stripping was encouraged. Somewhere deep inside I knew that if I allowed my emotions to come out concerning Divinity, then maybe I could define this life-long relationship with the Higher Power, figure out where Christianity fit in. New Glory was an outlet for that. As began dating Mike, the guitarist for the youth group, I thought, *life can't get any better.*

***

"She actually believes there is a whale in the Mississippi!" I heard someone shout out in laughter, snapping me out of my daydreaming. I turned to see who they were teasing, ah, *poor Wendy. A nice girl, but a little slow*, I reflected. Turning to face the party, I smiled. This was going to be one heck of a week.

It was a very hot July, and I was on my way to Oklahoma for a youth revival at Oral Roberts University. The large bus was stifling, loud, and crowded, but I was having a wonderful time. Never before in my life had I had so many friends. *Real friends*, I thought to myself, looking out over the Mississippi river. People that cared about me, as much as I cared about them. My thoughts drifted to Winter's Pass, and the careless religion they practiced. *Not here*, I thought triumphantly.

I smiled to myself as I cornered Tom on the bus.

"But what does it MEEEAAANNN??" I had whined to Tom for the fiftieth time.

"Tara, speaking in tongues is not something you can make happen, it is a gift from God. Please quit asking me about it. All you can do is ask for it. Let go, Tara, and God will fulfill your prayers." Tom was patient with me, but I knew I was getting on his nerves, I had been bugging him for months. I was determined to learn everything about speaking in tongues I could get my hands on.

Basically the story goes like this…..a bunch of apostles including Paul were waiting in the "upper room" for Jesus, when all of the sudden they spoke with tongues of "fire". It was the spiritual equivalent of a Red Bull, supercharging you, and giving you the ability for the "Holy Spirit to pray through you". New Glory said that the ability to speak in tongues was a gift from God, and they called it being "filled with the Holy Spirit", or "baptized in the Holy Spirit".

Gifts of the spirit were cool, a nice perk of belonging to this new church. There were actually GIFTS. They didn't want to take things away; they wanted to give me something. I found it consistent with the "celebrate life" mentality that these people seemed to have. Fun, gifts, the Lord wanted us to have it all.

*"Being **slain in the Spirit** is a term related to the charismatic movement and Pentecostalism which describes a religious behavior in which a person loses motor control over their body and falls to the floor during an event they perceive as a personal encounter with God's glory and power, usually associated with occasions of public prayer*

ministry when the laying on of hands is practiced."

I had plenty of experience with the other gifts. I remember the first time I saw people getting "slain in the spirit", it was a little freaky. People going up to the front of the church, the pastor walking around and laying their hands on the person's heads, and the congregation member falling to the floor. They dropped like dominoes. I used to think *not everyone feels like they can't stand up, there is no way*. But that is what it was supposed to be about….the power of the Lord was so strong that when they prayed for you it pulsed like a God-laser beam out of their hands and into you, you couldn't help but fall. There were a few big, burly dudes that caught you and gently laid you to the ground, and there was also a stack of shiny purple cloths that a designated woman would cover your legs with if you were wearing a skirt. It was a production.

I tried it for the first time after I'd been going there a while.

It's now or never.

The front of the church was a little intimidating. I could see an eager line of people standing there praying, hands outstretched, eyes closed, looking as if they were fighting some imaginary brain-worm. Pastor Sam and Pastor Bill worked in tandem, praying for every other person, weaving in and out of the bodies, some standing, some lying down, mumbling gibberish. As I walked to the front it dawned on me that I should have gotten up sooner. The area was so packed I felt like I was at a concert looking for a good view of the stage. I ended up being on the vestiges of the altar, and wondering if they were coming my way.

What if it doesn't work? I wondered. I kept my eyes

closed to show that I was ready. Would I feel a zing, a pop, a hit? Would it be more like warm apple butter being poured over my head? Would their hands be sweaty? I tried to focus on God as they made it over to me.

Soon they were next to me, and I could smell the pastor's cologne as he prayed over the woman to my right. I tried to detect the moment when she fell if there was any extra power coming off of him; I didn't feel anything. I had no time to ponder this, because before I knew it his big, heavy hands were I on me, and a person came up behind me to catch. I waited. He prayed harder. I felt slightly intimidated, like I was supposed to perform, but nothing happened. I felt his intensity, but nothing from the Holy Spirit. I waited more, and I could tell he was getting frustrated.

Would I fall anyway? I guess that was the question. Would I wait for the "spirit of God" or would I fake it if it didn't work? I didn't want to fake it, but I knew most people did. I guess in the end it was nice to just lie there and pray. I'd always preferred reclining to sitting or standing anyway ....maybe I was Roman in a past life.

So I fell. It was kinda fun, but I felt like a fraud. When the woman came and placed the purple cloth over my skirt, it was heavier that I thought it would be. My thoughts as I lay there blasphemously drifted to what was for lunch, or whether Mike would be at the pizza joint or the hairs that were growing out of Pastor Sam's nose that I tried not to notice. I guess I wasn't holy enough.

I didn't care too much about being slain in the spirit, though. I had some of the other gifts, most importantly, the gift of prophecy (which would turn out to be a natural psychic gifting in later years), and tongues.......... tongues fascinated me.

I didn't like the fact that I'd been praying about tongues for months "God if this is real and you want me to have it, then I want it, but I'm not going to fake it", and nothing happened. All my friends had given me advice, and prayed for me. People had said to just start praying, and it will come out, I did, and nothing came out but English words. I even tried a couple of times; mumbling a bit, seeing if it would "open the gate". All I felt was foolish.

But some people DID fake it, I even fancied that I could tell the difference. I kept this observation to myself, and just watched the congregation on Sunday morning, spotting who I thought was faking it and who was not-you could tell by the way it sounded. Real speaking in tongues was varied. It had a different sound that was exclusive to each person, kind of like an accent. It actually sounded like a repetitive language. The people who were faking it seemed to only have one or two syllables they kept repeating. That was another difference, the people who really had it, seemed to actually have something speaking through them, they opened their mouths, and someone else's words came out. With the people who faked it, it seemed like THEY were speaking the words. I was absolutely sure I didn't want this. If it wasn't real, and God didn't want me to have it, I rationalized, then I wasn't going to do it. Period.

We arrived at ORU, tired but excited. The university was packed. I had never seen so many kids before, there were thousands. Unpacking my things in our dorm room, we started getting ready for the evening church service. I wondered, *would tonight be the night?* The services were supposed to be the highlight of our days at camp, lessons, games, and then a big blowout at night. They didn't disappoint. When I first stepped into the college auditorium, filled with church groups from all across the country, my mouth dropped open. Music rang through the wide open space like a flock of doves released from heaven, pure white wings whispering against our seeking faces. As the first strains of the guitar started, I knew I was in for a ride.

Needless to say the service was amazing. At the end, a time they call "altar call", I went up hoping it would happen. But nothing did. Nothing. The promise of a week's worth of chances to be "filled with the spirit" kept me from moping on the way back to our dorms.

As the days and more importantly, nights went by and nothing continued to happen, I started getting worried. It wasn't that I didn't trust God, I just thought maybe the problem was with ME? Members of my youth group started to look at me funny. I thought, *half of you wouldn't have it either, if you didn't fake it*. I was getting a little bitter.

I started examining my life, and questioning. Was it the fact that I still questioned everything, including authority? That was still too ingrained in me, I would never lose that, I prospected. Was it the fact that I judged people? I had started inspecting each of my friends lives, and doing a checks and balances thing. Elizabeth. Unequally yoked (she was dating a half- hearted Christian) check for the cons list. Brought up in the church. Check for the pro's list. SHE was spirit filled. *What did she have that I didn't? Was I just not holy enough?* All my friends offered support, but Tom was the only one that made sense.

"Tara, you just have to trust God." He said, sitting me down after lunch, obviously worried about how obsessive I'd gotten. "I promise you that there is nothing WRONG with you. God loves us all the same. When it is time, He will answer your prayer. Trust, let go. You have to let go." Tom always knew exactly what to say. I felt at ease, even though this was Friday, and the last night we were here, I didn't care. I trusted God and that was there long before I had joined this church. I went outside and prayed.

Standing in the open Oklahoma field, I looked up to the dark blue expansive sky.

"God, I'm sorry that I have tried to figure this out myself. I'm sorry that I have tried to make it happen. The truth is, outside of all these people, and all this commotion, and even outside of this wonderful new church, I trust you, as I have done all my life. I give this back to you, and I'm not even going to think about it anymore." Walking away, I felt like a huge burden had been lifted off of me. I let go.

"Lord, if anyone wants to accept you as their savior let them come to the front" the singer was sweaty and out of breath. The service had been intense, and the music even more so. The room vibrated with electricity, and the sound of weeping accompanied the wailing guitar, and rhythm of the drums. The auditorium of thousands was swaying, crying, dancing, and praying out loud. I was at peace, having let go of my desire, and had been free to enjoy the service. In fact, I hadn't even thought of it once.

"Now Lord, if there be any who have special requests let them come forth now." The small space at the front of the stage was rushed. The thought entered my mind. *Maybe I should go? Nah, it is too crowded. Besides, I have given up on trying with the intensity of my prayers to make it happen. I will just sit here and enjoy this.* Satisfied with the results of my dialogue with myself, I wrapped my sweater around me tighter in the chilly auditorium, and settled into watching, a silent prayer in my mind.

Something caught my eye. It was my friend Rachel, one row down, looking at me with bug eyes, pointing to the front. *Go,* she was silently mouthing. I looked over at Tom, he gave me a knowing smile, and nodded. *What can it hurt,* I thought.

Making my way to the front was difficult. There were so many kids praying, kneeling, singing, and oblivious to anyone around them, much less one who was trying to get by. I finally made it to a small clearing I had spotted, a little annoyed with all the maneuvering I had to do. *Let go,* I said to myself. This had become my little mantra. Letting go had given me peace, it had made sense to me. I took a deep breath, and let it out. I slowly lifted my hands, opened my mouth and said,"God"......all of the sudden it was as if the sky had opened up to me. I saw God, and He was smiling. It felt like I knew every inch of something as vast as the ocean. I had never felt anything like it, and at that moment lost all idea of time, name, or body. I only wanted to be with him. It was when I became aware of my surroundings, I realized that I had fallen to the floor, and I was speaking in tongues. I couldn't believe it. I heard it come out of my mouth, as if someone was speaking through me.

I remembered the rest of that night, like one remembers big days in their life. Your wedding day, the birth of your children. Every detail, feeling, word spoken, sticking out with the mental headline proclaiming the title of the day. "Today is my wedding day!" or in my case, "today I know without the shadow of a doubt there is a God!"

As we went back to our dorm rooms, I was afraid to breathe for fear that it had all been a dream. It wasn't the fact that I could speak in tongues, which seemed like a side effect. For a moment, when I was standing up at the altar, it seemed like God showed himself to me. It was as if the heavens had split open. Being the realist that I am, it was exactly as I wanted it. I was positively sure that months later, when it was just a memory, small pieces of doubt creeping into my mind, there was nothing that I could have blamed, or named as an illusion. I wasn't fasting. I wasn't expecting anything, I wasn't emotionally worked up. I wasn't tired, I was perfectly sober, almost bored. God knew how it had to be for me. I had trusted, and let go. It was one of the most remarkable experiences of my life, and my first real sensory connection with God since feeling the waves of the earth 10 years earlier. Something deep within me was satisfied.

Let me tell you that this thing really freaking happened to me, and now, as a Witch, I STILL pray in tongues. It was a natural occurrence for me, and still feels very natural and spiritual to me. Back then though, disappointingly enough, no one seemed to share my enthusiasm "but it was reeeeeal" I would say, almost bursting with joy at the recollection of the meeting, my eyes glazed over in otherworldly bliss. I wanted the person I was talking to, to share what I had felt. To KNOW. All I got was a vague, uncomfortable smile, or among my most zealous of friends a distracted hallelujah.

Unfortunately I was a huge influence on my younger siblings. I managed to drag my very resigned sister, Vanessa, into the church, and my dad promptly freaked out when I brought Ness home one night after she had "received the Holy Spirit". She was bent over double, and mumbling and laughing. She had had a real experience, but coming from her, someone who is not comfortable showing that much emotion, they thought she had been drugged. They sat me down, and tried to get through my thick tunnel-vision brain just why this would scare them. My dad had even gotten out the little doctor light thingy from his kit, and checked her pupils. My poor parents. I should have been beat for what I put them through.

But it gets worse for them. The rest of my high school years were a parade of school days and church nights. My days out of school were spent doing outreach concerts, home Bible study groups and endless prayer sessions. My parents and siblings put up with the Christian Joy Mask I wore, and every life situation that was given to me I turned into a reason to talk about, sing about or cry about God. My experience with speaking in tongues had given me a confidence…a surety that what I was doing was the only way. It had poured gasoline on an already raging fire.

OH MY GOD was I obnoxious. Let me just apologize to anyone who had to put up with me for that chunk of my life. I was out of my element when I wasn't at church, so like the proverbial round peg into a square hole, I tried to make everything a rush of Christian excitement. In high school they didn't know what to do with me; the bad girl had changed into this weepy,crazy-eyed Jesus freak. No one at my high school had seen anything like it. I was always crying about some awesome thing that God had done for me, quoting Bible verses, or droning on and on about Jesus-this-and-that. So they made me class chaplain, and once a week I got up in front of the class and had "devotions". I think they did this to get rid of me, or give me a formal outlet for all that blabbering. Most of the time, when I was preaching everyone was busy setting Taco Bell wrappers on fire (very popular when I was in high school, they light up pretty fast), or talking loudly. I can't blame them, who would want to hear the over-the-top Christian weirdo get up and cry for the thousandth time. This was High School for God's sake.

As the years went on I became so intolerable that I ended up sitting by myself in the lunchroom, I had chased away all my friends. This was a Christian school, and no one wanted to sit next to the Christian. Yes, I was that obnoxious.

I wore the most annoying T-shirts. They had phrases like "Jesus, the real thing" written with the backdrop of the Coca-Cola logo. Then there was the really cool "Pick Three, Father, Son and Holy Spirit" one, which looked like a lottery pick, complete with balls and all. It wasn't enough that my mouth couldn't stop sharing the "truth", now my clothes had to talk, too. As high school graduation approached I started cultivating a vision of being a minister, having my own church. I dared not mention this to anyone yet, because

1. My family, namely my dad would never go for it, and

2. I wasn't sure if it was what God had "called" me to do.

Nevertheless, it was what I wanted.

I was such a fanatic, what else would the world do with me? I had structured my life, and friends so that I didn't fit anywhere but the church. As my peers were weighing their options in life "should I major in Psych?" or "I wonder if I should accept that scholarship?" I had cornered myself into one option.

Lifelong service to God in the ministry.

Chapter Three

"The shadow-the energetic counterforce of God- loves
to play in the fields of religion."
-Marianne Williamson, *The Shadow Effect:*
Illuminating the Hidden Power of Your True Self

"Are you sure you want to do this?" My Bible college
counselor squeaked as I gathered up the paperwork.

The small mouse of a man had no idea what I was up
against. But I felt confident, I had done two years of
community college like my parents wanted….surely they
would support me going to Bible College. It had been a
long two years. Everything I did, from my job at
Applebee's, where the other employees kept a safe distance
from me, to community college where I had regular
arguments about the validity of the Bible with my World
Literature teacher, a small Jamaican woman, I was
becoming more and more sure that Bible college was for
me.

It could all be summed up in two words: Baked Beans.

It was my crazy, red haired, multiple dog scented
English teacher. She had written a story about Baked Beans
that had gotten published, and that was all we heard about.
Day after day we argued in class, she was one of those
teachers that liked to discuss anything and everything with
us. She wanted to know our business, and my business was
the Lord, so I gave it to her, and I think she liked having an
antagonist. We'd argue, me for amusement and to pass time
in class, her because she had some real beef with
Christianity, and I was the closest thing in her liberal,

coffee house, artsy- fartsy world that came near that. I felt her anger, and chalked it up to her lost soul, but the fact that she didn't get to me bothered her. One day she took it too far.

It was a regular community college day. Sociology with the boring teacher, but sitting next to the cute guy, skip world history because the teacher was a flake, biology with the eccentric girl studying to be a mortician, finishing with the crazy redhead teacher that would argue with me all through class. Then off to my job at the Christian radio station.

"Look at the princess" she said under her breath as I walked in.

She is especially prickly today.

We opened our books as she approached the podium. I could feel her boring a hole into my head as we flipped to the page detailing Sylvia Plath. She wanted to fight, and frankly it was getting old, I was losing steam. She tried to pull me into an argument.

"Sylvia was an atheist, everyone read the chapter on her, except you, Tara. I know that is against your religion." The class laughed. I said nothing. *Weak, lady that was weak.*

Blah blah blah, she went on. The class was about to wrap up when I raised my hand. I had a question about an upcoming assignment. She was waiting to pounce.

"When is the assignment on Tolkien due?" I questioned.

"Like you care. Whatever you turn in will be crap anyway" she said.

My mouth dropped open momentarily, and then fury came over me. She wouldn't treat me like that because I had allowed myself to become her punching bag. I quickly retorted.

"YOU WILL NOT TALK TO ME LIKE THAT IN FRONT OF THE CLASS!" I yelled. The class gasped.

She kept it up "it's not like you pay attention."

I stood up, shouting now "what you think of my performance in this class is between you and me, you WILL NOT talk like that in front of anyone but me, if that is your opinion!"

The bell rang.

"See me in an hour, Tara" she said as I stormed out.

When I came back something had obviously changed, because her tone was much calmer and with overtones of fear. I'm sure she thought good and hard about losing her job for talking about another student in front of a class.

"I'm sorry."

"Apology accepted."

And that was that. The rest of the semester we kept it light. I decided not to air my opinions and she decided not to ask- but I was still the Christian girl. I had what it took to be a minister, the heart, the zeal, the mouth. Why was I still mainstream? Why was I not following my dream?

I don't belong here. I thought for the millionth time.

A year later and I was staring out of a small airplane window over the Atlantic, thinking about what had gotten me to that point with doubt, and fear. I was on my way to Bible College in Germany. What was I doing? Living for a year with the assistant pastor and their five children in Heidelberg, Germany, and studying with Wolfgang and Hilde, the pastors at New Life Christian Center had *sounded* good when I signed up. My church had offered the option and it seemed like a perfect fit. I had given up everything to go; a house I loved, a car I loved, and a promising job in radio as a disk jockey, all to follow my new dream of being a minister.

The decision had been hardest on my father. Having been reared from childhood to get my doctorate, my parents had scrimped and saved to eventually amass a promising sum of money large enough to send all four of us all the way through college. I had heard the word college all my life; I knew that my dad was a doctor, and the question of "what do you want to be when you grow up?" was never really asked. All the answers ended in PHD. After high school, I had done two years of community college and hated every minute of it, schlepping my way through all the preliminary classes. I didn't know why I was there, and I didn't want to be there, I wanted to be in Bible College. I was envious of my peer's parents for being *so proud* that so and so has decided to "follow the Lord", and go to Bible college. All I got when I asked my dad about sending me to The Institute of Biblical Studies was an endless stream of teasing, with references to kindergarten, and coloring all day.

In his mind going was useless. In my mind it was the only thing I could see. I pictured him finally respecting me when I had a big church, and he saw how much good I was doing in the world. He pictured me successful, and taken care of financially. Growing up in poverty he had worked all of his life so we could go to college, and I was now telling him that I didn't want to go. It was a slap in the face, the highest of insults-in his mind Bible College was not college.

Finally after much arguing and tears they had realized that my mind was made up. They had even offered to pay, surprising me at the last minute. They wanted me to "get it out of my system", and then come back and go to "real" school. The Institute of Biblical Studies was only two years of study, with the third year being an optional apprenticeship in one of our sister churches. There were churches in Belgium, Russia, Australia, and Germany. They figured I was taking a three year detour.

Going from a regular college to Bible College had been like whiplash. The classes sounded interesting enough but the teachers were another story; they were a motley-crew of pastors, excited new converts, old-timers, and sometimes ordinary church goers, who they pulled out of the crowd to fill a spot. It wasn't accredited so it didn't really matter who taught.

If they needed someone for, say, a class on the Tribulation, (a very serious subject matter about the end of the world) for some unexplainable reason, they used someone like Mrs.Topples-a very dumb, khaki wearing, manicured soccer mommy.

The first day I went to the class I was baffled.

"Um, o.k. lets open the book" she said, picking at her hot pink nails. I half expected her to be holding the book upside down.

"Can anyone tell me about the Tribulation?" she asked to no one in particular.

I raised my hand.

"Yes, Tara" she waved an emery board at me. She was NOT doing her nails while we were talking about the apocalypse...yes, she was.

"The Tribulation is the period of time that God gives everyone to get it together, before he comes back, and before everyone who hasn't accepted him goes to Hell. It is a really rough time, where Christians will be persecuted, like in the times of Nero."

"Right-O" she said almost joyfully, as if I had said that that the Tribulation was the time when God handed out free bubble gum to anyone who asked for it.

These classes were the hardest. Most of those picked-out- of- the- congregation teachers couldn't teach a fly how to land on a pile of crap. A few of the teachers were very qualified, though. My favorite class was taught by an old school, jump-up-and-let-me-hear-ya- testify! African - American pastor named Antoine. This guy was awesome, and we had him first thing in the morning. It was a good thing, too- saved me a lot of money on coffee. You had to be awake in his class, because he liked to yell, and jump on things. He taught The Gospels class.

Every sleepy cold morning, I trudged into the conference center, and tried to keep my eyes open. Antoine strutted in like it was Sunday morning, and we were his ever- loving congregation. He was always impeccably dressed, wearing his best suit, and smelling like a department store perfume section.

"And Jesus, DROOOVVVEE the money changers out of the temple! He DROVVVEEE them out. Who do you need to DRIIIVVVEE out of your life?!" and with that he literally jumped several feet in the air and onto the desktop next to me. I don't think I heard a word he said after that, because I kept praying that he wouldn't slide off the wood colored plastic, or the thing wouldn't crack in two. My heart always beat hard in those classes.

The new convert teachers were the worst, even harder to follow than the dumb blondes. I never trusted those people. Like Don, who taught, for some ungodly reason, Biblical Greek, and Hebrew. This guy, a year before was barely sober, he was a heavy drug abuser, and womanizer. Then he miraculously got saved. And miraculously they let him teach something that a PHD should have been teaching.

"So the Greek spoken during Jesus time was called Kainte" he very clearly mispronounced. I let it go, thinking it was an oversight.

"Anyway, Kainte was what a good portion of the New Testament is written in" he said, in the same tone you would sell someone a stolen gold watch.

"Um, Don isn't that Kione Greek? I don't think there is a T or an A, either." Even I knew that.

"What do you mean?" He said intimidatingly, jutting his chin out.

"Nothing" I said. I decided to leave it alone, after all he looked like he wanted to beat me up.

For what it's worth, he married a woman in the church, and they proceeded to have three cute little kids, then he left her and the kids for another woman in the church. Haven't seen hide nor hair of him since.

New Glory was started by a bunch of ex-hippies during the Jesus movement of the sixties. The original 10 or 15 remained, and they were the most fun of the teachers we had. Most of them had seriously damaged brain cells with the amounts of drugs they had ingested, and they loved to tell stories about it. For instance, the music minister at one point in a fit of religious fervor in 1968 insisted that Jesus told him to sell all his belongings, except his guitar, and dig a hole in the ground and wait. I swear I am not making this up. I used to ask him how long he sat there before he realized that maybe his vision was drug induced. He actually stuck it out a few days in the hole, singing Michael Row Your Boat Ashore, waiting for the halo to be visible in the sky.

These George Carlin burn-outs taught a few of the

classes at IBS.There was Miranda, with hair down to her butt, and a misty voice, who repeated herself often, and loved to start talking about random unrelated things. She wore gypsy-style earrings, and taught Covenants class.

Linda's hair was prematurely white as a ghost. She had the emotional range of a marshmallow, and often made things up. She taught an Origins of the Bible class.

"God said that if you don't go to church every Sunday then you are going to Hell" she would say, out of the blue.

I raised my hand. (I did that a lot)

"Excuse me, where does it say that in the Bible?" I asked knowing full well that there wasn't such a thing in there. Our church didn't even teach that, she was just loopy. She told me once that her hair was white because she had smoked so much dope in her time. Like the music minister who lived in a hole in the ground she almost seemed proud of her story, and repeated it often.

Sometimes one teacher would contradict another in the next class. It was mayhem, and truthfully I didn't learn jack. I hoped very hard that actually living with the pastors in Germany would teach me something worthwhile. Something practical. I wanted to see how it worked on a day to day basis.

Now let me say that even though it was a shoddy operation I wasn't exactly a model student. It was hard to drag my princess ass out of bed every day, and show up on time. Some of my zeal had been zapped by the monotony of the contradicting information, and by the impersonal nature of it, but even with my heart in the right place, I paled in comparison to some of my more devoted classmates- these were the star students.

Erin was a goofy but loveable tall brunette who naively believed everything that came out of their mouths. She drew stick figures and silly pictures on my notebook, and we laughed in between classes.

Ken was a quiet businessman whose real calling was in the world of commerce. Laptop and cell phone in hand, he dutifully fulfilled his two year Bible college duty to God, like a Mormon completing his required time on the mission field.

Jerry was a hard talking ex-Navy Seal from New Jersey who got up at four am to run miles before rolling into our eight am class bright eyed and bushy tailed and with the cholesterol of a four year old. I still remember the clipped, nasal way he said my name.

Yep, those were the stars. I had heart, but I was sloppy, this placed me somewhere between them and the second raters, like Ronnie, a handsome dark skinned man with a large family. He had the most realistic approach, and raised his hand rhythmically with mine. Straight out of high school, Mena was the daughter of a deacon. She clearly did not want to be there, and later dropped out. At the bottom of the ladder was Trish, a chain smoking older woman. She was hard, argumentative and prideful, and most of the teachers avoided her.

We were a handful of tropical, fresh and saltwater fish swimming in the same tank.

In hindsight I'm amazed at how supportive my parents were. They eventually got used to the idea, and started to support me, once they realized how serious I was. I blew through the first two years of IBS, being labeled the zealous, but slightly rebellious and sloppy student. No one questioned my love for God, but when I questioned the many inconsistencies in the teachings, I got more than one frown.

The illusion of New Glory had started to unravel itself when I entered the college. I was IN and got to see the day to day workings of the pastors. What I imagined as intense counseling sessions, leading people closer to God, became the reality of daily lunches at the local pizza joint lasting for hours. Instances of "rebuking dissention" in the church, sent up warning flags in my mind. Pastor Sam had even called an entire family up in front of the church for "speaking out against him". It turned my stomach. Still I chose to trust them, believing that they were who they said they were. Besides, I had invested too much to turn back now.

When the two years were done, I took the plunge. I decided on a third year, as a live-in apprentice, it *had* to teach me something. It was a scary, well-thought –out well planned decision. I was giving up life as I knew it to go. I was moving away from the life I knew to start a life I fantasized about. I sold my car, a little red Honda that I loved. I quit my radio job, and shunned the other offers I had from mainstream stations. I had parties, I cried a lot, I was ready to start a new life. And I had crystal clear visions of this life….. I wanted my own church. I would be the pastor and people would come there to be healed, fixed. It would be a refuge. I had no clue how to pastor, run a church, etc, so that is why I went to Germany. To learn how.

Chapter Four

"But thus do I council you, my friends: distrust all in whom the impulse to punish is powerful!"
- Friedrich Nietzsche

Stepping off the plane in Heidelburg, I was relieved to be away from the miserable thing with its foreign smells and uncomfortable seats. It had been a long, loud, smelly ride. I was happy to see the pleasant faces of the German pastors, Hilde and Wolfgang coming towards me. I knew little of them, briefly meeting the couple once, thinking that they would be great to learn from.

Hilde was a small woman with a slight hunch in her back. She had a perma-smile, and carefully teased dyed blond hair. She looked like somebody's clueless grandmother. Wolfgang was, at first look, a very unattractive man. He had buck teeth, a large bulbous nose, and small beady eyes. But he was kind, and the more you talked to him, the more you saw what was inside, a kind hearted, albeit somewhat skittish man.

The reunion was a little awkward, me with my bags, and weariness. I managed a stinky hug, and as we turned to walk toward the bus Hilde turned to me with a disapproving frown, and said "Tara, how did you gain so much weight?" I was shocked at the greeting. My jet-lagged mind struggled to answer, knowing only obedience, not wanting to rock the boat with a sharp reply, this being my only chance at the ministry.

"Um", I said, trying not to cry. "Um, I gained weight because I took the night shift at the radio station, and I…. um….ate a lot." It was true. I had been on the air six pm to midnight spinning the latest in Christian contemporary music at the small FM station. My career was great, but I was lonely. Because of the hours I worked I never saw my friends or family, so I ate, and put on a good thirty pounds.

Lying in the bed that night I thought about the comment, it was one of the only things she had said to me since my arrival. Over a silent dinner of wurst, senf, and brot, I got the feeling that they were disappointed with me. I had only been there a few hours and I was starting to wonder if I had made a big, costly mistake. The pastors didn't seem to want me, and I didn't know what to do, her comment made my insecurity even worse. I was afraid to eat around her at dinner, only eating one sausage, and one piece of bread, not wanting to invite more criticism. I'd only been in Germany for a couple hours, and already it was not turning out like I'd hoped.

God please help me, I prayed, and my tears dripped down onto the pillow.

Thankfully, as the morning light shone through my window, I woke up feeling hope, and a renewed sense of conviction. *I don't care what she thinks*, I said to myself. It was plain even with my blinders of Christian love, to see what that woman was about. The perma smile was just that. A camouflage. Her smile was the phosphorescent light dangling from the antenna of an angler fish…look at the pretty light…keep looking, and the last thing you remember is the jaws closing around you in darkness. The slight skittishness I had detected in her husband was because she was in control, and he probably didn't take a crap without her permission. I couldn't believe I hadn't gotten to know them better! I shut it out of my mind that the first thing I felt in Germany was disappointment. This *had* to work, I had nothing else.

No. I am going to do this, I thought, determinedly, *after all God is much bigger than that woman.* I ran to the window, eager to see my first daylight glimpse of Deutschland, my initial excitement returning. It looked like a fairy tale with red roofs, centuries-old houses, and an air of history staring right back at me.

I got up and went for a walk. It was breathtakingly beautiful. We were surrounded by little shops, and picturesque houses. I felt like someone in Lederhosen would walk up to me and hand me a stein at any moment, it looked like a postcard. Everything in Germany was smaller- the ceilings, the doors, the stairs, even the refrigerator was half-sized.

For the first few weeks, you would think I had moved to Mongolia as hard a time as I had adapting to life there. I pushed on doors that said pull. I completely missed signs that said "warning stairs!" or, "do not enter!", and when I did speak German, I tried to say things like "I'm tired", and instead I said "I'm stewed fruit".....but the doorknobs were the hardest. I'm not really that dumb, but man, those doorknobs confused me. I was still staying with Hilde and Wolfgang the first time I locked myself in the bathroom. I did my thing, and flushed, washed my hands, and then turned the handle. Nothing. Ten minutes of jiggling and I decided that I would have to be humiliated and call for help.

"Um...help" I said weakly and pitifully.

Then louder, because the mice hadn't even heard that first excuse for a cry, I said, "I'm locked in the bathroom, please let me out."

I heard Hilde creaking up the stairs. The hilarity of the situation struck me. Maybe this would win them back, endear them to the American who can't figure out how to open a door. I giggled a bit, watching the latch turn. The door opened to a grim-faced Hilde.

"You turn it to the right" she spat. Then shuffled back down the stairs to her oven full of children, no doubt.

I couldn't wait to get out of their house and go meet the people I was to stay with permanently, the assistant pastors, Donald and Renate' Burchett.

Knock knock. Hilde had dropped me off at the small house on Messer Strasse, and not even waited until the door opened. I stood at the door with my bags, wishing in my heart that the experience here would be much better than it had been with the Wicked Witch of the Old Country. *Good riddance,* I thought, as she sped off. My fist was getting ready for another round of knocking when a small, plain woman with blond hair, a hard set mouth, and tired eyes opened the door a crack, and stared at me through the opening.

"Oh" she said, in a small annoyed voice. "They didn't say you would be so pretty." It wasn't a complement in any way, it was obvious that she had a problem with pretty. Thrown off a bit with the lack of hospitality in this country I tried to make small talk, pushing my way in the door. *Problem with pretty or not, I'm coming in*, I thought. *You aren't going to ruin this for me, too.*

"Elizabeth said she had a great time here." I said, cheerfully fake, putting my bags to the side. My friend Liz had spent a year there earlier as a secretary. She sang the families praises constantly.

"Yeah, we loved her" Renate' replied, a bit of warmth coming into her eyes. She looked me up and down, quietly deciding that if I knew Elizabeth, maybe I wasn't so bad.

"Follow me", she said, "I'll show you where you will

sleep." I guess I had passed the test. Too fat, too pretty, I didn't care. I was in Germany, and I was going to make this work.

The idea was that I would stay with this family, and baby-sit some here and there…maybe a few nights a week, in exchange for living there. I thought it was a great deal, being fed and housed for just a little babysitting time. My counselor at the church said "you are to be at the church most of the time, Tara. Babysitting is only something you do when you are home in the evenings, or when there is nothing else to do." I don't think the idea sat well with him, but I wasn't worried. I figured staying with the pastors would be a great experience. I had never lived with a family in the ministry, I couldn't wait to see what their daily life consisted of. I expected to see the love of Jesus in every aspect of their lives. I looked forward to Bible readings as a family; to the new ways they had found to worship God in their everyday lives. I wondered how it would differ from my own upbringing.

Three weeks had passed. Babysitting was my daily life. I took care of their five kids for hours every day. When I went to the church, I stacked and stapled papers, and helped the wild looking grounds keeper, Dirk. Once we took trash to the dump. German dumps are the cleanest things, not a speck of dirt anywhere. He didn't speak English, so we got by on the little German I had taken in a crash course before I'd left. He pointed to each dumpster, and asked me to say what went in it. We laughed out loud, the joke of me learning about trash crossing the boundaries of language. To this day, I know a lot of German words for trash.

I rarely saw Hilde or Wolfgang. *What do they DO all day?*, I thought after not seeing them for a month. At least at New Glory, the pastors pretended to work sometimes, sitting in their offices making phone calls. I found myself wandering around looking for things to do. Usually the one cleaning job they gave me lasted only an hour or two.....one can only shampoo carpets for so long.

Finally it came, my first ministry job. The woman's name was Gerda, and her little six year old son Andreas accompanied her. Hilde had told me that Andreas's father had beaten her, so she came to the church looking for help. Gerda was hideous. She had two teeth, and a face that looked like Sloth on the The Goonies. Her hair was dyed black, and had the consistency of burnt straw, her body was like a man's with broad shoulders, and no hips- and she was dirt poor. My assignment was to "spend time" with her. I was excited, surely the fact that they gave her to me meant that this was a big assignment. She needed so much love and compassion, and I wanted to give her everything I had.

The first day we spent together we walked along the Neckar River. She talked and talked, and frankly, I had no idea what she was saying. When she would pause, I would say "ya", and that seemed to work. I don't know if she knew I didn't understand her, or if she didn't care. She seemed to just need someone to talk to, and talk she did. Nonstop for hours, without taking a breath, her toothless mouth working and working around shriveled lips. I was a little disappointed when I realized that I wouldn't get to teach her anything. I rebuked myself for being so prideful, thankful that she had someone to talk to, she obviously needed it.

At night I prayed for her and her son, pleading with God to help them. I didn't know her exact situation, Hilde never mentioned it, but I knew that she had been through a lot. I grew to love her, and respect her. It is amazing that without the boundaries of words things can be so clear- I started to *see* her, it was as if I knew what was inside her. I realized that she was a strong woman, her face becoming less and less repulsive as I got to know her….in the end I thought her beautiful. I suspected in the back of my mind that Hilde and Wolfgang thought she was trash, and that they had pushed her off on me so they wouldn't have to deal with her. Since she had no money I guess they thought she had nothing to offer.

Living with the new family, I was starting to see what the church people were all about. Donald and Renate' were horrible. Renate' was absolutely miserable, and her husband was an immature idiot. Neither of them were even the least bit happy. Their marriage was falling apart and Renate' seemed to think that I could help, the rare moments she opened up to me were like a dying man gasping for his last breath. She was bone tired, ignored by her moronic husband, and weighted down by too many kids. They had only planned for two kids, when the first two came, she was content. When she found out she was pregnant with a third, she was depressed. When she saw on the ultrasound that it was triplets "I thought my life was over" she'd say in her heavy German accent. Renate' played a push-pull game with me. At times she wanted to get close, and made a feeble attempt to talk, closely guarding her words, other times her hatred of me was almost tangible. I found myself getting out of that miserable, joyless house every second I could. The minute my babysitting was done, I bolted for the door, sometimes just walking for hours, to be anywhere but there.

Any attempts at friendship with Renate' were destroyed one night while we were sitting around after dinner. I didn't want to play family with them, I just wanted to get up, do the dishes, and start the process of getting the kids to bed. But Donald, like the attention seeking imbecile that he was, had pulled a puppet out of somewhere and proceeded to try to make us laugh. It was an Old World German puppet with a scary Stephen -King – come -alive -and -eat –you-while-you-sleep face. One of those things you'd pay a couple of hundred for in a tourist shop, then hide in a drawer once you got it home. As he put it on his hand, I thought *are you kidding?.....now I have to try to laugh at this fool.* He started making the stupid thing dance in a not funny at all way, and accompanied it with a poor man's Howie Mandel impression. I chuckled out of duty, which was a huge mistake, because the more I fake laughed, the more he was too stupid to see that I was trying to be nice, and the more it egged him on. And Renate' who probably had never laughed in her life glared at me in a jealous rage, because I was the only one laughing. After that evening, she was under the mistaken assumption that I wanted something to do with her idiot of a husband, and she hated me to her very core. If I could go back in time, I would have copied the "watching paint dry" stare that the rest of his family reserved for his ridiculous attempts at humor.

What further endeared me to this family was the way they tried to sabotage my *trying* to learn German. I took a month long course in German before I'd left, and at every turn tried to learn more. I wanted Renate to speak it with me, but since Donald was British, she spoke mostly English. If I tried to speak German to her she would either A. laugh, then leave the room, or B. answer me in English.

Most of the German I learned those first months was from the kids. I learned really useful things like how to say

Winnie the Pooh in German. It is Winne Pooh. Or the over used "vorsichtig!" which means "be careful!", or my favorite, "Meerschweinchen" which means Guinea Pig. I talked about those Meerschweinchen a lot because the Burchett family had about four of the poor things kept in a cage in the living room. After the kids went to bed I got to fish out all the toys that the triplets had dropped in the cage during the day while I wasn't looking. I could just see the German vet explaining why one of the Meerschweinchen had died suddenly. "We sink we found a Leggo in zie windpipe." Those oversized rats owe their life to me.

The really sad thing is, I *wanted* to like Renate'. I felt like that underneath all the fatigue, all the remorse at the life's path she chose, that she was once a happy, fun, probably interesting person. But she had long ago buried that person, and didn't even bother to put flowers on the grave, so any trying on my part only hurt matters. It was becoming crystal clear to me that Christianity didn't save you from real life.

***

And to think I'd worried about gaining weight, I thought as I snuck downstairs to steal some food. I remembered Liz working me up about the abundance of good food in this house, and what a great cook Renate' was. She had gained a good 30 lbs, living here. *Oh but Liz*, I thought sarcastically, *that was before Trennkost. Freakin' Trennkost. These people are going to starve me to death*. I reached into the drawer where she kept the chocolate, and grabbed some Milka, trying not to make a sound.

Mmmmm, erdbeer. I think that means strawberry. Gotta hand it to these Germans, they really know how to do some magical things with chocolate.

Liz had my mouth watering at the homemade bratwurst, tales of Maultauschen suppe- a kind of soup with little meat pockets in it, spatzle, sauerkraut right out of the barrel, and wonderful subtly sweet poppy seed pastries. Homemade bread from the bakery that morning......but noooooo. Dinner turned out to be a child's portion of eggs, with some red peppers. I finished it in three bites. Seriously.

Trennkost was a kind of food combining diet that they just so happened to start the week I got there. My stomach growled for the pizza which I'd heard Renate' made dressing to go on. Dressing! The picture painted was one of luxurious comfort food. Sautéed noodles with Butterkase', a yummy buttery cheese melted over the top. I'm a girl who likes to eat. But with Trennkost, dinner was pretty meager, and boring. Salads. Gritty gristly meat. More salads. These people liked to eat, too. Having to eat some crappy diet made them grumpier than usual and I think they resented having to feed me.

I looked at the pathetic remnants of the secret junk food drawer. A few crumbly pretzels. Some kinder chocolate left over from one of the kid's parties at school. A few misshapen cookies. Surely she'd notice that I was sneaking down every night after bed, just to satiate my growling stomach? Maybe she was doing the same? *I need to work up the courage to approach one of those wurst stands on the street. Maybe if I just say, "wurst please," then there won't be a repeat of that horrid McDonalds experience.*

You'd think that eating at a McDonalds in Germany, a purely American institution wouldn't be that traumatic of an experience, but I couldn't have run out of that place fast enough.

I was walking again. Trying to make the most of the hour I had left before I had to go back to the house and take care of the kids. My stomach was still growling from breakfast. I spotted the McDonalds.

Aww yeah, baby. I can do this, I made my way confidently in the front door. I looked around. Besides some strange color coded trashcans, and no plastic packaging to be seen, McDonalds looked the same. It even smelled better, like a clean version of the old favorite. I walked to the front and got in line, my hopes being raised by the clearly displayed value meals before me. I was starving from the pathetic breakfast at the Burchetts.

Menu 1- coke, fries and chicken sandwich. *Sounds good to me.*

O.k., so I didn't speak much German. Surely they would know what I meant if I just said "Menu 1, coke" I would even say the one in German. *Eins.*

I looked like a foreigner. My eyes were too open, my expression too American. People were staring in their German way.

I looked at the checkout girl, cloaked in the garish McDonald's uniform, and covered in pimples and piercings. *Please be helpful.*

"Hi", I said cheerfully, and much too American..... "Menu eins." I sheepishly pointed to the sign. She rattled something off in German that I couldn't tell if it was a question or an answer. More people were looking. I smiled again, and pointed.

"Menu eins, coke." *Please don't be mean. Help a sista out.*

She laughed and rattled something off again. I didn't understand. What was the deal? This wasn't rocket science.

Was she saying that they were out of coke? Did I want to supersize? That I had to say it in German? That my ass was fat and I didn't need any fries? What? It was starting to really get to me. There was now a clear divide. All the cashiers had stopped what they were doing, and were in on the joke, and on the other side of the counter (which was starting to look very big and yellow, and menacing) was me, and all the patrons that were bored enough to watch me make a fool out of myself. I decided to give it a go one more time.

I didn't smile this time, and gave her my best stop – giving- me- a –hard- time- you- know -what -it -is-I -want face.

I picked up the cardboard sign and shook it for emphasis "MENU EINS" I said clearly, pointing. Then under my breath, *"it's a freaking chicken sandwich, fries and a coke. What is so hard about that?"*

This sent the whole German Arches team into fits of laughter. I turned, and exited.

As I walked home I wished for a friend in this country. Wasn't I supposed to be meeting people? Making friends? Someone who didn't treat me like an obligation that they wished they hadn't said yes to? Living like this was getting old, I was so overwhelmed. Was I doing something wrong? Was it them? Was it me? Something was going wrong, but I didn't know where to point the finger. I was confused, and I couldn't ignore it any longer. *What am I doing here?* I asked God over and over. I asked anyone who would listen.

I thought that if I showed up, if I sacrificed, that God would fill in the blanks. That he would give me my big church, that I would be "called". That my perfect mate would show up, and I would live the rest of my perfect life helping people be perfect in my perfect church. I felt like my heart was right, I couldn't understand why nothing was going like it was supposed to. Wasn't there a shortage of people who wanted to give up everything to serve? I had proven that I meant it, giving up my job, my home, moving to a blasted other country for God's sake. Why wasn't God using me? Why did the pastors dislike me? Why did they avoid me? I was the most confused I had ever been in my life.

"Everything happens for a reason." People like to say that when you are panicking because your life appears to be falling apart. It is a catch phrase, like at a funeral when they say "they are in a better place."

Shut up.

Those are things people say to make *themselves* feel better. I gave up everything. Everything. Not just before I went to Germany, but way back in high school when I placed the God-cloak on, and allowed it to be who I was. I fought my parents, isolated myself, and made a fool of myself, all for what? The big pay off, the pot of gold at the end of the rainbow was not there. The glowing pictures they painted of Bible College were not true. It was a lie. I was lost.

There was no more work to be done at the church. Weeks would pass, and I would do nothing but take care of kids. I would call the church in the morning, hoping that there would be work to do, but Hilde and Wolfgang were always mysteriously gone. I prayed and prayed, trying to be content, and trust, but inside I was panicking. My big Bible college education was nothing but a glorified babysitting job. I became immensely depressed, faking sickness for days at a time, just to shut out the world.

Then one fateful day, Wolfgang called me out of the

blue and took me on a road trip. Frankfurt was a big city, and we were on the way there to visit a pastor that they knew. I guessed that because it was a day trip that Hilde and Wolfgang had decided to drag me along, I didn't really care why. I was just happy to be away from Renate' and the kids for a day.

"First we were going to pick up Kurt and Giselle", said Hilde from the front seat of the van. "Kurt is going to be the youth pastor one day Tara, he is a very spiritual man." (he was my age) Hilde said in a dramatic voice. "His girlfriend Giselle will probably be his wife, and she is someone you should model yourself after." I ignored her comment. When she did speak to me it was belittling, and I had gotten used to it.

As they climbed into the car, I studied them. They were a very German looking couple; both blond, blue eyed, and very tall, I instantly decided that I didn't care for Giselle. She had a snotty expression, and something about her didn't feel right. But Kurt, even though he seemed pretty fluent in church-speak, had a gleam in his eye. I could tell he was different. We awkwardly began to talk, and he gave me his history.

Kurt Mennaz was born in a small town in former East Germany. I listened with wide eyes as he told me the life he grew up in- Russian was his secondary language, and capitalism, and democracy were taught as poisonous to society. As he started his story I think I expected some silly romanticized idea of a poor repressed person rescued by the freedom of capitalism. Yeah, right...... Kurt was about as repressed as a stripper.

When the wall came down, he came to Heidelberg, found the church, and began to work on his English; it was perfect, only the slightest accent detectable. Kurt wasn't a typical German. He liked to laugh, and was very mischievous. He WAS intensely spiritual, one of the only people there I had encountered, he had the kind of spirituality that I felt on the inside. He wasn't stuffy, or too serious, and I knew immediately that we were going to get into a lot of trouble together.

Getting out of the car after the silent ride home Hilde spoke.

"I want you to spent time with Kurt", she said spinning away from me, and walking toward the front door. It was the first thing that Hilde had ever said to me that made me happy.

The next day, I made my way to Kurt's apartment. He lived in town, and his apartment was situated right over a Greek restaurant. We were going to spend the day together and "get to know each other". I, for once, was looking forward to it.

"So where are we going?" I asked Kurt, when I noticed that we seemed to be heading in a definite direction.

"I am going to sell you to the Turks", he said, stone faced.

"Ha-ha", I laughed, and prayed that he was kidding. Surely he was kidding. He looked very serious. I had only met this guy once. Maybe he was psycho.

Twenty more minutes of walking at a very brisk pace, and I asked again, "where did you say we were going?"

"I told you, I am taking you to the Turks to sell. You are Armenian and American, and you will fetch a high price." I stared at him. I didn't know where I was, but I could make a run for it. It seemed ludicrous, but he was so serious that I believed him. He must have seen the look of terror in my face, because he burst out in short guffaws.

"Blode Ami, (stupid American) I am not going to sell

you to the Turks, we are going to go eat some good food."
At that moment I didn't know if I liked him, or hated him.
Ninety-nine percent of the Germans I'd met had little to no
sense of humor, and I had gotten used to not smiling, so
this sudden barrage of sarcasm, good-natured mockery, and
practical joke meanness took me completely off guard.

"I'm sorry", he said sincerely,"it was just too easy."
He smiled at me, and won me back. *What a strange person*,
I thought. Intensely serious, or intensely silly. Warm
hearted or cold as ice. Great to talk to, but completely
guarded. Taking ahold of this new opportunity, I started a
conversation, one I would have never been able to have
with any Germans I had met so far.

"So tell me what German's think of Americans." I was
going to show him that I was a thinkin' girl, and not a
"blode Ami". He cautiously looked over at me, realizing
that I was trying to be real with him.

Never one to mince words he said "we think you are
fat, rich, and stupid."

I fired back. "Well guess what the stereotypical
American idea of a German is?"

"What?" he said, not entirely ready to hear it.

"We think you are cold, heartless, mechanical, almost
robotic, and freakin' weird." I also said that I thought that
they had no sense of humor, and could count on one hand
the number of smiles I had seen while I'd been there. Of
course, I was laying it on really thick to test him.

"Oh, yeah, and there is the smell…" I said, relentless. I
had to hold my breath whenever I walked into a room the
smell of body odor was so bad.

"Do you know how you can spot an American on the
street?" he said, tossing it back to me. "He is the one with
the idiotic self-obsessed grin. You Americans never stop

grinning or thinking that the whole world is yours for the taking. The constant smiling is obnoxious and fake."

"Whoa, wait a minute. You don't even know me, I'm not like that. What if I judged you by your stereotype?" Kurt actually smelled really good.

"We ARE cold, and we LIKE order. We have a saying -*alles in ordnung*. It means everything in order, everything in its place…... we have no place for silly emotions." He had his head held high for a moment, then cocked it to the side, and winked at me.

I stood in front of the restaurant, hands on my hips. This guy was infuriating in a way that only a younger brother can get to you. One minute he is hugging you, the other he is putting fake plastic doggy doo-doo on your seat. But I had to admit, I was having fun, having the first real conversation I'd had since I'd been there. We ate a great meal and then went back to his apartment.

I loved his apartment. It looked like a Witch's cottage, with bunches of dried herbs hanging up, and mysterious pots and bottles of brown liquid. We'd sat up and drank coffee that night, laughing till our stomach's ached. We clicked right away, and immediately started hanging out. As the months went on, at night I'd walk a couple of miles to Kurt's apartment. Giselle lived with him, a fact that the church didn't know, and I promised to keep my mouth shut. So much for being "someone I should model myself after". If the church knew that they were "living in sin" the jig would be up. She also had an affinity for shoplifting.

Kurt loved to cook, and when we weren't making up goofy German/American word hybrids or seeing how far we could spit, he taught me how to make lebkukhen, sauerbraten, and schnitzel. Kurt enabled me to experience some of Germany outside of the church. He was a lot of fun and I felt as if I had always known him. In true German form, his favorite pastime was abusing me.

"Hey, what is it I am called again?" I asked when we were on another one of our walks.

"A *praktikantin*. It means an apprentice. You tell people that you are a praktikantin with the kirche, the church." He was buying us a bus ticket to go check out this new Chinese restaurant we'd heard about. We both loved to eat.

"How do you say,'I am a praktikantin, nice to meet you'?" I was looking for a reply to the endless questioning from everyone I met on why I was in Germany.

"Ich bin ein praktikantin, bitte schlagen sie mich."

"Cool, thanks Kurt." I practiced it aloud. "Ich bin ein practikantin, bitte schlagen sie mich" it had a good sound to it, and it was easy to remember. I decided to try it out at the youth meeting that night.

I spotted my first victims. One of the kids in the youth group had brought two of his friends who had never been to the church. We were standing in a large circle, everyone speaking rapid German. I could understand a lot, but still was very shy about speaking. I decided to make my debut.

I nudged Kurt, "o.k. I'm ready."

He was kind enough to announce that I had something to say. Everyone stopped talking and listened.

"Ich bin ein praktikantin, bitte schlagen sie mich", I said proudly and loud enough for the whole room to hear. There was a moment's stark silence. Then everyone doubled over in laughter, including Kurt.

I figured I must have messed up the words. *Let's see bitte means please, schlagen, I don't know what that means, and sie mich, means you me. Wait a minute. I think Kurt taught me something wrong. I'm gonna kill him.*

"Come here, you rat", I shouted after Kurt, as he took off running. I went up to Renate' who was in the other room.

"Renate' what does schlagen mean?" I was out of breath.

Irritated that I was bothering her, she said, "it means hit, or beat", then turned back to whatever it was that she was doing. So I had said to a whole crowd of people,"I am an apprentice, please hit me". It was the equivalent of the *kick me* sign secretly taped on someone's back.

I mumbled to myself walking away,"I'm gonna kill him, I swear." Even I had to admit that it was kinda funny, though.

***

"Let's have a Halloweeeen party!" Kurt was practically skipping down the sidewalk.

"Where are we going to get the stuff?" I was a bit skeptical. I knew that Germans didn't celebrate Halloween, and I hadn't seen one pumpkin, or bag of candy corn. But I also knew that once Kurt made his mind up about something, especially something concerning FUN of any kind, that it was a done deal. I was just along for the ride.

"What exactly do you want to do?" I sighed in defeat.

"Why don't you make chili and cupcakes? We can get a pumpkin, and we can dress up. You said Renate and Donald will be out of town, so we can all come over there, I'll invite August, Carl, Sasha, Dieter…..." He was making a mental party list.

"O.k., but we are going to need some items that will be difficult to get. Honey, I haven't even seen a pumpkin, and you know ya'll Germans aren't exactly fond of anything with food color. Where am I going to find orange food coloring, or the spices for the chili?" I was thinking of the time my mom sent me some berry blue Blow Pops, and everyone thought it was the weirdest thing that I would want to *eat* something blue.

"I know exactly where to get the pumpkin." We took a sharp turn in the other direction, and headed for a Turkish grocery.

"You, American?" the grocery clerk had recognized the obvious, and was delighted.

"Ya" I said, perusing the pinkish, powdery Turkish Delight candy. He was following me around the store.

"Las Vegas, New York?" he questioned.

"No, South Carolina." I felt kinda lame saying it.

"South Carolina?" he asked back.

"South Car-o-lina" I repeated. Then seeing he wasn't getting it, I looked around for a scrap of paper, and drew him a grade-school looking map of America, pointing to where South Carolina was.

"Oh" he said, still impressed.

"Found it" Kurt shouted from behind me. I spun around and there he was holding the ugliest monstrosity of a pumpkin I had ever seen. See, when he said that he knew exactly where to get a pumpkin I got excited. I absolutely love Halloween, and being a little homesick, couldn't wait to hold my own little orange orb. Couldn't wait to show Kurt how to carve it, couldn't wait for that familiar nasty smell when you open the thing up. Looked forward to roasting the seeds as I had done practically every year of my life.

And that wasn't going to happen.

Because this thing was for starters, white. Not pretty chic Martha Stewart "look at how chic I am I have a white pumpkin while everyone else has normal old orange ones. Watch me transform it with old news papers, and glitter…" No. This was almost iridescent white painted over sick- as-a-dog green. This was wanna –be white, but didn't quite make it; it was as big and misshapen as a troll. This was the most butt ugly pumpkin I had ever seen.

Kurt was ecstatic. "Look how big it is" he beamed.

"Yeah, it's great" I lied.

"Here hold it" he handed it to me. I concluded that it must be made of lead. I thought of the long walk back to the house.

"Let's take the bus today, Kurt."

Fifteen insisted upon gifts of Turkish Delight candy from the store clerk, and much hemming and hawing, and we were lugging the ass-end hideous thing up the hill toward Hauptstrasse. Kurt's enthusiasm was diminishing.

"Kurt, I gotta tell ya, this pumpkin is the ugliest thing I have ever seen. It looks like an old woman's rear end."

"Let's just leave it here" Kurt suggested, covered in sweat, his party attitude having been left back several blocks ago.

"Hell no, we are carving this thing if it is the last thing I do" I was huffing and puffing, lugging the thing towards the door.

"It kinda looks like your butt" Kurt said, taking a jab at me.

"No, it looks like your face" I said back, like the eight year old that I was.

Dropping the beast on the front porch and hoping that an angry mob with pitchforks didn't form around it, we headed back to town for food coloring, and spices.

"This will do" said Kurt holding up a small sliver of a packet.

"What is it?" I said, looking at the color, it vaguely resembled orange.

"It will have to do" he said hurriedly. "Let's buy it and get out of here, we have to go put our costumes on, we only have a couple of hours."

We made our second trip back home, and proceeded to get dressed for the party.

"O.k., I'm readddyyy." I shouted up at the top of the stairs. Kurt was getting ready to waltz down and present his costume.

My costume was the best I could come up with under the circumstances. I was a nerd. Or better yet, a practikantin. I had on an old white shirt of Kurt's with a pocketful of pens, nerd glasses, and a sign taped on my back that said "bitte schlagen sie mich" the phrase being wildly popular in the church these days.

"Here I comeeeeee." Kurt was so dramatic. He was a vision. Slowly gliding down the stairs, he was decked out in a sheer lavender chiffon sheet that covered his entire body, and he waved it around like he was Stevie Nicks. He had a sprig of lavender tucked behind each ear. He looked like a cross between a homeless gay man, a Roman emperor, and someone who was seriously mentally unstable.

"What are you?" I said, carefully.

"I'M A LAVENDER FAIRY!" he said with a whish and a swoop of his silkily clad arm. "I bestow lavender dreams on everyone I meet." As he said that he was busy (bestowing) brushing my off- center nerdling pig tails with lavender flowers.

Kurt was the funnest person alive.

"Hey I think someone is at the door" he shouted to me in the kitchen. The guests were starting to arrive.

So after the chili that no one ate because it was too spicy, and just too odd after Kurt insisted that I put CHIVES in it, then admitted later he mistakenly thought that chives meant something else in English, and the throw-up brown/orange colored cupcakes that everyone tentatively ate after scraping the icing off, we decided to carve the Great White Terror. It took three people and was so thick that we almost lost a finger or two. I think Kurt and I were the only ones having fun. Everyone else seemed confused as to why Americans would want to even so much as touch something as ridiculous as that pumpkin, or eat something that looked like vomit. When it was time to carve the pumpkin, it seemed natural to be taking a knife to the thing, like we were putting it out of its misery. When we finally lit it up it looked like Jason Voorhees without his mask on.

After everyone left we cleaned up.

"Let's get drunk" said a very tired Kurt, a bit of lavender still dangling from his ear.

"Sounds good to me, lavender fairy, where is the fig vodka?"

With my new friend, things were great. Otherwise all my plans were falling apart. I never went to the church anymore. Hilde would recite the daily mantra on the phone, "there isn't anything for you to do today, Tara", or I wouldn't hear from them for weeks at a time. Gerda was long gone, and I was trapped under Renate's desperate judgmental eye most of the day.

At night I was free. Kurt and I would meet halfway, and walk up to the turm. Buying a pack of cigarettes, we'd sit in the park, smoking and talking, only starting for home when our noses had turned to ice. Sometimes we drank, sipping vodka and bitter lemon, and staggering home. I'd tell them I was spending the night with Giselle, thankful for the relief. Sometimes we just went exploring, snow falling in the night streets, and he pushed me down in it whenever he got the chance. To the observer it looked like two lovers immensely enjoying each other's company, but it went much deeper than that. We were spiritual soul mates. There was no sexuality, just pure love and affection. We were both seeking, and subconsciously knew that we weren't going to find what we were looking for in the church. It was a hard pill to swallow, the hope we had put in Christianity was slowly being unraveled before our eyes. We were desperate and we only had each other. For every practical joke or Loki-like jab he took at me, there were hundreds of serious conversations about everything two people could possibly talk about. He was quickly becoming my closest friend.

Then one day, it was suggested that I should take a German class. When the papers for the Folks Hoch Schule were shoved in my face, I figured, *at least it will get me out of this house.* These people made no sense. They insisted that I needed to learn more German, but refused to speak it with me. I think they just wanted to get rid of me.

Donald dropped me off with a halt.

"This is the only time I will drive you, so I hope you memorized how to get here" he said, bothered with the unsavory task of taking me.

I heard him speed off as I walked up the long staircase into a large room crammed with people. It looked like the customs line at an airport. The room was filled with the din of 15 languages being spoken all at once. I was surrounded with people, all nationalities. There were a lot of Turks, the women wearing the hijab. I loved the sound of Turkish, and leaned in closer to listen as the two women next to me, obviously teenage girls, chattered excitedly.

A woman walked in with a handful of papers in her hand, and glanced over the boisterous group. I figured she must be the teacher. She was naturally thin with glossy brown curls, and high cheekbones. She looked like a beautiful vampire. Her skin was pale, the color of milk. She had prominent straight teeth, the look of ancient blood running through her veins, and a kind smile, not without a history of pain. She started whistling to get everyone's attention.

Now how is this going to work? I thought. *None of us speak German. Surely she doesn't speak everyone's language?* It was then that she began telling us her name. The only reason I knew this is that the said it in 10 different languages. "Meine name ist Sorina. My name is Sorina......." she shouted over the crowd.

Wow, I thought. *This woman can speak at least 12 different languages.* She divided us into groups, and motioned for us to follow her. As I settled down into my seat in the classroom, I looked around at my classmates. There was a large family of Greeks, thick as thieves, a Spanish dude wearing a Rancid T-shirt who was glaring at me, several Turks, a Saudi man named Paki who looked like a poster child for the Taliban, a round Ukrainian woman named Natasha, and me, the lone American, and English speaker.

Sorina was Romanian, (hence the vampire look) and other than not speaking Arabic, she could speak everyone's language in the group. I instantly loved my class. They were funny, real, and the first non-Christians I'd connected with in Deutschland. Between them and Kurt, I began to feel stronger.

A large part of Germany's population is Turkish. They were everywhere, the women with covered heads, walking behind the men, dark hair and Doner Kebabs everywhere. Within the Turkish population I found degrees of religious and cultural extremism. There were the men in all black, standing on the corner in Saint Jerome's square, smoking cigarette after cigarette, looking for the entire world like they were up to no good, their women walking with their covered heads down, hurrying as if they were afraid to stand out. But some women's heads weren't covered. Some looked me in the eye. Some pushed strollers alongside their men, laughing and enjoying the day. They were Muslims. Even though this was pre-9/11, there was still a fear in me when I realized that I was surrounded by Muslims. I had been taught that Muslims were violent and crazy, and this couldn't have been further from the truth. I made many Muslim friends, them being some of the warmest, nicest people I have ever met.

"You come for coffee" was one of the frequent invitations I received from perfect strangers. My favorite restaurant became a local Turkish place. Kurt and I would spend hours there sipping the green mint tea out of tiny glasses, and eating the heavenly bread. I am Armenian-American, so the warmth I felt from the Turkish people helped heal more than one part of me.

Before class we would all huddle around the door to the school, drinking coffee, trying to get warm, and chatting in our new language. It was broken at best, but Greek, Spaniard, Saudi, American, Turk, and Ukrainian tried to communicate. We were all just trying to do whatever it was we came to this country for. That feeling bound us.

We were all in Germany for different reasons. Some had married a German, like Paki, who had a pretty good command of the language. Some were transplants. Some like SomTang, who later joined the class from Thailand, was a mail order bride. She looked like a scared child.

Natasha had married a German man, the dynamics of which I never understood. She rambled on in this German/Ukrainian mix, as I intercepted an occasional "ya". She was definately one of my good friends, with natural platinum blond hair and a round shape typical of Russian decent. I wished she spoke some English, thinking she would have been killer to have a drink with. She looked like she loved to party.

Everyone loved Paki. He had a classic Arabic face, black eyes that were so dark they looked like they had been rimmed with kohl. He was hilarious. He spoke pretty good German, but when we got to the written part of the German language, Paki struggled. He was used to writing Arabic. He would write one poorly formed *R* on the board, then get frustrated and jovially start writing curse words in Arabic across the board, cursing who knows what. The class responded with cheers and laughter.

One day, when he approached me, I thought, *oh no, here comes another argument. If you could call it that.* I rolled my eyes playfully.

"What do YOU want?" I said mockingly in German.

"Would you eat the flesh of your brother?" he would say, pinching his brown hand. He wanted to continue an earlier argument about eating pork.

"Do you say your prayers?" I asked, knowing that he wasn't as devout as a Muslim as he said he was.

"Humph" he snorted, waving me off with a little boy smile, and changing the subject. We did this daily.

The Greeks taught us to curse. They were a large family, the Alexandros. They owned a Greek restaurant, and every member of the family worked there. Costas and Maria were the parents, Stepohs, and Nikos their funny, sweet teenage sons. They were the happiest family, always laughing, always joking. One morning, Costas, who wasn't used to getting up in front of people, awkwardly asked our teacher, Sorina, for help. He had something to say to the class. He held out his arms in an uneasy dramatic fashion (I learned that Greeks are very dramatic).

"You….come eat…. with…us family." He managed in German. Sorina told us all in our languages that the Alexandros family had invited us to their restaurant for an end of class party. They were closing the restaurant down for the day, and serving us a meal. Satisfied, Costas sat down. I smiled and nodded to him and Maria that I would gladly be there.

Noon. The meal was at noon. I rode with Mehmet and Ibrahim, two Turkish buddies who I sat next to in class, enjoying the loud Turkish pop music, and good company. When we arrived at the restaurant, the smell of delicious cooking filled the air. I sat down in one of the dark wooden seats, and Costas filled my glass with a sweet Greek wine, the color of morning light through a window. Then came the food, plate after plate. They had made what seemed like five plates of everything on their menu, I couldn't believe their generosity; they were as generous with their food as they were with their spirits. We stuffed ourselves with the best Greek food I had ever tasted, and it just kept coming and coming. Calamari, Slouvaki, Moussaka, anything you could think of. In thirty minute intervals, Costas filled up

116

our shot glasses with Ouzo, and led a toast. I was full and drunk. It was 1pm. After gagging down dessert, I was so full I couldn't move but I didn't want to offend them, I looked at Mehmet, thinking soon, he would motion for us to go. About that time Costas came out with six bottles of Ouzo, and somebody started fiddling with the stereo. *Oh shit*, I thought. This party is just starting.

A group of completely drunk foreigners trying to communicate is a sight. Or *sound* should I say. The more alcohol we ingested, the more we reverted to the age old trick of getting someone who doesn't speak your language to understand you….. Yell. Everything. If they look like they don't understand, yell louder. Yell in your own language, yell in any language, doesn't matter.

I kept my place at the seat between Ibrahim, and Mehmet, glad that they seemed to be watching over me, because of Emilio. He was a Portuguese Casanova that had just recently started coming to class. With Fabio hair, and a face like Michael Hutchence (Goddess rest his soul), I instantly saw through all those good looks. He was nasty, greasy and overtly sexual. The drunker he got the more he hit on me, pulling me down to whisper, or more like *slobber* sweet nothings into my ear. He was really getting on my nerves and I got sympathy looks from everyone. Language really is a primitive form of communication .Even though I never said it, and even if I could, no one would understand me, everyone knew what was going on.

"Pleees go out wit meeeee." He would say, sloppy-lipped, his eyes drooping from too much Ouzo.

"Emilio, you are getting on my nerves. Stop asking me."

Yuck. The thought of going out with him repulsed me, he had the morals of a tomcat. As he drank more, he started following me everywhere. It was starting to get ridiculous, and he wouldn't leave me alone. I was more annoyed then afraid, because so many of my friends had had enough of him too. Costas was about ready to jump him. Ibrahim and even the timid Mehmet looked like they wanted to beat the crap out of him. I waved to them, and flashed an I- can-handle- it smile. It was then that I did my first conscious spell.

Pass out. I thought. I pushed him down on a chair mentally.

A few minutes passed when I started thinking that it had been five minutes of peace without sour alcohol breath insisting that I, "Pleas pleas …but you are so booootifullllll". I looked over, and he was slumped down, passed out. *Cool*, I thought. *Now the party can go on.*

It was five pm, and we were all butt ass wasted. There were several circles happening. Maria was reading tea leaves, surrounded by a table full of people with an air of mystery hanging around them like a mist. There were several drunken conversations going on loudly, but amicably.

Poor SomTang, I wondered what she was thinking. It was bad enough being a mail order bride, but the contrast between Germany and Thailand had to be enormous, I was sure she was in shock. She was sitting alone at a table, looking lost. I wondered if she hated going to bed with that foreigner with the white skin every night. I wondered what she thought of her new country, and her new life. I decided to approach her. She spoke no German, only Thai. I sat down, placed my hand on hers and patted it, trying to mentally communicate how I knew it must be hard for her. She stared back with black, vacant eyes.

Natasha was following me around trying desperately to

communicate. I had given up on this a long time ago. I had no idea what language she was speaking. It would have been nice to talk to her, but it was impossible. So I just smiled at her, and spoke to her in English.

"I like you a lot Natasha, but I don't have a damn idea of what you are saying." She paused, grinned, and then took this as a reason to keep talking, which was fine with me, I liked having her around. She was just a fun kinda person.

Our attention was directed to a commotion at the front of the room. The two boys, Stephos and Nikos had started dancing, a slow, timeless Greek dance. The movements reminded me of a puppeteer, each flick of the wrist setting off a slow chain reaction. It was wonderful to watch. Then the music stopped, and someone changed the CD. I heard the unmistakable first strains of that old disco favorite, the Bee Gee's *Staying Alive*.

Bump chicka bump chicka ,well you can tell by the way I use my walk, I'm a woman's man, no time to talk.

Costas staggered up to me pointing "Americaner, tancen…. americaner, tancen". Then in English seeing that I wasn't grasping the concept "you American, dance". Horrified, I realized that he wanted me to get up in front of everyone and dance to the Bee Gee's.

No way, I thought. Partially because I was too drunk, partially because I hadn't danced to secular music in years, the only dancing I'd done being the River dance- like shuffle acceptable in church. Costas frowned, and then went to the back. A couple of people went up to the front and did a few hip thrusting moves, imitating what they thought was American style dancing, causing the whole party to die laughing.

Suddenly Costas got up and went to the kitchen. I

panicked, thinking that I couldn't possibly drink or eat any more. He came out with a very large stein. Upon closer inspection it appeared to be full of holes. The trick was that one of the holes stopped the beer from spilling, and you had to try to find out which one. We all took turns drinking from it, laughing uproarsly when beer went everywhere.

The party was winding down. Costas was sitting on a chair, head weaving in an inebriated bob. The Portuguese Wonder was out cold, lying on the floor. *Maybe he'll choke on his vomit,* I thought evilly. Mehmet and Ibrahim tugged on my arm. We looked at each other with an it's –time- to - go ocular exchange. Some things you just know. Lots of hugging and danke's, and we were back in the hotrod, speeding towards town, Turkish pop star Tarkan blaring. I was so drunk, and wondered how I was going to get past Renate'.

"I'm going to stay with Giselle tonight" I said to Renate' over the phone.

"Fine" she said, she didn't care. I went up the stairs to Kurt, eager to tell him of the party.

"Watch this" a cloud of smoke billowed up from the small charcoal.

"What do you think that smells like?" Kurt seemed hyper-focused.

"It smells like something I've always known" I said truthfully.

"It's Frankincense" he said, dramatically waving the smoke around. "Look what else I got." He pulled out a deck of Tarot cards.

"Kurt" I said scornfully, but longingly. "What are you doing? You are a youth leader" I said without conviction.

I didn't care anymore. *Christianity is a big joke*, I thought, then stopped myself, thinking it blasphemy.

I had seen so much I hadn't wanted to see.

New Life was a small congregation with a lot of poor people in it. Wolfgang and Hilde ate at restaurants every day. Every day. They spent money like it was water, living in a nice house, and driving everywhere, in a city where most people walked. They were fake. Pretending to care. Pretending to be devoted. Justifying their lives with exclamations of how tired they were from all the networking and fellowshipping. Taking long trips, always smiling, never letting anyone in. I started flinching at the sight of them. They were supposed to be "counseling" me, and that never happened. They were supposed to be "teaching" me, and that never happened. The Christians in Germany were cold, lifeless people. I hated the church, and hated everyone in it. I hated Renate' and Donald, and hated Hilde and Wolfgang. I knew that my dream was never going to happen, and I told myself that I didn't care.

Germany had its own beat. It was heard through the empty headphones that I constantly wore as I walked through the city. In Germany I walked everywhere I went. I might have graced a vehicle with my presence maybe twice. In addition to helping me lose some of the weight that Hilde so kindly pointed out, walking everywhere gave me time to think, to be aware of my own space. If you have never lived in a big city or anywhere in which walking is your main form of transportation, you are missing out. I was amazed at how in touch with the weather I became, how much I started to enjoy the cold air hitting my lungs in the morning as I made my way to the Hoch Schule, or over to Kurt's. I kept my headphones on, and with Fiona Apple, and U2 helping out, my awareness expanded. I had given up on Christianity, I knew that. I knew it in the way that I looked at the world. The world was right in front of me every day, not hidden behind the metal and plastic car doors. My bubble of isolation had burst. I watched who I was and who I was becoming.

Even thought I didn't realize it at the time, <u>I changed before my mind did</u>. I didn't squirm as I passed a bar, or pretend to be open and kind to people I passed on the street. I dropped the fake smile and didn't assume anymore that I was God's gift to society. I didn't think I was any better than the little old man selling wurst, with his tobacco stained beard, and greasy hands. When I passed a large group of Muslims, I didn't think fearful thoughts, or assume that I knew who they were. I just thought *those are people just like me. They cry, they laugh, they fall in and out of love; they need sleep at night, and food during the day. Maybe they are having a better day that I am...*

I was back to being plain old human again, and that part felt really, really good.

***

THERR IS SOME COKE IN THE FRIGE, AND SOME PIZZA I GOT FOR YOU. YOU AR FREE TO DO WHAT YOU WANT JUST FEED THE KAT FROM THE PACKAGE UNDER THE TOLET. PLESE SHAKE THE BOTTLE THAT SAYS "SWEDEKRAUT" THREE TIMES A DAY. THER IS SOME BRED FOR YOU IN THE THING THAT SAYS S BROTTOPF.
LOVE YOU STINKY,
KURT

I laughed out loud at the letter, and ran to the fridge to

check out the American goodies he had left for me, immediately popping the pizza in the oven, and cracking open the coke. Kurt and Giselle were visiting her parents for three days, and they had asked me to Kat sit. I was ecstatic.

No church. No babysitting. No Christianity. Peace and quiet.

Wandering around the apartment trying to figure out what to do with myself was the order of the day. I put on some music and danced, pleased to have my own space for a change. That wore thin after an hour, and exhausted, I filled the bathtub, which was a rare and luxurious treat, the cost of water being steep in Germany. I tried to relax, but the reality of my thoughts were prominent in the silence, and refused to be buried in activity. There was something that had been building up inside of me, something that was on the brink of coming out.

Kurt's bed was not at all soft. I tossed and turned and tried to get comfortable. I was surprised at my thoughts, expecting to soak up my new free time. Being alone with my inner turmoil made me feel far from peaceful, and I couldn't sleep. I had brought a book, one that Kurt had gotten for me. *The Mists of Avalon* by Marion Zimmer Bradley lay idly on the bookshelf. I had only brought it along because I was desperate for something new to read, even though I had never really been into fantasy. Thinking that it might bore me enough to fall asleep, I roughly grabbed the book.

Chapter one: "Morgane speaks. In my time I have been called many things, sister, lover, priestess, wise woman, witch."

I did not sleep that night, but read until my eyes closed at dawn. I awoke at two, only to fix myself something to eat, and continue reading. I was fascinated. In the story she spoke of the Goddess. She saw all gods as one. She did not dismiss the "pale god of Christianity", but embraced a tradition far older. I was introduced for the first time to the Divine Feminine. I was introduced to the Goddess.

When my parents called I made excuses to get off the phone. Somehow all of this tied in with the growing feeling inside of me. I finished the book at ten pm the next day, my mind swimming with thought. I had been taught that it was useless to try to hide from God, that he knew what was in your heart. I thought about all of the people in the church, and of Wolfgang and Hilde, their lives a lie because they were living someone else's set of rules, someone else's conviction. I thought of the wonderful friends I had at school, their Muslim faith being richer and more earnest than anyone I knew at the church. Something very rational clicked in me.

Who was I to say they were wrong?! That the whole world was wrong?!

Had I ever taken the time to stop and....... think? Think about what it was that I professed to believe?!

I slowly said it aloud, like I was hearing it the first time.

"I believe that a man named Jesus walked the earth and he was God. If you don't believe in Him only, and that the Bible is the true word of God that you are going to a place called Hell where you burn in tormented agony forever. That means the …Muslims, the …Hindus, the ….Buddhists… the …Jews… are all going to burn in tormented agony for eternity." The words rang flat and hollow in the empty apartment. I listened to how it sounded. I had been hearing it all my life, and had gotten used to it. I had never listened with an objective ear.

I had taken this label, this grouping of sentences and slapped it on the WHOLE world as an ultimatum. In my little tiny world with my little tiny experiences I was trying to say that I knew who God was, and better yet that if EVERYONE didn't believe as I did, that THEY would burn for ever and ever. Holy crap! Just who did I think I was?

I was just Tara from South Carolina. I didn't know what life was like in Cincinnati, Bombay, Siberia, and New Orleans. I didn't know other realities, just my own. *Oh my God, what have I been doing!?*

The idea suddenly became ludicrous, and self-centered. Maybe there was more than the Lion of the Tribe of Judah? Maybe God was also female? It made sense to have a Mother *and* a Father. Maybe I didn't know who God was….as a matter of fact I was sure I didn't know. I had always prayed, but had I ever thought about who I was praying to? Like the guy on the street who waves to you everyday and says "hi, Karen", and you think, *it's not Karen, jackass, it's Carol. It doesn't matter though, to him I'm Karen.* I had been praying to this Awareness I chose to call Jesus that I had precisely defined…and limited with my tiny little definitions.

My thoughts came rapid and true.

I rewound to my days at Winter's Pass, and wondered how life would have been different had God been considered male *and* female. Thought of New Glory, with their beliefs being the same as Winter's Pass, camouflaged in a whirlwind of emotion, and good music. Thought of my own power as a woman, and wondered why I had always felt the need to suppress it. I was amazed at the change in my thoughts when I imagined female energy, only Divine!

I thought of Kurt, trapped in the same thing I

was….someone else's definition of God. I started praying out loud, the great burden in my heart lifting as I spoke.

"God" I said assuredly. "God, I don't want to go to Hell, but I have to be honest with you. You know what I am thinking, what I'm feeling. I can't hide from you. I don't know about all this Christianity stuff. I don't know if I think that is the only way, and that the miserable people at church are going to heaven, and the warm hearted friends at school are going to Hell just because they call you a different name. I will admit, I like the idea of you being male and female. The truth is, I'd like to explore. Maybe Christianity isn't for me. Please lead me back to Christianity, if it is where the only truth lies, but I'd like to look for truth in other paths. I love you, thank you for listening."

I felt like I had given birth. The relief at finally putting words to all that I was carrying around satisfied, and revived me. All of the frustration, all of the shame, all of the confusion had been released. I felt great, but it also scared me. What was I going to do? I knew that in speaking that out I couldn't live a lie. In speaking those words I was responsible for them.

Kurt and Giselle came back the next day, and I returned to Renate' and the kids feeling free and full of anticipation.

***

"You are just not working out" Hilde said to me, in the first conversation we'd had in months. It had been three days since my decision. I was sitting in Wolfgang's office, having been told over the phone that they wanted to talk to me. Hilde looked at me defiantly, but with a bit of fear behind her eyes, like she was trying to hide something. Wolfgang shifted uncomfortably in his seat, and stared at his enormous shoes.

"I'm sorry?" I said, surprised. I couldn't believe my ears.

So this was how it would go down.

She started getting defensive.

"You.......you don't play an instrument, you don't sing" she was trying to make this seem like it was my fault. I switched into a different mode.

"You knew all that before I came over here, and it wasn't a problem then" I snapped, sitting straight back in my chair, crossing my legs. I was ready to fight. I wasn't going to let them off this easy. She took it as a sign of defiance, which it was.

"Renate and Donald aren't happy with you. Renate' said you tried to make her watch secular movies, and ....and you don't hang up your towels."

I laughed a mocking laugh. It was pathetic. I thought back to how Renate' had begged me to watch an old library copy of the musical *Hair* with her, dubbed over in German of course. I hadn't wanted to watch it, and sat there patiently while she stared at the screen, reminiscing about her youth. She had been talking about it for weeks, and practically commandeered the TV, pulling me down on the sofa. That was what they were referring to. This whole thing was ridiculous. I decided to go for the gold.

"Don't worry, Hilde, I'm not going to go home and tell pastor Sam that all you had me do was baby-sit when I was supposed to be learning" I said, a little snide. There was silence.

"Well, we have known Sam for a *long* time. He won't believe you, he will believe us" she said slowly, making sure I had heard all the words. I wasn't surprised at this. I wasn't surprised when she got up and walked away, leaving me with Wolfgang. After she left there was an awkward silence, then he looked at me, the first time for real. I saw the exhaustion in his eyes, I assumed from dealing with her for years.

"Tara, we just don't have anything for you to do. We should have planned this better. You were our first student from the college, and we should have known exactly what to have you do. There just isn't enough to do here." Finally the truth came out.

"You aren't happy here, either, are you?"

I sighed a sigh of defeat.

"No." I admitted. I didn't blame Wolfgang. Maybe for letting his wife have his balls, maybe for being stupid enough to let her run the show, but really I just pitied him. "It's alright" I told Wolfgang. "But I wish you would have been honest with me. I gave up everything to be here."

Walking home, I felt far from great. The reality of the situation hit me hard. WHAT was I going to do now? It felt like I had saved millions of dollars for years, only to have someone steal it all in a single moment. I had built my life up for nothing. I had given everything up for nothing. What life did I have to go home to? How was I going to face everyone at church? Was Hilde right? Would Sam not believe me? What would my parents say? I didn't want to leave Kurt, I felt like he understood me. I didn't have friends like him at home.

What would I do?

I was standing at the stoplight waiting for it to turn red so I could walk.

The feeling of hopelessness was unbearable. There was a bus coming, fast. *All I have to do is walk out in front of that bus, then it will be all over. I won't have to deal with it.* I wavered, my foot stepping onto the pavement. I thought of how much I loved my family, and like a splash of cold water, snapped out of my self-pity. It was the first time I had ever thought of suicide.

Instead, I got angry.

Screw em' all. These idiots aren't worth dying for.

Vehemently ironing. Ironing vehemently. This means I was standing in the Burchette's damp basement, mad as hell, feeling very sorry for myself, holding a hot piece of metal. I was also listening to Hole. Courtney Love's screeching lyrics matched what I wanted to scream at everyone. "Sooommeeday you will ache like I ache" I sang along. Placing the triplets starched Sunday dresses to the side, I gulped.

It was time to break the news to my parents. I put down the iron, turned down the volume, and dialed the long distance phone number.

"Hey honey, what's up" I heard my mom's familiar bright, articulate diction.

And I was four years old. The rest of the conversation came out in broken sobs.

"And then she said that Pastor Sam wouldn't believe me...*sob...choke....suck up snot....*"

My mom was quiet for a moment.

"I'm glad you are coming home, Tara. I never liked that bitch."

Whew, mom never curses.

"Don't worry about it, I will get you a plane ticket. Your father will hit the roof when he hears this, as much money as we have shelled out for this whole fiasco." Her tone was angry but controlled and at the same time dripping

129

sweet with motherly comfort. It was just what I needed, and it only made me cry harder.

They say that most of the anger people express is because they don't feel like they have permission to express what they really feel. Anger is a safe emotion. Anger makes you feel strong, makes you scary to others, puts up a big defense. I acted angry, but really I was scared, confused, hurt. I ain't a saint, but I would never do to someone what these people had done to me. I couldn't understand it. They were *pastors*, they were *leaders*. They at least could have been honest, instead of treating me like a roach problem. Ignore it, till it starts crawling up your leg.

Sitting there while the iron cooled, I wondered how many of my clothes I would give to Giselle. She would surely appreciate some American jeans....the Germans went crazy for American jeans. My heart broke when I thought of leaving Kurt.

Someone knocked on the door. I assumed it was one of the Burchette's trying to get their American slave to do something else.

Renate' opened the door. She wouldn't look at me. I could feel her relief in my leaving, but I also felt uneasiness from her. She fiddled with her fingers. Before I could protest she ran over to me, hugged me, and blurted out "I hope I haven't done anything to hurt you". Turning sharply away, she exited.

What was that all about? Hi, I'm going to beat you up with a baseball bat, then apologize? I didn't know if the statement was to soothe her conscience, or if some still-human part of her felt ashamed that things had gone so badly. Either way, I could allow myself to feel nothing but hot, blazing anger. Anger ran over me in seductive waves. I turned Hole back on and screamed along......

"Go on take everything, take everything, I want you to, go on take everything, take everything, I want you to!"

Chapter Five

"It's not that some people have willpower and some don't, it's that some people are ready to change and some are not."
- James Gordon, M.D.

The phone rang and rang. I was trying to call Pastor Sam for the third time. I had been back in America for a week, and was desperate to tell Sam of everything that had transpired. Kurt and I had said tearful goodbyes, and I hadn't even seen Wolfgang and Hilde before I'd left. They'd avoided me, getting someone else to drive me to the airport. Getting home I was eager to tell the truth to pastor Sam, confident that he would do something about it. I thought that maybe the example of Christianity in Germany was just a bad apple in an otherwise healthy bushel. But the cold truth was, he wasn't returning my calls. Other than an almost forced meeting with my counselor in which I angrily tried to make him tell me that what happened was wrong, I had talked to *no one* at the church. They avoided me like the plague. There were no phone calls. The veil was off, the truth came out. These people were just as selfish, and fake as Hilde, they had just been better at hiding it. ……..surprise!

Hurray for Tara, surely God is with you! When I left for Germany I had received tons of calls, cards, and going away parties. Now it was just the sound of crickets in an empty stadium. So I did the sensible thing, I quit going to church altogether, telling myself dramatically that I was angry at God. I had tried to figure out Christianity, and it had backfired, and knocked me to the ground.

Now please for a moment, let me whine. Imagine that *all your friends at the same time* quit talking to you. O.k., not all, maybe there are a few, when everyone else is not looking slink over and ask you "what happened?", like you had been in a bad accident, and had a big bandage on your head.

I didn't fit in anymore. Like the biker chick that shows up for the Saturday night ride wearing a baby blue cardigan sweater, I didn't belong. I had a big old scarlet *F* for failure placed on my chest. Now, did I make the decision to not fit in on my own? No. That decision was made for me. I imagined telling my story to all of my friends, Tom, Pastor Sam, Kore, all of the people I trusted, and basically had grown up with. I daydreamed about them telling me how sorry they were, and helping me get back on my feet with kind words, and something along the lines of "well, I guess it just wasn't God's will for you, Tara, it is o.k. There is nothing wrong with *you*; it just wasn't a good fit. What do you need right now?"

But when I got home, I was alone. Like I was being punished. The church really was a well oiled machine; it was a close knit hierarchy of steps and ladders. Everyone knew where they fit on the ladder. When I "failed" at Bible College, I went from climbing on the top ladder to falling straight to the ground. There was no-one to pick me up (this, in hindsight, was a good thing), but I was deeply hurt at the time. I had night after night of dreams involving me following people from the church around trying to tell them what had happened. In my dream they were deaf, ignoring me, or always absent.

So it made complete sense what I did with my life next.

"I heard you needed a roommate." Liz, my old friend from high school said, casually puffing a smoke. *This sounds like just what I need*, I thought.

"Yeah, I really need to get out of my parents house." It was humiliating enough that I had to come home, but to move back in with my parents, stuffed in an old room full of my childhood relics was worse. My car was sold, and I had no house/apartment/job. Every day I was serenaded with a chorus of "what are you going to do now?" I was dying to get out.

"I know of some apartments that are close" she said. I took the fact that she didn't even ask what had happened as a good sign.

If you would have told me that in six months time I would have been drinking every night at a local bar, daily smoking three packs of cigarettes, and smoking pot every day, I would have crucified you myself. But the truth is, I did not care. I didn't want to face what happened in Germany, and I had no idea what to do with my life. I was riddled with guilt, confusion, freedom and shame. All emotions that I had no idea what to do with. I had been making plans since sixteen and there I was at 23 with no focus.

All the figuring and looking for religious enlightenment had completely burnt me out. When it came time to make a decision once I was home, instead of pondering it for days in metaphysical agony, I just made a quick, normal decision like everyone else. And I had a lot of decisions to make. I had to get a job, make some money, and try to figure out what had just happened to me, I needed to make some new friends.

So I got a job as a waitress, and proceeded to live the nightlife. I made up for all my strict teenage years, partying like there was no tomorrow. I got high, and let little pieces of reflection come into my mind, slowly looking honestly at my *Christian* experience. Every time anyone asked me what had happened, I was so bitter, my tongue forked at the re-telling of the story. But even then, kindness was all around me. I was surrounded by wonderful new friends, and besides stupidly abusing my body, I couldn't remember when I'd had so much fun! God, (who I will also refer to as the Higher Power or the Goddess from now on) was there, and with all my delusions of name and practice cleared away, I was free to discover.

I got a Tarot deck, promising myself that this time, I would have that deck for life. I started practicing doing readings on my friends; late hours, and empty bottles lending to the openness needed for the fledgling readings. I started tentatively reading books about Paganism, the first being Phyllis Currott's *Book of Shadows*. I longed for the connection that she talked about. Her coven seemed to complement her personal path, rather than define it.

It seemed the women she practiced with held hands and walked toward the Higher Power together, instead of my view of Christianity, which no matter what anyone said, was experienced through the confines of the pastor and the churches rules. Here is God, he is this, and this, and this, and this is how you approach him. That was how I began to sum up Christianity.

To have the faith to have NO rules. To meet the Higher Power undefined. I toyed with that idea, it feeling so foreign to me, that I looked for rules to start with, falling back into an old pattern. I caught myself, not ever wanting to get back into organized religion, no matter what religion, and started from scratch again, only to look for more rules. I had lived by rules for so long, I wasn't sure if I knew how to exist without them.

Something like God, the Goddess, and the Higher Power is so indefinable, that man simply can't stand it. He has to find a way to make a neat little box to shove that in, too. I looked honestly at all religions. At the heart of them all was probably someone meaning well, someone with an honest experience. Then with time came the perversion. Money, power, ego identity, rules, all the downfall of what should be a beautiful thing. Could I live without religion? I went on the Wicca chat rooms only to see people arguing about the proper way to cast a circle. Disgusted, I logged off. Just like any other religion, any other reason to argue about triviality.

As I pounded beer after beer in my little apartment, and tried not to think about Germany, I came back down to earth. I looked for once at what was inside of me, what was in my heart. Instead of using something outside of me as a starting point, like the Bible, the church, I let go, and looked within. It was there that I found the small pea-sized remnants of my personal beliefs, so time battered, they were like a timid child, or an abused animal. I was trying to listen to someone that for years I had told to shut up. Every time I tried to lure them out with promises of listening they said "yeah, right, you will ignore me, just like you have for ages". I had suppressed, shoved, and beat them down, now I was calling them back like the prodigal son.

I know it sounds like a hokey candidate for an Oprah episode, but I met myself for the first time at my seventies style thrift store table in my little apartment complex. Sitting there staring at empty beer bottles, marijuana seeds scattered like tears, and the mountainous pile of cigarette butts, I heard a peep inside myself. And I went in to investigate.

It was quiet in there………. gentle…….. open………
loving…….. accepting.

Not at all like the loud mouth I had been. I seemed to put up with my rambling mind with peacefulness and maybe a little humor. I couldn't believe how open it was! It seemed to listen rather than talk. Instead of all the striving, and denying and pushing, I began to see how simple spirituality could be.

That was the beginning of the inner change. Complementing that was a completely different outer set of circumstances. One minute I am surrounded with hallelujahs, the next my restaurant manager boss is doing lines of coke in the bathroom, and my two female managers are groping each other in front of me. Talk about culture shock!

Day in and day out I went to work, got high, gobbled up books about Paganism, but avoided talking to others about it, and partied hard with a capital H. The restaurant I worked at was a Peyton place-they were a rough bunch. Even for normal non-church people, they were pretty rough. Most of the cooks were strung out on heroin. The dishwasher was a very angry looking fellow from Nicaragua, rumored to have slit a few throats. Everyone was openly sexual, they all slept with each other, and most people snorted coke like it was candy. The girl's bathroom smelled like vomit from all the bulimic waitresses. We passed around pills, joints, and leftover whiskey, making sure to share. My hands shook when I took food orders from too many pills, not enough sleep, and three peoples worth of booze. I was trying to shock my mind and body and I did.

Now let me say that I did not seek this out. I simply applied for the first waitressing job I could find, not knowing that this would become the norm for me. My stringent boundaries were all dropped the moment I had left the church, and I had no desire to make new ones. So I was like a child exploring life for the first time.

I certainly don't advocate drowning your sorrows in addictive substances, because I was lucky to have gotten out, but nose diving into this lifestyle was very freeing for me. I was SO SO SO angry, and I stayed high on something most of the time. For about two years in fact. It was enough time to start re-programming my brain, and get over being angry. Underneath all of the boozing, and toking, I was waking up. Maybe I couldn't have done it sober, I don't know.

I started to embrace circular time, instead of linear. I looked beneath what people did for the first time, and at the human underneath. I was learning to separate people from their actions, and drop the *bad* and *good* label I still liked to slap on everyone, and everything. I didn't judge the people who did heroin or coke, but saw that they were just people making choices. It all boiled down to that. People making choices, and whether or not they would face the consequences of their choices. I watched the heroin addicts lives go down the toilet and, stripped of all cosmic meaning, I just saw stupid decisions bringing miserable consequences. Nothing more, nothing less. God really had little to do with it. This caused me to switch from pushing my responsibility to the church, to learning that I was responsible for myself. No one was going to clean up after me.

I listened to my intuition, and begged it to be louder. Among the waitresses I developed a reputation for being someone you could talk to, and I had random people confessing things to me. I didn't ask for it, it seemed like everything else, to come to me. Here was what I wanted, to help people, and I got it. It was like a cruel joke from God/Goddess. Now, when I woke at two in the afternoon, pulled on my jeans from the night before, picking off any leftover sour cream and bacon bits, smoked a bowl and a few cigarettes, and went to work, *now* was when people needed me. Not when I went to Bible College, shunned almost everything pleasurable, and acted like a know-it-all-A-hole. Maybe I was more accessible once I dropped all the bullcrap. Go figure.

I decided that I liked the blanket of Paganism, knowing that it seemed to be the most undefined of defined belief systems. *After all, you have to call it something*, I rationalized. I liked the way Pagans claimed to embrace all religions, even though what I saw was far from that. There were plenty of religious-idiot pagans, too. I meditated on what religion means to mankind for months, and realized that *there is no answer*. No rule to make it all make sense. It was what it was to each individual. Like picking out a style of car that I fancied, I could pick a belief system that suited me.

God was all of it! I felt like I had just been handed a Gold God Visa card with a limitless balance, and told to shop till my heart's desire.

I decided to pick tidbits from all religions. A few Hindu Goddesses here, a Wiccan altar there, maybe a Buddhist chant, even a few Bible verses. I wanted to connect with the Higher Power in the way that made sense to me, in a way that came from my HEART. I didn't want to do anything out of habit, cultural pressure, or heritage. When I worshipped I wanted to *want* to do it, and not be forced or guilted into doing it.

The external things were just ways to make, or

enhance the already existing connection. The inspiration you got from looking at your altar, the peace from sitting under a tree, the wisdom from a timely Bible verse, the connection to the earth that came from a wild dance. God wasn't those things; they were just things that helped US. Damn, but I finally got it!

What I was doing just so happened to have a name. *Solitary eclectic Witch*. Solitary meaning alone, Eclectic meaning that I wasn't part of any religious organization, or better yet that I did what I wanted, and Witch, coming from the Anglo-Saxon word Wicce meaning "to bend or to shape", and also translated as "a Wise One, a Seer"..... I was a Witch, and I knew it. I had always been one.

I hid this knowledge in my heart, not ready to call myself anything. *The name doesn't matter anyway*, I said to myself.

Chapter Six

"Any fool can make a rule, and any fool will mind it."
- Thoreau

Now, this is where the story comes to a screeching
halt. The moment of truth. No matter what I have said
about all I went through, I'm sure some of you are saying
"how in the world do you go from Christianity to
Witchcraft?" One day she is a die-hard, give -up-
everything -for -the- cause Christian, next thing she is
completely comfortable calling herself a Witch. Is this
chick crazy or does she just need a title to function? Hello
Mrs. Identity crisis?!

The truth is neither. I have given you my basic
background in Christianity, but there is a lot I haven't told
you about my natural Pagan background (for goodness
sake, no wonder I was so confused).

For starters, while I was neck-deep in fanatical
Christendom as a child, my parents never denied me
knowledge. While my peer's folks were cutting articles out
of the newspaper that reeked of "the world" so their pure
children wouldn't be tainted by them, my parents
encouraged me to read everything I could get my hands on,
and to see the world as a potentially dangerous, but
fascinating place. My dad hoarded books of all kinds, and I
had to so much as stroll downstairs to pull a book off of the
shelf to learn about everything my heart desired. We
traveled a lot, visiting new cities, learning. I realized at a
young age that the world was much bigger than my small
sphere of influence in Anytown, USA.

As a family we were fascinated with the world, and

other cultures. Even to this day, when you walk in my parent's house, there are African ceremonial masks, large Tibetan Daikini statues, and every manner of Native American, Indian, and Chinese fetishes, dolls and wall hangings.

Also, we were weird. Like, New Age weird.

Burning incense in our house was the norm. I assume that most people's dealings with incense are of a let's-mask –the- pot -smoke nature. Or maybe a religious thing. My dad just liked the way it smelled. The scent of a stick of incense burning instantly transports me back to Saturday afternoons in the Garabedian household. Sometimes we would clean up the living room, and my sisters and I always fought for the coveted job of polishing the furniture. Whoever got that job got to piss around, and waste time, and whenever an adult walked by, you just pretended to polish. An hour or so of this and all the rest of the chores would be done. My dad would then light the requisite stick of incense, maybe Sandalwood (his favorite), or Amber or Patchouli. He would settle down to watch some old monster flick like *Mothra*, or *House of Wax,* while we played, and avoided looking at the TV. The smells pervaded the room. Wonderful woody incense and the lovely lemon smell of furniture polish, two of my favorite scents to this day.

Dad was always trying out some new health food craze. On us. Most fondly do I remember the grains phase. *Every night* for weeks we ate grains, which was a combination of millet, barley, and brown rice, cooked in my mom's worn out old pressure cooker. We drowned the grains in Kikkoman soy sauce, and livened things up by the whole family eating with chopsticks. Did I mention that my dad loves to eat with chopsticks? If you can eat it with chopsticks, he will try.

Anyway, there were the aforementioned grains, the seaweed soup, which mercifully wasn't pushed on us, but you could smell a mile away, the colloidal silver teaspoonfuls, the mysterious green/brownish liquid that even when masked in orange juice still tasted of leaves, and licorice.

We drank cup after cup of what we called "dirt tea" (which was Echinacea before it became hugely commercialized). There were lots and lots of vitamins, and no one in the household went without a daily vitamin pill, or two....or three. Some of the experiments were pleasant, like the honey phase, which involved a teaspoon of honey two times a day. I eagerly stood in line with my brother and sisters for the sticky sweet medicine. After dirt tea, honey was heaven.

We went to the symphony, we got our hands hennaed at the Indian festival, we stuffed ourselves with Spanakopita, and danced the along with the Lithuanians. Our vacations were to Arkansas to mine for gold or to New Orleans to Marie Laveau's grave. We went in every museum we could gain admission to. "People who went over Niagara Falls in a Barrel" "Cherokee Trail of Tears", "Women's Suffrage", and" Diseases of the Civil War". I was obsessed with mummies and Egyptology, and loved to go to the library and check out books on the black plague, and the Witch hunts.

The people I went to school with thought Chinese food was exotic, and wouldn't touch it....no wonder we didn't fit in.

We ate differently, didn't think like anyone that was in the church, knew of the world around us, were exposed to a little culture, and were encouraged to think outside ourselves. Oh yeah, then there was the acupuncture.

My dad studied acupuncture in China. I can remember the time my friend from Bible College walked in on me getting an acupuncture treatment. We were on our way to the International Food Festival for some Vietnamese food, and to watch belly dancers, and I didn't feel well. So, I was lying on the floor with about ten acupuncture needles sticking out of my FACE.

I could almost hear her thinking "this is sin, if I have ever seen it".

I knew that just because I didn't understand it, or grow up with it, or speak its language, or like the way it looked, sounded or smelled, that it wasn't *bad*. I saw it as something to discover. In hindsight I understand the reason Christianity didn't work for me.

You can't fit an open mind into a close minded religion.

Now I know that a lot of you are freaking out about that last statement. Let me clarify. Close minded means that the mind is closed about a particular subject. Christianity doesn't leave much room for interpretation, personal expression, or exploration. Those things are strongly discouraged. The moment you step out of the carefully set boundaries of the church you are given the boot.

Also, like the children that come out of the womb with a natural affinity for animals, or say, who gravitate to building blocks, and later become architects, I have always been fascinated by Witches. The hook nosed, green faced warty hag that forms most people's perception of a Witch never swayed me. I knew there was more, that she was just a small reflection of what a Witch was.

There was a hollowed out tree in our backyard. As a

child, I walked to the blackened hole, and threw in Bluet, Buttercups, stones, and any other natural, interesting things I found in the yard. I loved to play Witch. As I stirred the "cauldron" I was doing something. I wasn't sure what but I knew on a base level that I was trying to reach something. I felt that it was very close, and I was oft frustrated because I couldn't reach it.

Halloween (Witches call it Samhain meaning, *summer's end*) was a highly exciting, and equally frustrating event. I looked forward to it all year. I always felt that the night had layers and that I was only experiencing the outer layer. As we walked home from trick or treating, our bags full of candy, I knew that there was something else I should be doing, I just didn't know what. Voicing this would have been futile, as I wasn't sure what it was that I wanted to give voice to. It was a feeling, and a subconscious one at that.

In my tweens, when my concerns were how many pairs of jelly shoes I owned, and boys boys boys, we began receiving the Barnes and Noble catalogue in the mail. Running to the mailbox I snatched it up before any of my other family members could get to it. It had a New Age section, and there were REAL books on Witchcraft. I read the descriptions over and over again, hoping to find some clue, something that would help me make some sense of this strange obsession. I never spoke of it to my peers, one bad playground experience reminding me that not everyone thought it was fun to play "Witch". I was scared to ask my dad if I could buy one of the books fully realizing that the general consensus was that Witchcraft was evil, baby sacrificing business. I scavenged his bookshelves for anything that remotely spoke of Witchcraft. All I found was a dog eared copy of Ripley's Believe It or Not, the supernatural edition. It was full of ghost stories, complete with eerie illustrations. The only Witchcraft it had were disturbing spells involving dead men's hands, and rabbit feet. It grossed me out.

Finally, sheepishly I mentioned it to my dad.

"No, Tara, you don't want to fool with that." He said cautiously, not wanting to upset me, "black magic is bad. Voodoo stuff. Once you get into that, there is no going back."

I was confused. I didn't want to make anyone fall in love with me, and I certainly didn't want to harm anyone. I just wanted to know, why would someone call themselves a Witch? What did it mean? My books on Marie Laveau, the Voodoo Queen, showed her as a kind, but powerful person. There had to be more to it all than spook stories.

My grandma used to sit me down and tell me about my third eye. She knew who was at the door before looking, or who was about to call before the phone rang. Her book shelf had a copy of Sybil Leek's book *Diary of a Witch*. What was different about her? Did she see things? Know things? Could she talk to spirits? I wanted to know the mystery of it.

Finally in Germany when I discovered the missing piece, the Goddess connection, I understood. It was what I had been looking for. I understood that most of being a Witch is understanding the Flow. The natural ways, seen and unseen. People call it Energy, Chi, Prana, the life force in and around everything that has existence. It is timeless and wordless.

Energy was how that flowed together and what song it made. I was especially interested in the discordant notes. Pain and suffering, how did that fit? Who were these dark scary Goddesses that were in every culture throughout time? The Morrigan, who feasted on dead bodies in the war fields? The angry, sexual Lilith, much misaligned by patriarchal views, even my soon to be beloved Kali with Her sword that sliced through all ignorance. There was no shoving of people into one faced roles, denying the feminine in spirituality, telling us that we had to be nice girls and boys, and that everything else was outside of the will of God.

I had done the research, knew that pentacles weren't evil or scary, that they were power signs, to be used for protection, the five points referring to earth, air, fire ,water, and spirit. Most importantly I knew that Witches did not believe that some cloven hoofed, malevolent little red man was responsible for all the wrong in the world. Witches didn't believe in Satan.

So why after all that did I nose dive right into Christianity, even after I was informed about Paganism and had all the makings of a good Witch?

Fear. Inevitability. Fate. I needed to find God in Christianity to find out that God exists outside of Christianity. Even when I returned home from Germany, disgusted at all things Christian, I was shocked to find that my prayers were answered just as they were when I was Bible thumping. You see, as much as I wanted to pretend that I was angry with God, I still prayed, as I have my whole life.

God in the church felt the same as God outside of the church. Maybe God was who I believed he was. Maybe Divinity reflected humanity, and vice-versa. Maybe to learn more about God was to learn more about myself. Maybe God was like a jewel, each facet a different face. If I was Muslim I called Him Allah, if I was Christian I called Him Jesus, if I was a Sumerian field hand in 5326 B.C. I called

Her Inanna. When I called on Oya I got that face. When I called on Odin, I got that face. People have been doing it as long as mankind has existed on this earth.

And then the last truth of the matter is that some bit of rebelliousness in me liked to shock people, calling myself a Witch, at least I did at first.

My Christian identity had been a blanket. With the blanket removed I felt like an ant under a magnifying glass. There was nothing to take the focus off of real life, and everything in my brain, heart and soul was revealed. This was sacred, necessary. How would I help people change themselves, if I had been hiding from myself for so long? It occurred to me just how many pastors and spiritual leaders out there had been under the cloak as I was, most of them had never chosen to get out from under it. They crafted the world to fit them, instead of changing themselves to fit the world. I had to see it all. I had to feel its loss, see what it had done for me, what it had robbed me of.

In Christianity, when I tried to work through issues with my parents as everyone must throughout their lives, when it got too painful I pushed it into the *bad* category. *They are not serious, spirit filled Christians*, was my explanation to myself. I'm ashamed to admit most of this, but that is how I allowed myself to think. The world is made of many things, experiences, colors, sights, sounds, and most of all, people of every shape, size and race. It got scary for me. It is scary for most people. It is so much easier when something gets scary to tell yourself a story to make the perceived monsters go away, and religion did that for me, protected me. I knew the monsters were bad, and happily stayed in my little created bubble.

The view of "us against the world" is so easily

perpetuated when you create an environment to foster it. I had no contact with the outside world, and when I did, the uneasy feelings it created by shining a light on the possibility that, yes, I was a fanatic, were pushed aside once I was back in my safe haven. The people I knew, the church I knew, the friends I knew, the doctrine I knew, it cushioned me, cocooned me. When I felt like a fanatic after working at Applebee's, where it was obvious that I was the odd one in the bunch, I marched harder, prayed louder, spoke in tongues more, upped my time at the church to validate myself. In our group we prayed hard for those poor blind people that I worked with, instead of the poor blind me that was a seventeen year old fanatic preaching religion while bussing tables. The world was so big. The customers so varied, and all I saw was one thing. One way. It is so hard not to be disgusted with myself, to love my obsessive, scared Shadow, and understand why I let it take over.

Not seeing behind the scenes and coming to terms with who I really was made me have to do a lot of catching up in my early twenties. I had never partied as an adult, where there is no parent to catch you. I had never learned how to relate to people on a normal level. I was either trying to convert you, or in the Lord's army alongside you, banging the drum.

If the church was my previous avenue for salvation, then partying hard was my new one. I could abandon myself, get lost in the best of people at the moment, and the worst the next morning. I loved making friends with the cooks, or fellow waitresses. We were like a big family, and once again I was isolated. The hours that we worked were absurd, and exclusive; who wakes up at 2 in the afternoon, and doesn't get off work until 2am? We all did, and so we partied with each other. My sphere of influence narrowed again, this time out of necessity. If my mom asked me to go to church with her, I laughed. She wanted me to get up when? Eight am? I didn't go to bed until six am. Finding a man to relate to turned out to be challenging.

Upon my arrival home, I started dating a wonderful man named Scott. He lived in New York, and was funny, sweet and great to talk to. One problem (besides our long distance relationship), he still had one foot in the church, very firmly. I had taken both feet out. He knew me *before* when I was super Christian, so he thought that showing no interest in the church was just a phase I was going through. His upbringing was shitty at best, and he desperately needed the stability that the church provided. I knew he needed it, but I was sick to my core of church. We could talk about anything *but* the church. He bristled when I spoke anything that wasn't affirming to him, and I had nothing good to say about the church at all. This, added to the long distance between us had me wishing for a way out and mourning the relationship. I really cared about him, and really wanted to be with him, but it was quickly becoming apparent that it was not going to work. I had to hide my new path from him.

One night he found me out.

The black light made us all look good. *I guess that is the point of a club.* I ordered a Greyhound, and walked back over to my friends, joining the makeshift circle in the dark dance club. The music pulsed, and I longingly looked at the dance floor. *Maybe I can convince Scott to dance with me before he gets wasted.*

"Scott…dance with me" I said, swinging my arm around him.

"No" he said in his sharp New York accent "but you

go ahead, I'll just stay here". He patted me on the back. *I'll never get used to dating a northern man.* Southern men treated women very differently, chivalry and that whole thing. Scott often treated me like his buddy, and it was hard to get used to. Both had their merits, though, with southern men came an enormous amount of jealousy, and putting women on a pedestal as fainting southern coquettes had a tendency to make us into objects. At least northern men, despite the lack of passion, would let me go off and dance by myself without going green.

I squeezed past all the people to get to the dance floor, making my way to the middle. I was a decent dancer, not fabulous, mind you, but my recent bellydance classes were upping my skills. A handsome raven haired man joined me, and we started to dance. I would have quickly bowed out, he pretty much sucked as a dancer, but the conversation was so interesting.

"Hi I'm Dan."

"Hi Dan, I'm Tara" we yelled over the music.

"What do you do?" I asked him, straining to hear his answer.

"I work for a Pagan book publisher. I'm Pagan. Do you know what that means?"

My eyes widened. *Jackpot!*

"Me too, let's go talk off of the dance floor so I can hear you" I practically dragged him off the floor.

"You are Pagan too. Cool. Imagine that."

We were immersed in conversation when Scott started to walk towards us. *Crap.* He knew that I didn't want anything to do with Christianity anymore, but he was the only one I kept my new path from. I knew he'd hate it. Of course he walked up to us right as Dan said, "so how long have you been Pagan?"

Scott stopped in his tracks and his eyes narrowed as he waited for me to answer.

"Um….I…..a little while."

"Who is your friend, Tara?" Scott asked, not bothering to mask his displeasure.

"Uh….this is, uh, Dan….Dan this is my boyfriend, Scott."

"Nice to meet ya Dan" Scott said, grinding the words out of his mouth as if they were sand. We were at a nightclub getting drunk, and Scott was mad at me for not being a Christian. I was so tired of flimsy church idealism like this.

Dan the man was oblivious. "Anyway we have just published a new book on Witchcraft for solitaries, I can get my hands on a free copy, would you like one?" I cringed. He said the *W* word. As in Witchcraft. I sure as hell wasn't ready to break that one out on an unsuspecting Scott.

I couldn't take it. Standing between this very nice chatty Witch, and Scott who was trying to decide whether to punch Dan or break up with me…..I decided to bolt.

"I'm sorry Dan, I've gotta go to the bathroom."

I left the two of them behind, and raced to the bathroom. This sucked. With our long distance relationship I never saw Scott and now the rest of the weekend would be ruined.

The weekend went exactly as I'd anticipated. He ignored the issue, but distanced himself. How could I hide that part of myself from the man I loved? Face it or not, the relationship was going nowhere. So……I cheated on him. Nasty, yes, immature, yes. I didn't have the balls to break it off, so I insured a way out. I couldn't have a clear conscience and stay with him. Of course I broke his heart; he did not deserve that, at all. He was one of the best people I had ever dated, and he deserved the best. I gave him my worst, at a time when it was plain that the stars didn't jive for us. I'm so sorry, Scott. I'm still sorry.

He felt so fragile, and *I didn't want someone fragile*. I wanted a hard partier, with a kind heart, and a strong disposition. I wanted someone to follow me down my new pathway to enlightenment- drinking and doing drugs.........I wanted someone cool, cool like my dad. The kind of cool that is rebellious, the kind that says *I don't care*. My heart was battered and broken, and I needed someone who wanted to be numb along with me.

That person was right around the corner.

"Hi, my name is Tara" I said to the tall rust haired guy who was washing dishes.

"Oh, I know who you are" he said, snarky, and flirtatious. *Hmmmmmm......this guy puts out the right mix of cool, smart and nonchalantly nice.*

Luke, his name was Luke. He would soon have the title of *my first husband*.

Shortly afterward we started dating and started our habit of choosing our poison each night. Shrooms, a couple of cases of beer? We were in our mid-twenties, that dangerous time when, if you don't start in a real direction, your "I'm only going to party a few more years" becomes a lifestyle at thirty, your bane at forty ,and your death at fifty. The lifestyle at thirty was where his two best friends existed. Jeff and Rosemary.

This would have probably continued until I "found myself" or whatever. But I got pregnant. Getting pregnant in the middle of a drug and alcohol induced haze was like being slapped awake from a deep sleep. We were stunned, but we both wanted a life of substance, and frankly for me the partying was getting old…… so we decided to do it. Get married. Give it a shot.

I once heard an author say that you can't condense a marriage or a divorce into a few pages and even if you did, it wouldn't be a fair assessment, because it is only one point of view. I'm sure his is different, and if he wants to write a book, go ahead. But from my point of view, we really didn't know each other. The day I got pregnant, I quit it all-smoking, drinking, everything. And all of the sudden no one wanted to talk to me. All of our friends, the people we saw daily, hung out with, the people I cried on and sat with while they cried, the people I was supposedly close to. No one wanted anything to do with me once I couldn't drink or smoke or hit the bong. I thought that some of the friendships I had at least were based on more than getting effed up, but apparently not. Not a single person would hang out with me when there was nothing of an illegal or intoxicating nature being ingested. Pathetic, but I made that bed, and now I was being forced to lie in it.

I found myself on the computer a lot. Trying to remember who I was before the fanaticism, before the head-first partying. What did I like to do? I couldn't remember. Before, we didn't just go to the movies, we got high and went to the movies. We didn't just go to an amusement park, we got high and went to the amusement park. What did life look like before I put on church goggles, or beer goggles? Plain old living was something I had to re-learn, and now I had so much time I didn't know what to do with it. As my belly grew, and my brain-fog cleared, so did my memories of who I was before the church, before I was a party-girl. I liked herbs, I remembered that. My memories went to the little gardens I had as a child that grew Basil, Sage and Lemon Verbena. I

154

liked fashion, so I bought *Vogue* and renewed my interest in models and Versace. I used to gobble up books, so I renewed my stock, and spent a lot of time at bookstores. I loved crafts, so trips to the craft store became more frequent. Once I tried to remember it opened the floodgates, everything came back to me. All this added with plenty of time outside and my growing interest in Witchcraft, I started to re-discover my roots.

Luke grew worried with each passing day of my pregnancy, drowning himself in alcohol. I grew up in a stable home, he didn't. I think he doubted his ability to pull it off. The day the baby came was monumental- I fell in love with her, and out of love with him. The more I loved this new little person the more I realized that I didn't even know her father.

Luke, my husband, was smooth. He would flip his cigarettes out of the box, light them, and take an apathetic drag all with the flick of his wrist. He naturally gave out this "what you lookin' at?" look. Born in rural West Virginia I always thought he should have been born in Brooklyn. He was an excellent father, but as a couple we didn't quite cut it.

As the years passed, our life became a charade, a game. I called it "pass the baby". I'd wake up at three am for my morning show radio co-host job, wake up my daughter, drop her off at grandmas at four- thirty, go to work till noon, then pick her up. We'd play and nap till seven pm when Luke got home. Once he was home there was a standard conversation about how much she'd eaten, pooped, slept, which usually ended in an argument. I'd angrily hurry off to bed. Not to say that we wouldn't make feeble attempts at trying, but I was past the point of caring. I didn't want to talk to him; he didn't want to talk to me. I really think we were doomed from the start, we had no foundation. But marriage in my family was just something that you didn't leave, you just didn't.

As the years passed and my baby became a toddler I started to look at my life as a colossal fuck-up. I felt like I had failed at Germany, and the still-in-love state of marriage that my parents had after forty- five years together had never even started for me. I wanted out. I wanted to hit rewind, I wanted to be with the only things that comforted me, and made my heart sing. My daughter and my spiritual path.

As I cried in our bedroom for the thousandth time wondering how I got where I was, fanaticizing about taking my daughter and living any other life than the one I had, I slumped down on the bed.

I need help. Whoever you are, please help me. I need help.

My daughter's cry echoed from her bed, and I left my pity to live real life.

***

I sat up in the bed, covered in sweat. It took me a second to adjust to my familiar bedtime surroundings, and realize that I had fallen asleep with my daughter Willow in my arms. My heart beat with glee. I had had a dream, and even though I didn't know what it meant, my dream meant something.

It was hazy as most dreams are, and I appeared to be in a shop of sorts. Yet, I had the feeling of *really being there*, which later I would discover was the earmark of astral travel. The shop was full of beautiful items, and it felt peaceful. I browsed the perimeter of the store, and noticed that everything was rainbow colored. Not like a flag, with distinct colors, but like a shell or an oil spill, that when you turn your head rewards you with a color play. I picked up a wooden cane that was propped against the wall, amazed at all the colors. It seemed three dimensional. I was transfixed on the cane, turning it around in my hands, when I felt someone come up behind me. I heard a female voice say "can I help you?" I spun around, anxious to see who possessed the soft voice.

There was a woman standing before me. She looked like your grade school best friend's grandma, you know, the one that you didn't want to admit was just a tiny bit more hip than your own grandma. Her hair was dyed red, from a lifetime of dye jobs, and she had laugh lines layered like strata around her mouth.

She started talking, but I couldn't hear the words. Because I was staring at her robe……it kept changing colors, red, to green, to purple, to yellow. I had never seen color like that-each change seemed to be alive. Somehow the words and colors formed a certain rhythm. I felt like I could fall into that rhythm, and know. Know about life, love, and everything unseen. Her robe meant more than color…... it was life.

She held up an onion. "Peel this for Sara" she spoke as I started to drift awake.

Recalling the dream, my shaky hands dialed the phone. I had to talk to Kurt. We had been following a similar path, and I knew he would have some answers.

"She showed me a rainbow cane, and she had this rainbow robe that kept changing colors, and she told me to peel an onion for Sara." I was practically out of breath.

"Who is Sara?" Kurt said.

"This chick I work with."

"Is she sick?" he asked.

157

"Yeah, she has heart problems" I said, amazed that he would know that.

"Well the onion is a common healing spell. You visualize healing as you peel the layers."

My jaw dropped. Kurt didn't know that Sara had multiple problems, heart issues being the least of them. Her problems were certainly layered like an onion.

"What about the rest?" I wanted to know about the magical woman, the shop, and the rainbows.

"Baby, you met Iris, the Goddess of Rainbows!" I could hear him smiling.

I gushed, "I love you Kurt, you always manage to make everything right!" I was in utter amazement that Iris would actually want to talk to me! I could feel a renewed sense of hope coming on.

"Wait there is more" Kurt said with a twinkle in his voice, "she is also the Goddess of new beginnings."

New beginnings. I hung up the phone. All I could think about was how much I needed a new beginning, a fresh start. Sitting on the edge of the bed, with my new husband in the other room, I felt like I'd been heard. She, He, They, Whomever, had been listening. Thank Goddess, there was hope. I had just had my first Witchy dream since I was a child. I was hopping on the broomstick, and as soon as I learned to fly, I was taking my baby girl with me.

Chapter Seven

"You have brains in your head
You have feet in your shoes
And you can steer yourself
Any direction you choose."
- Dr. Seuss

O.k. let me stop for a minute and tell you a little bit about why I choose Witchcraft as a personal path, the car I choose drive to the Divine, if you will. This is for those of you who are still under the impression that it is nude, wanton Satan worship. Call it a little intro to Witchcraft primer.

I like to tell people that Witchcraft is the best self-help class you will ever take, or the most effective "find yourself" book that you will ever read.

There are the key words, like *spells, ritual, altar*, and all those other things we read about, or see in movies like *The Craft*. Those things took me a while to warm up to- I'll get to them later. But the real part of Witchcraft, *the power*, that is what I want to explain.

There is a general formula for life, no matter what path you are on-Christian, Jew, Atheist, Pagan. Life hands you opportunities to learn. You either learn, or you ignore the lesson, until it comes up again…and it always does. I believe because Witchcraft is ACTIVELY seeking personal growth, and no one is telling you your boundaries that this particular path helps speed up the process.

There is nothing- no mindset, doctrine, or person holding me back. The only "rule" is to not hurt or manipulate anyone else, and believe it or not, there is not some moral, righteous reason for that one "rule". It is actually pretty practical. Since we are all one, harming someone else is harming yourself- kinda counterproductive to screw it up if you ask me. Hexing does have its place, but trying to understand hexing is only for fully developed practitioners. When you finally do understand, you see that it is executed as a necessity and is not at all something you get pleasure out of. It certainly isn't just slapping someone with a magic hand when they piss you off.

So in Witchcraft, I am responsible for my own growth. I came to this incarnation as a Leo sun, Aries rising, Taurus moon...... this means that I have been forceful, and loud from birth. (My mom tells me that I used to stand up in my crib and say "and hereeees Johnny!") It also means I am very much into speed, and getting right to the point. I take my lions roar, bull horns and ram my ram's head into life (as you have previously seen). That is why this path works for me. Because at the end of the day, there is no Satan, no pastor, no doctrine I can blame anything on, or give accolades to. I am my best and worst of success and failure, it all falls in my lap.

But I can hear you saying "Witchcraft, a self-help tool? Seriously? I thought it was all about spells, and robes and junk". Let me educate.

Like the people that only go to church on Easter, or to Christmas Mass, then ignore the Divine in their lives for the rest of the year, then I would say that Witchcraft *is* all spells and outward stuff. For those people, it is just for looks. Let's leave them to their Walmart brand garb, and mindfully placed ornate daggers.

But if you want it to work.....if you want to get to the *heart* of it all, then we need to dig a little deeper.

Most people get involved in Witchcraft wondering if

they can influence some outside thing. Make so & so love them, get a new job, more money, etc. They want a quick fix or instant power over a situation that probably needs more than a magical band-aid. And believe me, sonny, there are PLENTY of books selling this form of fix-a-flat magic. Not to say that it doesn't work sometimes. If you get a newbie with a lot of emotional pull, who does a spell for more money, they might just create enough energy with their emotions and intent to get a surprise refund from the insurance company, or a $25.00 check from Aunt Clara. There is nothing wrong with this…... feel free to spell away. Do spells till your fingers are black with candle soot. Do spells till you feel like you can call yourself a Witch. Then try, just try to understand the *whys* of things. Try to see what is underneath it all.

Instead of just eating what is on your plate, think about where it came from, and who enabled it to get to you. If you never dig deep, you continue on the same mundane "I want this, so I will try to make it happen" mentality. It will only serve to frustrate you in the future. You will be missing the main point, which is that you will continue to look outside yourself for something to make you happy. The Goddess is within, the answers are within. More money, a new lover is nice, but in the end will neither add nor take away from the life that only you can create. Yeah, it sounds like a New Age catch phrase, but man, is it true. Are you even really satisfied when you get those new clothes, or lose those twenty pounds? Maybe for a small chunk of time, but eventually human need and want kicks in, and you are desiring something else with the same "when I just get this, then I will be happy" mindset. It is an endless cycle.

Maybe there is a *reason* that you don't have money.

Maybe more money is not the answer- maybe finding the root or the underlying cause of the problem is the answer. This is where Witchcraft comes in (and the time for spells that not only work, but give you a real understanding, and subsequently more power. Real power.)

Let's continue with the money problem. Say you have always had problems with money, and you find yourself needing more, yet again- the more you get, the more you need. You do a personal money spell, asking the Goddess (or whomever you call on) to help you with the real problem. Maybe you ask Brigit for healing. Maybe you ask Odin for wisdom. Maybe you ask Bast for some release, and to lighten up. Maybe you are crazy like me, and ask Kali to take Her sword and lop off the offending idea that is causing the problem. Sorta like the time you said you were tired and needed a break, got a 104 fever the next day, and spent two weeks in bed. Kali is not a time waster.

Let me tell you this path is not for the wimpy or weak. Chances are, if you ask you will receive. The Goddess will *show you* in many ways where things need to change in your life, or where your underlying unhealthy views of money are influencing your life. The power doesn't come from changing your surroundings, any coward can do that. It comes from changing yourself. It will show you what you are made of….it will be time to put on the Big Girl Pants.

Parental issues will come up; things will be dragged out of long forgotten parts of your psyche. Your spending habits will come into full view. A real money crisis might pop its head up, so your attention will be drawn to the immediate issue. With love and support, the Goddess will help you work through these things, but it is called *work* for a reason. Sometimes I think it should be called Witchwork

162

instead of Witchcraft. This path is not for the lazy or the fearful, and if you want Mc Religion served nicely with a side of fries, look elsewhere.

It is challenging, amazing, and a constant learning process. You never arrive, you are never better or worse than anyone else. You are just where you need to be. There are no steps and ladders, it is more like a journey in which sometimes we are resting, and sometimes we are running. Once you delve into energy, you will gain perspective and really learn something, it will scare you off, or you will get drunk off of the power of it, and miss the point. Most of us don't *choose* to be uncomfortable to learn. Most of our technological generation likes things the way we likes 'em.

Hopefully, you eventually *get it* that when you learn more about yourself, you let go of ego a little. The side effect of that is that you do gain power, and knowledge. When you have nothing to lose you have nothing to fear, the fearless have no boundaries. You will have a deeper understanding, although you won't feel a need to prove it, or blab it, or push it on anyone. The fumes from all this soul searching eventually create peace, and peace is what ya want. Peace is an inner knowing that no matter what the circumstances, you have that quiet place to go. The place where even if it feels bad, it is still o.k.....powerful, even.

You will be the guy in the room with the gun that he doesn't necessarily need to use, but is resting in the fact that it is there, nestled at his side.

That is why I chose Witchcraft particularly, because Witchcraft outside of black fingernails, and *Charmed* episodes is a very powerful place to dwell where I can learn to my heart's content. I want to learn and grow as much as I can while I'm here on this earth....and knowing that you have that Glock at your disposal rocks pretty hard, too.

163

When I got back from Germany, the biggest lesson, and one that I will probably be learning for the rest of my life, was to learn to trust my instincts and intuition. I wasn't "bad", I was connected to a source of constant wisdom, my inner voice. I needed to learn to hear and respect my inner voice on each aspect of my life, whether it be contact with the spirit world, friendships, unhealthy relationships, or simply being able to make a decision based on what was inside me, and not what someone else said I should be.

There seemed to be several problems. I had been a prisoner. Tell a man who has been locked up most of his life that he is now free to roam......see what that does to him. It ain't the picnic that it sounds like. Reminds me of the old man in the movie *The Shawshank Redemption*-he had been in prison most of his life, when he got out he hung himself. He just didn't know how to live "on the outside".

I was still approaching Paganism like I approached Christianity, still waiting for someone to tell me what to do. I had been programmed from childhood to do, say, and think what other people said to do, say, and think. If you walk into a church today and say "tell me how to live, tell me how to be a Christian", there will be a line at the door ready to dictate your life down to even what you must wear. I had heard this my whole life, and knew the rules better than anybody.

Concerning every aspect of my life, I had to learn how to *trust*. Trust the Goddess that I wouldn't end up in another Germany situation and trust myself, that the small yearnings in my heart weren't bad or wrong. I wanted out of my marriage. I judged that, and quickly dismissed it. I wanted a different career; I judged that and pushed it away. I wanted to learn more on my new path, and I still had some small buried part of me saying that what I was doing was wrong.

I wasn't thinking, yet. I was still acting on autopilot, taking internal orders from some idea of life that wasn't even mine.

Even though I had chilled out a lot on chasing God, I still was looking for a connection that I could live with, which left me with a lot of unanswered questions. I was only sure of a couple of things, things I had learned so far. I held on to these new realizations like precious gems.

I figured out that *if you are seeking you will find*. I ran after what I thought was God but there right in front of me was what I needed. Patiently waiting for me to chill out enough to get it. It took ALL THAT for me to realize that I didn't have to finish a marathon to get to the Higher Power; that the Goddess wanted a connection with me, as bad as I wanted one with Her. Thank goodness. I don't think the Universe would have tolerated any more striving from me, so I finally relaxed a bit.

I also learned that *spiritual experience is uniquely personal but social at the same time*. Most people have a connection, entirely their own, and most people feel the need to share this with others in some capacity. I didn't want anyone telling me what to do, but I did want someone to share this new path with.

So all that hemming and hawing and freaking out, Bible College, and buckets of tears and that is what I learned. I felt pretty proud of myself. I felt like I knew something others didn't. I felt like I had "been through it", like I "had some answers". Obviously I had never heard what Confucius had to say-"the beginning of wisdom is knowing that you know nothing".

God, I was a mess.

I wandered for the next couple of months, needing

more, but not knowing what it was. Salvation came in the form of four pink walls, and a 30% off sign.

***

Jingle Jingle. The doors to the Crystal Garden chimed gently as they opened. The familiar smell of Nag Champa hit me, and I instantly felt at ease. The Crystal Garden was a small New Age shop camouflaged in uptown colonial style snobbery. It sat awkwardly next to wine shops, and pricey stationary stores. I had started frequenting the store after accidentally discovering it while enjoying a languid Saturday shopping. Within a month of discovering the store, I was visiting there often; relieved to have a place I could go to be quiet. It became a second home, a place I felt accepted and understood. The Crystal Garden was a living, breathing extension of Marnie, the shop owner.

It was a beautiful store. Not aesthetically beautiful like the more high end shop across town, with their exorbitant prices, $400 Kwan Yin statues, and colorful chakra wheels.

The Crystal Garden was beautiful in the way that home feels like....warm, inviting, like someplace you could put your feet on the furniture, and wouldn't get yelled at. The walls were baby pink. There was always soft melodic New Age music playing, and the comforting smell of incense had worked its way into the drapes. The room hummed with a kind of powerful but respectful energy. It said "take your time; I'm here if you want me".

The bookcases were full of knowledge, and some silliness, too. Marnie had a little of everything. A little Witchcraft, a little New Age, a little Native American healing, a little herbalism, even a little cheese, like "Magic 1,2,3" and "Three Easy Steps to Psychic Ability".

But the most precious thing of all was the store cats. Marnie was a big softy, and an animal rescuer. So there was Mojo, a lion of a cat, who she had found abandoned in a parking lot, and Princess Pudding, who was a small tabby with a lame foot. She sort of dragged herself around the store with all the airs of royalty. The two cats checked out each person who came in the store and decided whether or not they liked you. Princess Pudding would wriggle back to Marnie and seem to report on whoever had entered, like some soft, fuzzy spy.

At the crux of the store were two high backed mauve armchairs. Marnie always occupied one of those, and the other begged to embrace you. The chairs were the stage for many wonderful conversations, and exploration of ideas. The chairs also faced Marnie's heart, her rocks.

In the middle of the store, there were two huge tables filled with every hue of stone imaginable.

My uncle was a rock hound so I grew up with rocks. Split geodes, Amethyst points, volcanic rock, and big hunks of Sandstone. I had always thought they were neat; a curiosity wedged in-between the books on the mahogany book shelf. They were pretty to play with, but I never got it. Now it was different- I was learning that everything had its own vibration of energy on the planet, and that energy could be transferred, especially from stones, or rocks. The wise old men and women of the natural world.

One day as we were chatting Marnie held up a green Calcite. It was the color of the Mediterranean, and smooth as silk. She showed me how to place it on my chakras for cleansing.

"Put it on your third eye" she said, chuckling.

"What am I supposed to do with it?" I said, momentarily feeling stupid for holding a rock to my head.

"Do nothing. Give it a few minutes and then remove it from your auric field. You can go place it on the table in the corner, then see if you feel different than when you started."

It was challenging to idly chat with my hand up in the air, but it is weird what you can get used to.

"O.k., it's been five minutes" Marnie said.

"Huh? Oh yeah, I know it sounds silly but I almost forgot!" I placed the rock on the table; it was warm from my body heat. Mojo looked up from his grooming and seemed to be listening.

I did feel different. It wasn't a head thing, my thoughts still swam around and around, but the Calcite had definitely affected my body. It felt like the first day of vacation when your body is starting to unwind, but your brain is still keyed up. I felt de-congested energetically.

"I could really get used to this, Marnie. What would happen if I did this over a period of time?" I was excited.

"Your body would change first, then your mind. To understand energy work, and how stones affect you, then you have to understand the energetic body. See it as a thing not separate from yourself, which needs rest, rejuvenation, periodic cleansing, and positive energy like your physical body and mind do." Marnie knew a lot about a lot.

"So different stones do different things?" I was curious.

"Yeah, follow me." She got up from behind the counter, and led me to one of her tables full of stones. It was a long banquet style table, with a backdrop of rich purple brocade. The multiple groupings of stones popped like a Jackson Pollack.

To the soundtrack of Buddhist chants we explored the many- colored baskets of rocks.

"Don't think about the meaning, or read the card at the bottom of each basket. Just place it in your hands, detach your mind, and listen with your instinct. See how it makes you feel. See if it changes your energetic current. Then read the card if you want to."

I picked up a murky forest green stone with bold splotches of red in it, and instantly felt grounded, like I had been dreaming, and I was just waking up to what was around me. Things felt very solid. I described the feeling to Marnie.

"Go ahead and read the card" she motioned toward the wicker basket.

"Bloodstone grounds, and clears the mind. Good for....."

"Wow. How cool is this!" I was a kid in a candy shop.

On the *yes* list: shimmery Labradorite, milky white Selenite, and rosy pink Rhodochrysite.

On the *no* list: translucent orange Carnelian, sunshine yellow Citrine, and pupil black Obsidian. When I picked up some marbled green Malachite, I felt like I would throw up.

"Whoa, what just happened?" I said, a little shaken.

"There is nothing wrong with the stone, Tara. Your needs change as you change, I guess you don't need Malachite today."

Rocks weren't the only thing Marnie taught me.

One particularly misty fall day, I bounced into the shop unable to wait for the soothing smell of incense, and the mini-vacation from stress with her rocks. She was standing in the corner over a bleached blond who was seated. Marnie had her hands on the woman's shoulders. They were both very still.

I walked the perimeter and tried not to stare. Whatever she was doing it looked important, and I didn't want to interfere. I eyed the woman as she briefly hugged Marnie and then left the store.

"What was that?" I said as soon as the woman was out of earshot.

"Reiki. I was giving the woman Reiki. She was having a bad day". Marnie said in her usual quiet way.

"Well, what is it?"

"It is channeled universal life energy. I am a Reiki master." She was moving around the shop placing books back on shelves, and tidying up.

"Sounds kinda hokey to me, Marnie. You know I hate stuff like that..." I caught myself. "I'm sorry to sound so brash. That didn't come out like I meant it to."

"Come here, Tara. I'll let you feel it. You are a pretty experience based person, so you can tell me what you think." She had me sit on the cushy chair reserved for customers.

"What do I do?" as I said it I realized that I asked her that often.

"Nothing, just sit there and relax". She placed her gentle hands on my shoulders.

I felt an immediate zing, then warmth, then little laser-like points of heat, and cool. As I was focusing on the feeling of it, I realized that I also felt like I was *filling up*. Like I had been half empty, or half tired, half full, half eaten, like a forgotten apple in a lunchbox. Reiki seemed to fill in the old parts with light, warmth, and something wonderful.

We spent the rest of the day talking about Reiki.

Paganism was so broad, so all encompassing. It offered so many things to learn about, sift through. Tarot, Reiki, stones and crystals, Pendulums, energy work, Herbalism,

Palmistry, Runes, Witchcraft, Chakras, angels, guides, meditation, candles, spells… some of it was Wiccan, some of it was Pagan, some of it was Native American, some of it was New Age. Some people called themselves psychics, some Witches, some Wiccans, some Healers, some Directors on the Most High Pathway of Light. Some of it made me laugh, some of it made me cry, some of it bored me, some of it blew me away. All of it was game. All of it was valid to someone.

I wanted to meet those "someones".

"I don't know anyone who practices but you, Marnie. I need to meet some people."

She smiled. "It's funny that you bring that up, I was thinking about bringing back Witches Night Out."

"That sounds cool." I envisioned a bonfire, black robes, and all of my new friends dancing merrily in a circle, or even better, a group of smart, witty women in black turtlenecks and bright silver pentacles laughing and sipping margarita's at a trendy restaurant.

"*My husband actually put his boline on my altar, can you believe it? Ha ha ha ha ha ha.*"

She would have white teeth, and answer any question I had about Witchcraft and be my bestest friend forever and ever.

"When does it start?" I was already there in my mind.

"Next Thursday if I can get the word out quick enough." She seemed amused at my excitement. As I left the store that day, my heart soared. Thursday couldn't come fast enough. I was relieved that come Thursday I could meet some people, ask some questions, and make a friend or two.

When the evening arrived, I felt privileged walking

into the Crystal Garden after hours. I pushed aside the closed sign, and walked to our meeting feeling secretive. It was like sneaking into an exclusive men's club, the invite was my VIP pass, my embroidered jacket and expensive cigar. *No one else can come to our club.* I told myself as I slid as quietly as possible through the front door, tinkling bells announcing my arrival.

"Hi Tara" Marnie said from the circle of chairs she had arranged in the center of the store. A few of the seats were already occupied. I looked without looking too hard.

One confused large woman in her late fifties. Check. A couple of Gothlings. Check. And whoa! What is he supposed to be? He looks like Robin Hood.

The guy looked like he had just stepped out of Sherwood Forest. I sat down next to the Goth couple and tried to look confident.

"Tara, this is Robin" she said pointing to "Robin". I tried not to laugh. I nodded in greeting, clenching my teeth.

"You are sitting next to Slade and his partner, Moth." I smiled at them, noticing the combat boots, spikes, and pitch black hair casually seated next to me. Your typical Goth kids, so non conformist, they managed to be conformist. They looked so much alike they could have been brother and sister.

"And this is Martha" she said, gesturing to the jumpy woman next to her.

"Everyone, this is Tara."

"Hi Tara" they said in unison. I felt like I was at an AA meeting.

"We are waiting on Rose and Lydia to show up, they said they were coming." Marnie glanced at the clock.

Oh great, I can't wait to see what they look like.

Thirteen minutes passed as I checked out the crowd.

Robin-of-the-Hood had on knee length, lace up beige suede boots, black tight jeans, and a peasant blouse a la Jerry Seinfeld's puffy shirt. There was a dagger placed in a leather belt at his waist, and yes, my friends, he was wearing a cape. A forest green cape made of some rough material. The small pouch of herbs at his neck smelled so strongly I could get a good whiff every time I turned my head. It was the smell of candlelit medieval apothecaries, and bent bearded wizards stirring boiling pots.

Guess that was what he was going for.

Robin was a thirtyish dude with black hair and pale skin. He was definitely of some foreign decent, eastern European, maybe. The energy coming off of him, despite his get-up, was focused, and powerful. I tried to keep an open mind.

What is the equivalent of this kind of *thing in the church?* Images of women with hair down to their waists, overstated crosses, no makeup, and floor length denim overall dresses. That was their costume, this was his.

Martha was seated across from me, and her energy was so frantic I was glad not to have sat next to her; it must have been an instinctual move on my part. She was fidgeting with a loose string on her canvas bag. Her legs were splayed open in vulnerable helplessness. The extra eighty or so pounds that she carried tried to escape from every extra opening in her clothes. She reminded me of a little Chihuahua that had lost its bark. I didn't know what was up with her, and I didn't want to know, I had enough problems of my own. For a moment I panicked at my apathy, then remembered in Witchcraft, it wasn't my responsibility to "save" anyone. She was responsible for herself, I was responsible for myself. *Whew*.

Rose and Lydia never showed, so we decided to start

without them.

"Thank you for all coming here" Marnie started. "I thought that as Witches, those of us who aren't in covens needed a place to meet and discuss our beliefs, experiences and support each other." Marnie looked tired, I knew she had opened and closed the shop without a break for weeks. This was a real sacrifice for her, and I was infinitely grateful.

"Anyone want to start?"

Start what? What is it that we are going to start?

The fact that my hip Witches with Gucci bags weren't coming didn't bother me. I knew that the socio-economic boundaries of Pagans were much larger than that of Christianity. There were rich and poor Pagans, celebrities, and the furthest fringes of society. I was cool with it.

The Goth people glowered in easy angst. That was probably how they always looked. *Even brushing their teeth is depressing to watch, I suppose.*

I hoped that they were real Goth, not just teddy bears on the inside that needed protection from the real world in the form of black lipstick and tattoos. Most of the really Goth people I knew looked like Donald Trump or Rachael Ray on the outside-they didn't need to flaunt it.

Everyone was silent for a moment.

Martha spoke. It came out so fast and jumbled that she sounded like an auctioneer.

"I got a divorce after I became a Witch, we were on two different wavelengths."

Robin said nothing. The Goth kids said nothing. Completely out of character, I said nothing. I had been burned too many times to spill my guts to people I didn't know. Marnie spiked the awkward silence with wisdom.

"Sometimes when one person in a marriage or intimate

relationship decides to change or grow, the other person is faced with a choice. Grow with their mate, or stay the same. If they choose to remain stagnant then the relationship will fall apart. It is just as Martha described it, two actual different energy wavelengths. When you make a choice to grow, no matter what the consequences, your vibration changes. You actually vibrate at a more accelerated rate."

She made Martha sound like a rocket scientist, I loved Marnie for that.

Moth was half reclining on the floor in Roman fashion. "I see fairies."

WHAT?

"Yeah" Slade said, trying not to be out done, "I see 'em too."

Maybe I overestimated the Gothlings. I was just getting into this stuff, I wasn't ready for fairies yet.

"Good topic" Marnie said, taking away the random sporadic nature of the "conversation". "Let's talk about the spirit world."

No one spoke. I was beginning to see the reason that we were all solitaries. I'm sure Robin's practice included damp mossy woods, and balefires. The Goths probably had Marylyn Manson or Massive Attack playing, as they sprawled out before a large black altar with pewter chalices, and maybe some bloodletting. And Martha, well, I didn't even want to go there.

I glanced at the clock. This was like pulling teeth, hopefully it would be over soon. I looked at the rest of my cronies. Robin appeared to be out of body, the Goth twins had said all they were going to say tonight, and Martha was still riding the high of being called out by the teacher. Marnie let the silence continue for a brief moment.

"I brought a DVD that I'd like you all to watch." She popped it in and lowered the lights, I was relieved. *Thank Goddess that is over.*

I didn't focus on the movie. It was a sad but slanted documentary about two murdered little boys in a small town. Their murders were pinned on the only practicing Pagan in the area.

As I sat there in the bookstore I knew and loved with the lights dimmed, I felt like it was closing time in a dance club or bar. The lights had been turned on full force to reveal a used up place with cigarette burns, vomit stains, and no neon lights to create an atmosphere.

This was just a room. With no fluorescent lights to highlight the iridescent shine of the amethyst, they were just dull rocks. With no enchanting incense with names like Night Queen or Fire Goddess burning, I could smell the Taco Bell that Marnie had for dinner.

This was just a room.

Move all this stuff out and it would be an empty room with nail holes in the wall and falling pieces of plaster.

Where was the magic? It had always felt so comforting and wonderful, and magical whenever I was there. Where was the magic contained?

I guessed it was in Marnie, maybe she wielded it all. Maybe she was Merlin, was Morgaine, was BrunHilde, was the one who controlled the switch. Maybe I should place my hope in her? What was frustrating, though, was that she refused to "lead" me.

Marnie never told me how to do anything, instead, she led me to my own experiences. She became a confidant and a teacher. I rambled and she listened. After my long winded emotional diatribe she would say one sentence. One non-directional, un opinionated sentence like "Tara, you need to trust yourself". For some reason, it always seemed to go to the heart of whatever I had been going on and on about. Instead of giving answers that existed outside of myself, she forced me to look inward. She was infinitely patient, and infinitely kind to me, and everyone else she encountered.

I started confiding in her about how I felt about my marriage. She never judged, or addressed anything but my own feelings about myself. When I told her about my background in the church, and how women were basically powerless, she disappeared and came back with a book.

"Read this. It will change your life" she said, handing it to me.

I read the title *Mysteries of the Dark Moon* by Demetra George, and then thanked her about fifteen times. I couldn't wait to get home and read it. I knew that if she gave it to me, that it was the right timing, she had an excellent sense of what I needed at the time. The one simple thing she would tell me would hit me like an arrow, and I would chew on it for weeks.

Marnie was one of those people who could be easily overlooked. Like the loud politician next to the humble soup kitchen volunteer, her simple wisdom was often ignored by the constant stream of new Witch teenagers who wanted instant power, and identity. The calico-clad unassuming woman wearing glasses in the corner just did not fit in with their cat-head sized pewter pentacles and Witch-chic clothing.

"I am LOOK-ing for a book on hexing" the smart mouthed teenager would predictably say.

"I don't sell those kinds of books" Marnie would quietly reply. Then with a proud huff the wanna- be Witch would storm out.

The store attracted all kinds.

There were the New Agers, with their hazy blue and green cotton dresses, and vague jargon. They seemed more interested in how something appeared than the thing itself.

"I had a session with Max the Skull (a zillion year old Mayan crystal skull reported to have magical healing powers)" they would say proudly to Marnie.

"Well, how was it?" she would ask, in a natural progression of conversation.

"Um, well, it was nice…hey did you get the new Sylvia Brown book in?" they would say changing the subject. Their lives were full of fake one-upmanship not unlike a pissing contest between weight lifters.

"Dude, the other day I lifted an extra 75 pounds…WITHOUT A SPOTTER." The sweaty bulked out Joe boasted.

"Well, I did 55 extra quad blasters, and all I'd eaten was a protein shake. Dude, I THREW up afterwards." Sweaty bulked out Joe number two would counter, then follow with an exaggerated high-five.

I was reminded of this kind of thing when I hung around and listened to the New Agers try to outdo each other. How many forms of reiki you could do, who had you met, how long could you meditate, how many sweat lodges had you been to, what was the name of the spirit you channeled... all the while their lives were teeming with the glaring faults that plagued the unaware. Alcoholism, severe obesity, sheer neglect for anything in the earthly realm.

How could you have your head in the clouds, and completely ignore your feet? It was the kind of devil-may-care blind spiritualism, that I had seen, even imitated in the church. I accepted the New Agers as an obvious part of the package. You get that kind in any religion, any belief system.

There were many people that came to the store just for help; I called them the Broken People. They were people who came in the store just looking for something, someone to take the pain away. It broke my heart when they walked in looking lost. These were regular people, with mothers that were dying of cancer, babies that had been stillborn, or marriages that had unexpectedly fallen apart. Life had been hard to them, and they were just looking for a book or a crystal that would heal their wounded hearts. Sometimes they found peace, sometimes not. Sometimes they hopped between churches, the bookstore, and anyone else that offered an explanation of the Divine. It was sad, but I felt that I could more easily relate to them than the fluffy New Agers, or the downright ridiculous pretender Witches.

***

I stood at my sink, hands immersed in the warmth of the dishwater....o.k. the torment of the dishwater. I did it like my mom, liking her dish and even bathwater scalding hot. It burned me through my gloves and the slight masochist that I am, I liked it. The smell of Palmolive drifted up to my nose, making tiny bubbles in the air. I was alone in the house with only the dim kitchen light illuminating the sink. I could feel my feel stick to the linoleum as I shifted them, taking the pressure off of my back.

I don't even remember what I was thinking about when it happened.

Someone came up behind me. A definite presence. I did a mental check, nope, I was alone in the house, and expecting no one. I froze, daring not to turn around. This wasn't just a fuzzy feeling, I was sure of it……someone was plainly standing behind me. I turned around and as I did, a strong orange aura hit my eyes, it was the color of the setting sun, and felt as intense. There was a woman standing in my kitchen. She had red hair the same color as her glow, and a face that looked familiar. Her eyes held so much wisdom, and so much love. I didn't notice her clothes particularly, just that they were long, and covered most of her body.

"My name is Rachel and I am here to help you" she said. Her mouth moved, but the sound came from somewhere else. This was intense, and even though I felt nothing but pure radiance and peace from her it didn't diminish the fact that there was a spirit woman standing in my kitchen. Like most normal people, I panicked.

"Leave, leave, and don't come back" I shouted, my hands shaking. I could barely talk I was so scared. A deep overwhelming sadness so full it almost brought me to tears filled the room. She lowered her head and faded away, leaving me standing in the middle of the kitchen, dripping water everywhere. After her warming orange light faded I was sad too, as the only light left was the flat fluorescent one. I sat on the floor for a while, focused on the sadness I felt as she left, as I tried to calm my beating heart.

When I related the story to Marnie the next day, her reaction surprised me. It was one of anger, pity and a little jealousy.

"You are the only one I know, Tara, who would send a spirit guide away." She shook her head in disappointment.

I felt bad. I didn't understand, but by Marnie's reaction was beginning to feel the weight of what I'd done. I remembered the sadness in the room I'd felt when I forced the spirit lady to leave, and it was all out of my fear and ignorance.

I caught up with Marnie as she went to the storeroom for some supplies.

"Marnie, wait, can you please explain this to me?" The panicky feeling returned, the more I thought about it. Man, I'd screwed this one up. Rachel had stated her intention, she even followed her name with it. "My name is Rachel, and I'm here to help." It was plain as day, she had no intentions of hurting me, it was just a new thing for me, being around spirits and I didn't know how to handle it.

Hearing the New Agers talk about spirit guides had turned me off, it seemed a trophy they'd earned when they bragged about their guides. Why would I need a guide? I don't need someone to help me along, I can get to the Divine on my own. Thanks anyway. Spirit guides seemed an eerie side dish to the main course, and an unnecessary one.

Marnie turned around, and looked at me, her frustration subsiding when she realized that I honestly had no idea.

"What are spirit guides for? It *scares* me, Marnie. I have gone through pastors and people to get to the Goddess for so long that I get cold feet easily."

She plopped down on her chair, and sighed. "They are like friends on the other side, Tara. The thing is you have them whether you are aware of them or not. How bout angels, guardian angels?....same thing, basically."

Crap. What had I done?

"What do they do?"

"They help you, bring you information, give you advice, suggestions, and guide you. They are GUIDES, not controlling power freaks. They are like tour guides, they GUIDE you" she articulated. "Don't worry, maybe she will come back."

Oh, I pulled out all the stops. Begged her to come back, lit candles, apologized.

But she never came back.

In Bible College they used to say "it is relationship, not religion". But I still didn't know where to locate the Divine, to have a relationship with Him, Her or Whomever. I looked at the ceiling, and prayed, then felt dumb. It is so archaic to think that God "lives" in heaven. Like if you are God that you are stuck in something that is compartmentalized. My neck started hurting from looking up.

I memorized pictures of the Goddess and sat before my altar trying to hold the image in my mind, thinking that if I lost the image, then I would lose the connection. I imagined Her right in front of me. I prayed to the Trees, the Sun, the Moon, the Air, trying to find where She was.

I wanted to deepen my relationship, I wanted to *see* and *hear* the spirit world. I wanted Her to show Herself to me. Now that I had no boundaries, there was no one showing me that in I Jehoshaphat 12 verse 4 that "thou shalt not asketh to see me", I could ask for something that was in my heart. Anything that was in my heart. Didn't mean I would always get it, and that was o.k. I trusted Her enough to know that if I didn't get it, then it was a sign I shouldn't have it. Thank God I didn't get my big church and congregation. Boy, would that have been a mess.

What was wrong with me wanting to see Her? I wanted to locate Her. I knew that the Higher Power had heard me, which had been evident all of my life, I felt like the request was a pure one. I didn't have anyone to brag to, so it wasn't to have a spiritual experience. It wasn't to prove anything. My heart was fully devoted to the Goddess without a doubt, I knew what faith meant.

I guess it was curiosity. I had felt the waves of the earth, and seen God that night I prayed in tongues.....both experiences had left me with a brand, a sort of spiritual tattoo that I could never remove. I wanted to see Her. I wanted it with all my heart. Wanted to know that this new slight feeling of doubt about the Goddess was just jitters from the aftermath of Germany. I felt like it was, but I wanted to EXPERIENCE Her.

"LILITH".......I whispered the name aloud. I was reading the book that Marnie had given me, and kept getting stuck on the chapter about Lilith. As a little girl I'd been fascinated with archeology, and mythology, I had seen pictures of Lilith with fangs, and disheveled hair, and as a child I was afraid. This time, though, I was fascinated; this was the fourth time I had read the chapter. She was amazing. Not the semen sucking, bloodthirsty demon, that patriarchy had made her into, but a woman who stood up for herself. *Something I desperately need to do*, I thought.

She was

angry.......sexy.......strong.......ANGRY.......angry like I wanted to allow myself to be. It was becoming clear to me the underlying views I had about my own sex, about being a woman. Winter's Pass with their endless women must submit idealism, my mother, who gave up everything to make her marriage strong, and now I was in a marriage where I realized I never talked back. I had no idea that I was as wimpy as I was. I was so unhappy in my marriage, but felt because of the antiquated fifties mentality that I was raised with, that there was "no way out". I needed Lilith.

Basically the story goes like this. Adam wanted to

always have sex in the missionary position, and one day Lilith, his wife, said "hey let me get on top this time".

He said "no way, chicks are supposed to be on the bottom, because we men are supposed to dominate".

She said "Fuck you, if you don't let me get on top, I'm going to run away, and do what I want to do". And She did. I couldn't read the story enough. I desired to have the strength to say no, to say "kiss my ass, I'm not your slave!" I needed Her. As I reached for the bedroom lamp switch and closed the book, I said Her name once again, to the darkness….."LILITH". Then I sunk into a deep sleep.

Luke must be drunk! Was the first thought that came screaming into my head. *Why else would he be WALKING on the bed?* His weight was causing the bed and my body to sink down with every footstep. It was pitch black in the room, and I was so startled from sleep, that I hadn't had time to get angry at him, I was just trying to get my bearings. Then it stopped suddenly, and I looked above me.

It was HER. It was Lilith, I knew it with every fiber in my being. I was frozen with fear. She looked like a big black moving mass that was brown around the edges, formless, except for two distinct cat- like eyes. She moved like a cosmic dance, as if each part of her was a galaxy within a galaxy, I felt her vastness. It was almost too much to handle for my physical body. I was very conscious of the weight of my body, keeping me from leaving with Her right then. Nothing else mattered. I wanted to mesh with her, to go with Her, it was the most natural, most intense yearning.

She was about two feet from my face, and She was looking at me. My heart was beating out of my chest. She didn't say, but rather impressed on me to not be afraid, I heard Her from inside myself. Her presence felt so gentle and powerful at the same time-I knew Her as the all powerful creatrix, I could see the swirling primordial oceans, and hear her thunderous voice. I also felt her delicate whisper, a rose petal brushing against your skin in a silent room. She was breathtaking.

I instinctively took one deep breath, and as I fully let go, She melded into me, went into my body. I watched as I seemed to separate from my body, and with feet as light as air, walked around the room. I stepped on top of the bookcases, and stuck close to the wall, circling several more times. As quickly and dramatically as She had arrived, She left. I found myself back in my body.

As I turned the light on and stared at my surroundings, I cherished that burning feeling, that aware, raw, magnetized energy that was still all over me. That night I fell in love with the Goddess.

That night changed everything.

Chapter Eight

"Nearly all men can stand adversity, but if you want to test a man's character, give him power."
- Abraham Lincoln

You've seen 'em. The reject, awkward, greasy -haired videogame nerds playing Magic at the local Comic book store. Their girlfriends are always Witches- tattooed, pink haired pixies with Hot Topic clothes and pentacles. Most of them have no idea what they are doing. I actually heard one of them tell a boyfriend *while he was breaking up with her*, that she was going to "banish" him. Didn't he just break up with her? *Whew.* So yeah I was a Witch, but I didn't want to be that. There is some part in every person, that when you say,"I'm a Witch", or "I do magick" (it's even worse when you spell it like that), there is some small voice that recalls the nerdlicious rejects at the comic book store, Star Wars convention, or high school dark corner. Their scent is unforgettable, it reeks of someone so in their own head, that they neglect things like, hygiene, and um....reality. They name their cats Taliesin, and say things like "may the force be with you" seriously.

In practicing Witchcraft there is some part of your sarcastic, cynical self that you have to let go of and just believe for God's sake, but I didn't want to let go too much. Get in too far, so far that I would forget myself again like I did in Christianity. Maybe that is why Rosemary came into my life.

I was lonely. I really didn't have any friends, having missed those crucial years when you are supposed to be learning social skills. I spent those years scaring people off.

I certainly had never had any close female friends. Most women in high school, and college wanted to talk about boys, makeup, and other girly things. The dark eyed serious dame talking about God was about as good a fit in their little cliques as two left shoes…..but now that I had evened out a bit, I was ready for a friend.

I thought it would be nice to have someone who was my peer to bounce ideas off of, to talk about Witchy things with. Someone to have fun with, someone to hang out with. I loved talking to Marnie, and spending time at the Crystal Garden, but it ended there. Marnie had a life of her own. When it came time to go out on Friday nights, my default setting was drinking with Luke, and our friends, Jeff and Rosemary. Rosemary seemed like a good candidate since we already spent so much time together. She was a lot of fun when we went out, and although our conversation never went any deeper than the occasional my- boyfriend -sucks crying session, I felt in my heart that there was more to her than her outward appearance suggested. Her boyfriend was my husband's best friend, so I wondered when we were having a normal drunken Friday what would happen if I mentioned to her that I'd been exploring Witchcraft.

She was throwing darts at a dartboard in one of the better local breweries that we frequented. The boys were outside on the restaurant's patio, smoking cigarettes, I figured now was my chance. We were both a little tipsy, so the worst thing that could happen….*well, she could be a Christian and I could offend her for life. Nah, she doesn't seem like the type. Still, you can't tell sometimes……….. God, Tara, just go ask her.* I joined her at the dartboard.

Never one for tact I just blurted it out.

"Hey did you know that I am a Witch?" I gulped.
Mental note, go back to high school and repeat. Learn tact.

"Really? I have always wanted to do that." she seemed excited. I exhaled.

"Yeah, let's go get another beer, and talk about it" I said, practically leaping to the bar.

And as they say, the tide turned again.

***

"Read as much as you can, discarding negative or disturbing information. Learn by doing, and the Goddess and God will bless you with all that you truly need."

I put my new Scott Cunningham book down, and glanced at the clock. Rosemary would be here in ten minutes. *Was this a mistake?* I had the vague feeling that she thought I knew a lot more about this stuff than I did, I was still groping my way through it. Other than reading, I'd done nothing. That first act, whether it be a spell done after Luke was asleep, or tinkering with the idea of casting a circle, I knew that my first official act of Witchcraft would be it. Would seal my exit from Christianity now and forever.

Besides, I thought picking up the book from the floor and turning to where I'd left off, *all I've carried with me into my new awareness is a feeling, and a few fuzzy pre-teen years of freedom, before I tangled myself in Christianity*. I wasn't sure what to do. Was the magic in the doing? All the books I read were about doing, but no one addressed the why? Or the feeling, or the underlying pulse that I longed to know.

"I'm hereeee" I heard Rosemary shout as she came down the hall. "Wow! I've never been in your bedroom before" she said, surveying the room.

This wasn't our bedroom, it was MY bedroom. The

walls were crimson, a stark contrast to the dull white of the rest of the house. I had everything I loved in that room, and the colorful scarves that hung over the bed were a transport to any continent that required an afternoon refuge from the sun. My Tarot was spread on the dresser without shame, and the woman with the dark eyes, and snake coiled about her waist looked down at me from her place next to the armoire. Nope, no hiding here. I often retreated to this room, preferring it to the rest of the house. Luke had even escaped by taking all his things out of the room "to give me more space". He did nothing but sleep in there. I guess I had already moved out, in theory.

"This place is magical" she said, taking a deep breath and smelling the rain from the open windows, and the Isis incense that I burned. She looked at the pile of books at my feet.

"God, have you read all those?" Rosemary wasn't much of a reader.

"Yeah, I have amassed quite a collection, this is Doreen Valiente, here is some Raymond Buckland, I've got Gerald Gardner, here is some Patricia Telesco, and all the rest is good ole Scott Cunningham, my favorite."

"Wow" she said, looking at the covers of the books, an array of pentacles, Witches, and mystical symbols. Some part of me took comfort in those symbols, knowing that they were the keys. If I could only get the sigils off of the page, I knew they'd unlock the understanding I needed.

"I used to have an Ouija board" she said, squatting down on the floor, putting her purse to the side.

I figured she'd start with the "wow" stuff. Séances', psychics, crystal balls, Ouija boards, all the spirit world, and in my mind secondary to what I was trying to get to, which was the practice of it all. How you lived from day to day. Why did you do spells, when did you do them, could you really pray to any God or Goddess you wanted? How did it change you? I was trying to get back to the experience on the grass so many years ago....

If I did all these things carefully outlined on the pages of the forbidden books that lay at my feet, would they really show me the way? Or was it up to me? I was afraid. Afraid to try. I'd tried before and threw myself in one hundred and ten percent and it had hurt me, bad.

"So are we gonna do some of this stuff or what? I'm not much of a reader, so you'll have to tell me what to do" she seemed eager.

How would I explain everything I'd been through? How would I explain that this was like walking down the aisle and saying *I do* again, after getting out of a terrible marriage? I really think I lacked the courage.

"Hey, how long do you have? Do you have to be anywhere tonight?"

"No, girl, I'm yours. I told Jeff that I'd be a while" she said.

"You want a glass of wine? I've got a bottle of red. Merlot, I think."

"Yeah, that'd be great!" I could see her energy shift to a better place. I knew that a night of drinking wine and talking, to her, was way better than looking over stuffy old books.

"O.k. this is going to be a long story, but if you are as interested in Witchcraft as I am, I need to tell you where I came from, so you can understand."

She filled her glass, and listened with rapt attention.

"So yes, I am a Witch, and yes, I probably always have been one, but let's just say ....I took a ....detour" and I spilled it all out, all the tears, all the bonds, all the pain. For the first time, like it was history, I told MY story.

When I was done, I felt new, felt like I'd unloaded a heavy burden. I sipped my wine as I waited for her response.

"Wow" she said again. I knew she'd listened intently, I knew she'd shared the story, known the story.

"I had no idea" she said, almost tearful.

Relieved that I'd shared it with someone, I could continue. "Now do you understand that I'm a little hesitant to move beyond the, just- reading- about- stuff stage?"

"You just need to take the plunge, come on, hand me a book." She wasn't afraid, at all.

I reluctantly handed over the candle magic book.

"Ooh, perfect" she said, opening to a random page and skimming the contents. "Do you have any candles?"

"Yeah, I'm prepared, I just haven't made the first move." I'd been stocking candles, stones, and statues for months.

"Um, this says that you can do anything you want, any spell you want with a candle. Listen to these color meanings: red means physical energy, passion, fire, sexuality, pink is friendship, compassion, puppy, and emotional aspects of love, orange means encouragement, flow, nourishment, yellow is changes, learning, harmony, confidence, green means luck, employment, prosperity, growth, blue is health, intuition, tranquility, rest, dreams, clear speech, and purple is power, intuition, the spirit world, clairvoyance." She took a sip of wine and cleared her throat.

"How bout yellow? Sounds like you need to have the confidence to follow your path, and allow yourself to make mistakes. I know you've been through a lot, honey, but it wasn't God, or the Goddess, it was people. The cool thing about being a solitary though, is it sounds like the mistakes you make are your own, you don't drag anyone else down with you. Don't worry, I'll do it with you, I could use some confidence." She cleared a place on the carpet between us where we sat cross-legged.

"Yeah good point." *Maybe that is what I'm afraid of.*

"So let's do this thing" she said, reaching for her purse. "I think I have a lighter."

We are going to do this, we are really going to do this.

"Can you go get your yellow candle?" she said to me. I think I was frozen.

"Yeah" I said mechanically.

We placed the candle in the center of us, on the floor. "Do you think this is alright? The books say…"

"Who cares what the books say, Tara, does this feel right to you?" she almost yelled at me, and the tone of her voice took my timidity away.

I closed my eyes, and tuned into my senses. I smelled the bright sunshine- like fragrance of the candle, heard the hum of the TV in the other room. Felt. *What do I feel?* I took myself away from my mind that had been engaged in the world of ritual tools, planetary charts, opening circles, and candle placement on the altar. I dove into the quiet place inside myself, past all of the pain, past all of the disappointment, all of the hurt, all of the feelings of failure that still burned within me every day. I went to the quiet place that I discovered in my little apartment, and tuned into what she felt.

Peace. Excitement. Like the christening of a ship ready to set sail. I felt that this was the beginning of a long journey. I felt my fragments come together as one single note. It wasn't the candle itself, it was my intent, and my intent was to connect with the Divine in a way that pleased me. This pleased me.

When I opened my eyes, I felt like a new person.

"Yeah, I'm ready."

"What do you want to do?" This time she looked to me for answers.

"I want to…..to…hold the candle in my palms and think, feel my will. Let's both do that."

I handed the candle to her. She closed her eyes, and concentrated. I felt her energy stream out and flow in a cloud around her. She opened her eyes and handed the candle to me, it was warm. I held it in the center of my palms. I reached invisible antenna out and in to the Goddess. I felt my will, my power chakra at the apex of my ribcage, it was sensitive to the touch. The candle flame would ignite the will I was ready to unlock. The will that I had handed over to so many people, to so many institutions, I was ready to claim it as my own. I placed the candle in the center of our little circle, and said a quick prayer for protection. As we opened ourselves to the spirit world, and took the walls down that we'd built up to protect our battered courage, our wills that at some point we'd given to another, I knew we'd be vulnerable. I suddenly understood the casting of the circle for protection. Doing this, we let our guard down. It made sense!

I spoke, our eyes centered on the flame she held, "this flame burns with our will, the will we reclaim". She lit the flame in an act that made me feel like we'd done this for centuries. It felt right, it felt good. I felt the energy we'd put into the candle go into some hot motion as the flame danced merrily. This was the beginning of something new, and very good.

It was pretty much set in stone after that. When she called the next week with a suggestion, I was game.

The local paper would jump on this one.

<u>Witches Caught Casting Spells on Local Golf Course Green</u>

Rosemary and I knew that there was a possibility that we could get caught, so we opted for jeans instead of robes. If we had to, we could make a quick getaway. This was a relief, because I didn't own a robe, and didn't know if I wanted to, it seemed too fussy for me. But fanfare-loving Rosemary seemed enchanted by the idea.

We were stumbling through the dark, having decided to try our hand at ritual together. We were going to do it….cast a circle, the whole nine. The only place we knew to practice was the golf course that bordered our little community living suburb. So there we were at nine pm walking on a dimly lit path strewn with autumn leaves. It was the full moon on Halloween, and the first one in fifty years. The large disc looked down on us, shedding just enough light for us to make our way to the sand. Rosemary set her bag down, and kicked her shoes off. It was biting cold outside.

"Come on, take off your shoes" she said, plopping down on the scratchy grass.

"Are you kidding?" I wasn't sure that I could concentrate on magic if I was nearing frostbite. Still, not wanting to be a party pooper, I gave in. For a moment neither of us knew what to do.

"First the salt" Rosemary said leaping up from the ground with a sudden air of ceremony. I shuffled over to the bag, feeling very witchy, and cold. But Witchy.

"How do you wanna do this?" I said, small grains of salt spilling out of my hand. I looked down at the green. I wasn't a horticultist, but I was pretty sure that salt wasn't good for grass. A flash of guilt ran through me…..*crap I didn't think of that. Oh, well, it is the off season. The neighbors are gonna love seeing a circle burned into the grass. Hee hee let's just hope we don't get caught.*

Surrounding us was the auburn glow of lights from the houses, dimmed in the anticipation of bedtime. I imagined mommies tucking their little ones into bed, dinner dishes being cleaned up, maybe a little late night internet surfing. They had no clue what was going on in their upper middle class backyard. I chuckled again at the thought.

"Let's just make a circle" she said, wanting to get on with it.

Tracing deliberate steps we sprinkled salt clockwise for protection. After picking up our representation of the Elements, I had Earth and Fire (a candle and some dirt), and she had Water and Air (some incense, and a little bowl of water), I turned to the North. Time to open the circle.

"Um, powers of the North, and um, Earth, please protect us, and give us wisdom….thanks." I knew it wasn't fancy, but it was the best I could do on the spot. Rosemary was next.

"Powers of the East and Air enlighten us with your wisdom, and protect us this night!" She waved the stick of Nag Champa around with flair. I glanced over at her, her eyes shut tight, the concentration pouring out of her like the stream of smoke from the stick gripped firmly in her hand.

Trying harder for my next one, I gathered myself. "Powers of the South and Fire!" I said with my radio voice, pulling from my diaphragm for power.

"Burn with us tonight and bestow your wisdom, (dramatic pause) we invite you into our circle!" I held up the candle to the oncoming wind.

I felt like an idiot. *What am I doing? I am acting like a jackass. This isn't a contest...we aren't trying to outdo each other. I need to concentrate, and not care how it sounds... something to work on next time, if there is a next time.*

I turned my attention to the now cast circle.

I don't know what I expected, but it felt different from anything I had ever done. It was very.......real.....very... solid. I wasn't in my head, I was right there.

I swear it got warmer once the circle was cast.

"Do you feel that?" Rosemary said, removing a sweater.

"How can I not?" I said, feeling comfortable for the first time that night. I was chilled, but not freezing any more. I could almost see the bubble that surrounded us, and it had a red sheen to it.

I reached in my magenta Indian beaded bag and fumbled for the slips of paper and black and orange candles I had brought for the actual spell. It was hard to see in the dark, and I kept waiting for some angry suburbanite to come out of his house with a flashlight and a "what are ya'll kids up to?". No way did either of us want that to happen.

The spell was perfect. It was simple- write on two slips of paper. On one put what you want to enter your life, and on the other, put what you want to go away. We burnt the "go away" stuff in the black candle flame and the new wishes in the orange.

Putting action to our desires made them all the more real. Watching the paper get eaten up by the humble candle flames, I felt the prayers go into motion. It was a satisfying feeling.

After our "cakes and wine" (two Miller Lites, and a

handful of saltines) we packed up camp. Making the walk back to the house I reflected. Even though the whole thing had turned out well, I couldn't quite concentrate knowing that anyone could walk in on us. I thought about the warmth once the circle was cast, and the effect our togetherness had on the happenings inside it. I knew what I wanted to do differently: be even more real, drop some of the flowery stuff, and stay true to my heart. It felt like trying on a new suit. One that I had picked out myself, loved the color, etc, but once I actually tried it on had to get used to the way it felt. A bit of adjusting here, taking it in an inch there, and it was just about perfect.

Tallying all my feelings I labeled the whole thing as a success. *I definitely want to do that again,* I thought as I warmed up my car to go home. Driving through the dark winding suburb, I ruminated on the differences between what I had just done, and my experiences in the church.

In church, we avoided anything earthly. With our eyes shut tight, we tried as hard as we could to transport ourselves out of this world and into God's dimension. The talk of "when we all get to heaven" was constant. We wanted out of our dirty bodies, and our dirty lives….we wanted the cleanliness of God. The clear blue sky, the white robed God-not the pregnant Goddess, the bleeding Goddess, Mother Earth. The dirty, dark skinned, bloody Mother. After doing our circle, I was struck with the...realness of it…the earthiness of it. The Christian God represented escape, the Goddess was reality. If God was in heaven then the Goddess was the earth.

In our circle, we focused on the earth, the elements, the Goddess in ourselves. We focused on the thing itself, the nature of Water, Earth, Air and Fire. It made total sense why the church dismissed sex, our bodies, even wanted an escape from death- a pristine eternal life. Because our bodies/emotions/desires were part of the earth, anything earthly was seen as far from God.

Some small part of me knew that this would be a process. The terrible condemning voice of the church wouldn't go away, it almost seemed to cloud my thinking. It was like the guy loudly talking through the movie you really wanted to see. I had to do something about it.

"I want to go to church." Luke said,surprising me one Saturday morning.

"Why?" I had absolutely no desire to go, and unless he had a good reason, it wasn't happening.

"I think it would be good for us, good for Willow".

I was surprised. My parents had been hounding us to go to church, and I always brushed them off. Them I could understand, but Luke? Luke who was not raised in the church, Luke who had no previous interest in going to church? I was very suspicious.

"Honestly, what's the deal? You never cared enough before to go."

"I talked to your dad."

I rolled my eyes, it made sense. Dad was a big proponent of the "church is good for family togetherness" thing.

"Nope, not going. You know what I've been through. I thought about it for a moment."The only place I'd go is to a Unitarian church." I remembered my uncle's funeral at his Unitarian church, and I was impressed with the openness and large pictures of Jesus where he appeared to be made of rainbows- it was Baptist with a New Age flair. Even though it was church, I could swallow it.

"Fine, I'll go on the internet and look." He ran for the

den.

I cleaned up the breakfast dishes, scraping the leftover eggs into the garbage disposal before they'd stink up the house.

"There aren't any on this side of town." he yelled from the other room. "But I did find something else."

I walked into the den, hands wet with dishwater.

"What."

"It's called Free Will Baptist…. apparently they let you do whatever you want."

I vaguely remembered a friend talking about how much he loved that church. *Maybe I'll like it,* I thought. *Maybe I'll melt when I set foot on the church grounds,* I thought more realistically.

"Alright, I'll go on three conditions. 1. If I don't like it I don't go back, period. 2. If they do or say anything that makes me feel uncomfortable, I get up and leave. 3. You always consult me about Willow going. I don't want her ever going to a church without my consent."

"Fine. I agree" he said happily.

I can't believe I'm doing this.

It was a nice Sunday morning. Willow had her usual runny nose, a little more than was in my comfort zone for taking her out, but I'd promised. I said I'd give the church a try.

Open minded, I've got to be open minded. As we drove into the parking lot, I felt sick.

"I don't want to do this!" I said suddenly to Luke as I gripped his hand. "I don't belong here, I'm a Witch!"

"Look, you are just panicking because this is the first time you've been to church since you left. They won't know you are a Witch unless you tell them. I'll be fine, I remember your conditions." He was calm. I guess it rubbed off on me, because I calmed down too.

We went into the average sized church, and into the nursery. At first glance I was struck by the glaring misery of the woman sitting in the corner rocking chair, holding a sleeping baby.

"Hi," I whispered "we are new here, um, do I have to sign anything? Who will be taking care of my little girl? Her name is Willow." I wasn't sure that I wanted to turn over my kid to people I didn't know.

"I will" she said, and tried to smile, but it came out so forced that it made her look even more miserable. I felt so sorry for this woman. She wore a navy sailor -type dress with a large collar, hose and scuffed white pumps. Her brown hair was bobbed, and the circles around her eyes were big black beacons, showing against her forlorn face. The more she talked the more I got the feeling that this was her. How she normally was. The frown had turned into a mask, and the mask had turned into her face.

I reluctantly handed her Willow, and she informed me that her husband was preaching on discipline today and that we would enjoy it. *Her husband…that would make her the pastor's wife. Awesome. The pastor's wife is miserable. Mark one for leaving right now.*

Luke and I walked into the sanctuary and chose a seat in the back. Looking into his face I saw that he felt as reluctant as I. He leaned over and whispered "isn't the pastor's wife supposed to be syrupy sweet, and full of hugs and stuff?"

"Yeah, the ones I knew were" I whispered back.

The pastor took the stage. My momma taught me not to judge a book by its cover, but let me say that the instant I saw this man I didn't like him, at all. He was average height with a brown comb over and ruddy completion. He had a plastered patronizing grin on his face, and large sweeping movements that pastors often develop from having to be seen on stage. He was a low rent pastor. Not attractive, not charismatic, not articulate. He was beyond sloppy seconds; he was leftover Chinese food thirds.

"Blah blah blah….hymnal to page 420….blah blah…welcome new people" at this everyone turned to look at us.

If I'd had a broom I'd have flown out of there.

We sang a couple of songs in which an astonished Luke admitted later "I realized just how long you'd been in the church when I watched you sing all three verses of four songs without the songbook." I replied "what, did you think I made all that up?"

During our whispering the pastor walked into the stage.

Great. The part I've been waiting for. Now I can see what this joker is all about.

He adjusted his tie and introduced himself and his family. Pastor Blah Blah, Mrs. Blah, Blah, (she is doing her DUTY in the nursery), and our two sons, Jake 16, and Jon 18. They sat on the front row and waved at the congregation.

The sermon started with a few points about God's punishment for sin. *Good way to win my heart, dude. Keep it up.* Then continued with the fact that God always punishes, and we'd better expect it if we sinned. *Yeah whatever. Only 20 more minutes of this drivel and I can go get my kid.* He called his son, the 16 year old, on stage. *What is going on now?* Luke looked at me quizzically, now that he thought if it took place in a church I knew what it meant. I shrugged at him; I had no idea what this guy was doing. Maybe his son was going to sing a song or something.

The tall sandy haired boy took the stage, his face beet red in embarrassment.

"Now bend over, Jake" Pastor Blah Blah gestured to his son.

WHAT? I was getting extremely uncomfortable. Even in what I was used to, this was odd. The boys face, I thought it impossible, but it got even more red. He looked for a minute like he might say no, but years of robotic obedience had trained him. He bent at the waist, shoving his butt at his dad.

"God always punishes" Pastor Crazy said as he picked up a large binder.

What the hell is going on? I looked at the poor boy, and around the congregation. They had the church face on- I couldn't tell what they were thinking.

"And the punishment hurts!" with that he took the thick binder with both hands and spanked his 16 year old boy with it, putting all of his might into it. On stage. In front of everybody. *Whap!* It made an audible sound as it echoed through the auditorium. The boy had to struggle to remain upright from the force of the strike.

"When God punishes" *Whap!* Another smack with the binder. Jake staggered again.

"You know it!" *Bam!* and another. *I can't take much more of this.* The young man was now crying. I wanted to rescue him, and beat the hell out of the pastor. *How bout when Tara punishes, you asshole.*

I was nudging Luke so hard I probably bruised him. We were getting ready to stand up and get out of this egomaniac-child abusing- freak- show that called itself a church, when he stopped, and like clockwork dismissed the thoroughly life- scarred, humiliated boy, and said the closing prayer. We picked up Willow and left. Not a word was spoken the whole way home, and it was never mentioned again……it took me a long time to not spit on that church when I drove by it.

I still do it sometimes for fun.

The whole thing was good for me, it was like going back to a bad relationship that maybe after time passed, you forget how bad it really was, and only fantasize about the "good times".

I decided to call Kurt.

"Hey, I'm not sure how to put this…..well, I'm having a hard time letting go of some things, and from the way it feels, it is so ingrained in me that it will never go away, but I think I hate Christianity now, and want to be rid of it."

He immediately knew what I was talking about.

"Two months ago I did a spell to let go of the chains of Christianity. It really changed me, would you like to do it?"

That is what I loved about Kurt, his straightforwardness. A European thing.

I took a deep breath. "Yeah, tell me what it entails."
I'll write it down, and then decide whether or not I want to do it.

"Well it is very secret, so don't write it down. It is something I learned from my coven." I shuddered at the word, I didn't know much about covens. "You will know when and if it is right for you, Tara."

I believed him.

As I hung up, I felt the strand of my past that still connected me. If I said goodbye to Christianity for good where would that leave me? Even though I was loving being free, and loving my new path, I knew that if I said goodbye for good, then that would be it. I'd not only say goodbye to Christianity but more importantly, to my past. Accept that the whole thing was gone from me forever, my friends, my whole way of life. I had long since discarded it, and the thought of going back to that made me feel dizzy, but to formally do it, formally say goodbye, what stripped down feeling would that leave me with?

"I took Willow to church"

"You what!" I shrieked. I had just gotten off of my Sunday morning shift at the radio station. While I was at work, Luke had taken her to the Baptist church his mother went to. I was beyond angry.

"You know how I feel about that! I can't believe you didn't ask me first!"

"Well, I knew you'd say no. Besides, I'm never going back. You won't believe what happened." He seemed angry himself. I'd been so angry that I hadn't noticed it.

"Well?" I said, holding my daughter close. She was still dressed in church clothes. She looked up at me with her big brown eyes, her nose running as it always did. An innocent, fragile little flower.

"The church was fine…boring, actually. I just went because my mom asked us to go; it was a spur of the moment thing. I didn't want to bother you while you were on the air."

I waited for him to finish, and wondered why he seemed so upset.

"Afterwards the pastor came up to introduce himself to Willow and me. He asked about her, and I told him that she was hearing impaired, and a very weak, sick child. Then he asked about you, why you didn't come. I told him that you were a Witch."

"You what? Why would you do that!?"

"Please let me finish! Anyway, when I told him that you were a Witch, he said that God's punishment for you practicing Witchcraft was Willow's disability."

I reached behind me for the chair, shocked. I sat down, my knees knocking in disbelief and rage. How could someone say that about my daughter? About any child? My sweet, precious, sickly daughter had been in and out of the hospital since she was born, and wore hearing aids in both ears. All of the times she'd had surgery, all of the times I had to hold her down while they put an IV in or watched them wheel her into surgery, and her nothing but pure innocence. I couldn't believe the bare ignorance. How dare him! I was beyond words. There were so many things wrong with this that I didn't know where to start, I just couldn't understand that kind of thinking.

I looked up at Luke. Willow had totted off, and found a toy to play with.

"I know" he said, incredulous, understanding my loss for words.

So this, this weak putrid example of Christianity was what I was reluctant to leave behind?

Fuck that.

I did the spell to release myself as soon as I could be alone.

Soon after, everything became an act of worship. With Rosemary and the teasing smell of Nag Champa in the background, I began to explore myself as a Witch. It was personal, Rosemary playing the part of the talent coach, urging the young dancer out of her shell. I'm sure she got a lot out of it as well, but in my view she helped me far more than I helped her.

With her everything became magical; or rather I began

to see the magic in everything. It all overlapped my emerging feminine on the march, in the same step as my awareness of the Goddess in my life. We were the Goddess. Walks in the woods, the thrum of the birds call came from the well inside my own belly. Branches configured in delicate greeting. As we danced at a party, a circle formed around us. The rhythm of our bodies accompanying the haunting melody, we became something much larger than two girls swaying to a slow beat. We expanded not up to heaven, but deep down and wide out until we absorbed all that was around, and under us, all amalgamated into a big, moist, clumped powdery bowl of dirt brown cake mix. A mix of humanity and the Divine. The Divine wasn't in heaven shaking a big stick, She was right here, around us, in us.

We/the Goddess were the beat. We were the anger in the singer's voice at the injustice done to women, the tortured moan from her lips, the small voice that mimicked her girlhood. We moved and the world moved. We were the Goddess.

And thankfully, the voice of institutional patriarchy got quieter and quieter in my head, until one day, I couldn't hear it anymore.

***

My dad thinks it's ghetto to have your car smell like anything other than car. I really like the coconut- scented, translucent blue dolphins that you hang from your rear view mirror. They make your car smell like Malibu rum. But dad hates 'em. I wondered what kind of shit-fit he'd have if he ever got in Rosemary's car.

"Do you know where this place is?" I said, breathing in fake Patchouli and candied strawberries.

She adjusted the mirror.

"Yeah, it is downtown. I looked it up online.It's called Earth Mother."

I couldn't figure out what was wrong with her today. This was the tenth or so time that we had been somewhere, done something that was Witchcraft related, and I got the feeling that she was already getting bored with it. Like one of those people who skydives, and halfway to the ground is yawning and thinking of what to do next. I didn't like the way it made me feel. Like it was MY fault that we were out on a gorgeous Saturday, driving to one of the new Witchcraft shops in town. That somehow if it wasn't perfect, and amazing, and when we left if she wouldn't be able to shoot blue lightning out of her fingertips that she would be upset the rest of the day. A kind of passive-aggressive upset. She wouldn't lash out, but everything we did for the rest of the day would have an "I'm just waiting for this to be over" quality. It was exhausting.

I really hope this place is cool. I surveyed the front door.

Yeah, I don't know about this. I didn't like the way it felt the minute I stepped through the threshold.

Rosemary sashayed past me, and over to the Pagan jewelry. I looked around the store. It looked like it was trying to cover up something. The colors were a muted brown, and an earthy green, and there were pretty twisted branches, and bamboo stalks everywhere. There was peaceful what I like to call "outside" music playing-it sounded like running water and birds chirping. But damn if it didn't feel like it was screaming red and black to me. I didn't like it at all, and I didn't care if they were giving away the entire works of Scott Cunningham for free, I wanted to leave. We'd been there thirty seconds, and I was ready to run for the door.

A nervous looking clerk approached me. He was sketchy, and sweaty. Scary skinny and with dark circles under his eyes, he looked very out of place. He was wearing what looked like a borrowed cheesecloth batik shirt, and someone else's rune jewelry around his neck. Even he looked out of place.

"Can I help you?" he twitched.

I looked at him out of the side of my eye, I knew what he was up to. *This will be easy to figure out.*

"Hi" I said, "nice place you've got here."

That was all it took. He spilled his contents like an overturned milk jug.

"This is my wife's place" he blurted like he hadn't talked to someone in years.

"I actually work at Sears- I only fill in when she can't run the shop. I don't really like being downtown, I think it is a bad area, and we have had some problems with the previous owners." He looked regretful, like he'd said too much. "Anyway, is there anything you are looking for?" He tried to switch back into sales clerk mode.

God, that was easy.

"What do you mean problems with the previous owners?" I tried to spot Rosemary…she was engrossed in a deck of Oracle cards.

"Oh, it was nothing" he said, then pretended to dust an imaginary shelf. "My wife will be in soon, she is the one with all the answers."

Great. I wasn't sure that I wanted to wait that long. I didn't have time to start worrying about some nasty spirit following us home from the store, though, when the Witch Princess herself glided through the doors.

Head held high, she was obviously, unlike her husband

"into all this". She had on enough silver jewelry to sink a ship. Her floor length black cotton dress, and long braided hair screamed Witch. She clearly identified with the position.

"Excuse me, I have a questi…" I tried to catch her majesty as she walked, or rather, ran past me to the back. *Twitchy husband, creepy store, bitch owner. And why are we here again? I have had enough of this, time to collect my friend and leave.* Besides, I had the feeling that I'd been in the shop before, and it wasn't a pleasant feeling. I had to do what I dreaded. Interrupt Rosemary, who clearly was oblivious and having a great time.

"Hey hon" I said, trying to sound casual. "You ready to go?"

She was cross legged on the ground, engrossed in a book on ritual. There was a pile of books next to her.

"Huh? Um….no…what did you say?" she said, nose still in the book.

I knelt on the ground. "Rosemary, something is wrong in here."

That got her attention. She put the book down.

"Don't you feel it? Like all this is covering up something, you know wolf in sheep's clothing, that whole thing?"

Rosemary loved drama, especially when it came to the spirit world. And wanting stimulation of some kind, or a story to tell everyone, she jumped right on the concept.

"Yeah, I think it's haunted. Over there in the corner, near the candles, I thought I felt something brush my shoulder." Her eyes were as wide as beach balls.

Whatever.

"It is nasty in here, let's leave before we bring something home with us." I helped her put the books back on the shelf.

Princess Witch was suddenly focused on us.

"Can I help you with anything?" she said, fake friendly and much too close for comfort.

How can I ask her what is wrong with this place? I have to be sly about it…I have to….

Rosemary interrupted my thoughts. "Is this place haunted?" she asked Miss Witch bluntly.

So much for worming my way into that one.

"Yeah" the woman sighed, as if she was talking about a plumbing problem. "It used to be a Voodoo shop, and when they couldn't make their payments and I bought the store, they cursed me, and the shop. I have had nightmares for weeks, and business has been really bad."

For once both Rosemary and I were speechless. We stood there with our mouths hanging open. I remembered the feeling that I was seeing red and black everywhere.

"Hey, what color did these walls used to be?" I asked, already knowing the answer.

"They were this awful loud red with a black stripe underneath. We had the hardest time painting over them, we had to use four coats…..it was like they didn't want to be covered. One of the painters even fell off of the ladder and broke his leg. We had to start the whole thing all over again, and hire new painters."

I didn't have a problem with Voodoo, I knew there were good practitioners as well as bad, but I wasn't about to be on the receiving end of any dark magic, no matter where it came from.

We heard her last sentence as we were half out of the door, me dragging a stunned Rosemary out behind me.

"Ya'll come back, we don't get many people in here" she yelled after us.

Fifteen minutes down the road, and you would have thought that Rosemary had solved "the case of the haunted shop".

"I knew something was wrong the minute I walked in there." She rambled. At least she was happy. I didn't care who she thought did what, I was just glad to be out of there. All I wanted at that moment was to take a cleansing bath. As she recounted her version of the story I rolled the window down, and asked the wind to blow over me and cleanse me.

Rosemary has her story, her excitement. But why, when I try to meet other Pagans does it always end up like this? I keep meeting losers. Players. That Witch Woman was all show and no soul.

Goddess, I'm starting to get frustrated.

That night over take-out egg rolls and fried rice, we sat on the carpet and traded psychic stories.

"I have always been psychic." Rosemary claimed. I knew what was coming next. It was her favorite story to tell, and I was going to hear it again for the tenth time.

She smoothed the carpet with her free hand. "Once when I was staying over at my cousin's house, she decided to have her boyfriend over. Her mom would never had allowed it, so he snuck in the window when everyone was asleep."

I patiently listened for the rest of the story.

"We hung out for an hour, drinking sips of her mom's bottle of Southern Comfort. All of the sudden I had a permonition!" She held her hands up in the air in a halting motion. I tried to suppress a chuckle at her mispronunciation.

"I told him, I said, 'tonight you will get caught sneaking out. When the clock chimes four your mother will be sitting on her chair wearing her pink bathrobe and drinking coffee. You will try to sneak in the house, and she will be sitting there, waiting for you. You will never see my cousin again'. He was kind of a rough dude, so he just looked at me funny, we smoked some pot, and he went home. I forgot all about it."

She leaned in towards me, forgetting about the food in front of her.

"The next part was the crazy part, my cousin didn't speak to me for weeks afterwards. At eight the next morning, the doorbell rang. Her mom said it was for us. When we came to the door, there he was. He said 'Witch! You are a Witch! How did you know all that? I got home an as soon as I walked in the door the clock rang four, my momma was sitting there jus like you said she wuz. That was the scariest damn thing I'd ever heared of. I never want to come to this Witch house agin!'"

I always liked hearing the story, so I didn't mind hearing it again. Rosemary had a flair for drama, and she could tell a good story. But while Rosemary's psychic abilities came in short pops mine were more like a steady stream, or a slow consistent drip.

I always knew stuff. It just wasn't that dramatic. It was more like when things happened, I watched them take place like a movie I'd already seen. It wasn't impressive because I was used to it, and I never vocalized it. Usually it was mundane things. I knew who would be absent from school. That my mom would be singing a certain song when I woke up. What someone would say next, or sometimes what they were thinking. I thought about the time I purchased a little red Tiffany style lamp for my grandmother's birthday. From the moment I picked it up in the store, to watching the clerk packing it up, all I could see were pieces of it lying on the floor. When I got home I carefully placed it out of the way by putting it on a table in an uninhabited room after she had unwrapped it. Five minutes later it was lying on the floor in pieces. No scary music, no drama, just broken like I knew it would be. Little things like that, and it happened all the time. Why bore someone with that?

So after Rosemary's exciting story, I really had nothing to add. The one thing I could think of didn't sound as cool once I said it out loud.

"Um," I said dipping my eggroll in some sweet and sour sauce, "I used to share a room with my two sisters, they were younger and had to go to bed earlier than me. So I'd lie in bed and listen to Metallica on my headphones. My mom had hung a little wind chime right over the bed….I remember we got it on a trip to Florida, and it had little plastic oranges on it…anyway, I used to make it move with my mind."

Rosemary looked unimpressed. I remembered turning it clockwise, stopping it, and then turning it counterclockwise. I thought it was pretty cool.

Who cares…….. this isn't a pissing contest. Too often I noticed that Rosemary and I were trying to one-up each other. I wasn't in the mood.

We'd had enough excitement for the day.

"Hey, do you wanna go to the Beltane festival in Columbus?" I had called Rosemary in hopes of having a driving pal. We were calling ourselves Witches, much to the dismay of our significant others. I had come out of the broom closet.

The Beltane festival was our first large-scale mingling with other Pagans. It was a big step, and I knew it. I was hoping to meet someone I could "learn" from, and was still too thick to realize that I had been learning all along, and was learning now. Guess you can't teach an old dog new tricks.

We had gone to our favorite thrift shop earlier in the week to find the perfect Beltane dresses. We both had images of Heart's Anne and Nancy Wilson in their seventies gypsy inspired dresses, instantly winning the friendship of other Witches with our beautiful flowing attire, and hip attitude.

The day turned out to be cold and rainy. Our gowns were turned in for Birks and army green cargo pants. The whole drive up we fantasized about what a spiritual experience it was going to be. Rosemary was sure she had a strong feeling that it was a blessed event, with twists and turns of fate to unfold.

It actually royally sucked.

The Beltane festival was everything I hated about religion. Our first contact was at the registration desk (a cafeteria table poorly set on a sloping hill, with careless papers slung all over it). We were barely greeted. A tired, middle- aged woman wearing a cheap burgundy crushed velvet cloak approached the desk. Her attitude was horrible.

"Whole day" she barely squeezed the words out, as if it pained her to talk.

"Yes, two please" I said with a smile. *Come on, you guys are supposed to be Witchy, not pretentious.*

"That'll be twenty dollars apiece" she said with obvious satisfaction.

Rosemary looked at me. The website had said nothing about an admission price. I apologetically looked at her as we both dug through our cotton tie-die bags for the precious cash. I smelled a rat.

A two minute walk down the hill past the miserable woman, and my hopes lifted. From afar it looked like a medieval bazaar, with artisans selling their wares. I even heard what sounded like bellydance music.

"I'm excited" Rosemary said, forgetting about the long gone 20 dollars.

"Me too" I said surveying the landscape, wondering where to go first. We were starting to come out of the funk imposed on us by the registrar.

"Let's split up" Rosemary suggested. This was a good idea because shopping with Rosemary was like looking after a four year old, her excitement got the best of her. I immediately made my way to the Athame dealers. An Athame was something that a lot of Witches used. It is a knife, usually double bladed, and with a black handle. It was never used for cutting, and mostly used in a symbolic way...... I couldn't think of one reason for me to use one. I hated anything that even hinted at religion, and all that formal pointing and stuff made me uncomfortable. Maybe sometime down the road I might consider one, but at the moment I looked at the beautiful handcrafted knives with their alabaster handles, and doubted if there was any room in my magical practice for them. I chatted with the salespeople who were the only ones there who seemed to have a decent attitude.

Leaving the stand empty handed, I skimmed the other booths. Hair braiding stands, feather wings stands, herbalists, period clothing sellers, even the one belly dancer, dancing in between a row of merchants, seemed apathetic. Bored. Some even looked at us with contempt. I had really hoped to make some friends, some

215

acquaintances, someone who could tell me what this was all ABOUT. I was still waiting for canned answers. I wandered around hoping to see a friendly face.

Rosemary and I found each other after about ten minutes realizing that it was not what we had hoped for. After accidentally walking into a lame-o renaissance style knighting of sorts, we decided to head home. Thank goodness for Rosemary's positive attitude, because I was ready to spit in all their faces. I was busy bitching about our lost money and time, when I looked over at her, and she was doing a goofy two-step. I relaxed, she was right-those people weren't worth it. I should have known better to expect a lot from what was basically a bungee jump right back into organized religion.

We giggled all the way through our dinner at Mi Pueblo, and all the way home. Popping open some wine and dancing to the new CD we bought, I was having a great time. As I was rolling on the floor laughing at another one of Rosemary's antics, I thought, *this is what Witches should be, not those ridiculous people putting on a show.*

Part of me wanted to believe that Witchcraft and Paganism was special. Right. The best. That Witches had the corner on the market, the truth. It was painfully obvious to me after the Beltane fiasco, that these were just people like the people in the church that I had known. Same shit, different religion. I didn't want to believe it, I wanted to distance myself from all of that. I wanted to believe that Witches were cool, open minded, accepting people who weren't at all self- aggrandizing, or haughty or rude or smug. I wanted to believe that Witchcraft changed people the way that the church claimed Christianity changed people. But there was no change that didn't take place from within. Religious or not, Witch or not, Christian or not-people were people. The mindset of having "the way" was entrenched in me, and it would be a while before I fully let go of it, but I made a vow never to go back to that large of a gathering. I was afraid to see more of the same, afraid that it would ruin it for me. I was thankful for Rosemary, and thankful that we were practicing together. She brought a sense of mystery, a sense of fun to our circles.

As it turned out each meeting with Rosemary was drastically different. I think we did everything wrong those first few times.

Rosemary was unbridled, and I was a killjoy.

"Tra-la-la-la-la-la-la!" *I am so excited about this.* I thought as I unpacked my Yule goodies from the car.

We definitely learned from that first ritual. *No freezing cold. No paranoia, this time we will have more than some crackers and warm beer.* At Samhain the night had been freezing, but somehow the beer was warm. *Figures.*

Struggling, I made my way to Rosemary's front door. She came and opened it, looking very festive with a red, green and silver sparkly head band. I wiggled the leaves of my poinsettia choker at her. She laughed. Her mood matched my own.

"I'm so excited!" she said grabbing a box, "let me carry some of that."

I had been put in charge of the cakes and wine. I will admit I went a little crazy. $75 dollars at Costco crazy. I had enough little mushroom puffs and mini-spinach quiches to choke a horse, or feed a small army. Three different kinds of flavored pound cake. Lots of red wine, and even a bottle of mead. I thought the mead seemed medieval and perfect for our first Yule ritual. I could die stuffed full of phyllo dough, and lemon poppy seed cake. Fine with me.

"I'm starving, let's have something to eat first" I said, eyeing the frozen hors d' oeuvres'.

"Girl, you read my mind" Rosemary said as she heated up the oven, and went to look for the wine cork.

"To us…Witches!" she said holding up a full wine glass, and handing me the same.

"To our first Yule celebration!" I said, clinking the glass against hers.

We downed half the glass. So much for class.

"I had an idea for our ritual." Rosemary led me into the living room, where we decided that our festivities would take place.

"How bout we use this to make a circle?" She held up a large garland of fake evergreen, with little red plastic berries.

"What do you mean?"

"Like this." She got to work making a large circle out of the fake greenery.

That was going to be our circle. I pontificated for a moment.

The circle is supposed to protect, to contain energy. It is supposed to be something borne out of our combined energy, not something made in China…………I am such a stick in the mud. Who cares? What does it matter any way? Those yahoos who wrote that it isn't a good idea to drink and do ritual were wrong, too. I feel wonderful- relaxed, warm and fuzzy. This is going to be a powerful night!

"Tha'll be lovely honey, I like our little Yule circle."
"Good!" Rosemary said, "Are you ready for a refill? I think I smell the bacon and cheddar rounds." We took our empty

glasses to the kitchen.

"You know, every book I've ever read says not to do drugs or drink while you do ritual. They say ,like, one glass of wine is o.k., but any more than that, and you get out of control." This was my third glass. Rosemary's fourth.

"Look at all this food" she said, picking off a melted piece of cheese and tossing it into her mouth, "by the time we stuff ourselves, we won't be tipsy anymore."

"That makes sense" I said, as we loaded our plates, and made our way to the green plastic circle.

"I guesh we are shtarting with cakesh and wine tonight" I slurred.

Rosemary had one foot outside of the circle, and her empty plate lay next to her. So did two empty wine bottles.

"Hey....where is that mead?"

"It'sh in the bedroom, no, the kitchen." Holy crap was I drunk. How long was cakes and wine supposed to last? We hadn't done anything except down bottle after bottle of wine and stuff ourselves. Food soaks up alcohol, sure, but nothing can stand up to three bottles of wine. The food was simply outnumbered.

Rosemary returned with the mead.

"Have you ever had this?" she said, admiring the scrolled lettering on the bottle, and weaving a little bit.

"No, have you?" I had moved into a much more comfortable reclining position, not minding at all that the circle of Yule greenery had turned into sort of a wonky U shape.

"No, but it smells soooo witchy" she said, opening the bottle.

The smell of something spicy and bubbly filled the room.

"Mmmmmmmm....this ish good."

"Goes down smooth" I said, draining my glass.

"I know letsh chant!" I was feeling kinda stupid that all we'd done was drink, and eat, and drink.......I had to do something.

"What do you want to say?" Rosemary let out a belch.

I sat up, with a sudden purpose, forming the scratchy evergreen into a circle again.

"How bout 'Isis, Astarte, hear us today' ?" I felt inspired.

"O.k" Rosemary said, clearly going along with what I wanted to do. She would have been content drinking the rest of the night.

"Come on, it'll be fun, turn and face me." We positioned ourselves in the circle, sitting so we could look into each other's eyes.

"Now, let's focus" I closed my eyes. Bad idea. The room was swimming, and I felt queasy. Rosemary wasted about as much time on this notion as I had.

"I don't wanna .....do that." She was trying to get her bearings. Head in her hands, she was rocking back and forth. I really wanted to do something other than get sloppy, but the mead was kicking in and I could feel it.

"Come on" I whined. "Let's just try it once".

Rosemary tried to will herself to sit up.

I started," Isis, Astarte...Rosemary, you are supposed to be chanting."

She giggled. *Great*, we had gone from two Witches celebrating Yule, to one bossy drunk, and one ready-to-pass-out drunk. We got one chant out, and Rosemary burst into laughter. I gave up. It was pointless. We became a living illustration on why-it-isn't-a –good-idea-to-get-drunk-and-practice-Witchcraft.

All those stupid books were right on that one.

Rosemary was my new teacher. I came to realize this in later years, once she was gone. I was still looking for a preacher style/textbook teacher- one who I was sure would answer all my questions. Rosemary wasn't like that. Witchcraft isn't like that. There aren't blanket answers to questions; each person's experience is entirely personal. There are only individual answers, not all-encompassing group answers.

Even though we both considered ourselves mainly solitaries, I had someone else I knew who practiced Witchcraft. This in itself is a way to learn. Phone conversations, sharing on insights, even seeing how someone else does their altar, or meditation space. In watching them you learn who YOU are, and sometimes who you want to be. This is where real teaching begins. It is comparison and contrast, a personal spiritual practice is a living breathing thing, and sharing that, even verbally can be a great way to learn about yourself, and the Universe.

Born into an awful situation, Rosemary had two switches, *on* and *off*. *On* was what made everyone love her. She was a friendly, energetic, petite bubbly blond. She was fun-loving, imaginative, child-like and compassionate (we practically had to pull her away from homeless people) she appeared to not be afraid of anything. Not only was she a blast to be around, but her biggest asset was that when you talked, Rosemary listened. Really listened. It was like she listened with every part of herself.

Her *off* switch was scary. She would switch off suddenly and without warning, although as our friendship progressed I found that I could see it coming days ahead of time. She would go berserk, screaming, crying, throwing things, delusionally overreacting, or just shutting down to the point of being comatose. These times were worth it though, because it was so rewarding to be her friend.

As a Witch, Rosemary taught me a lot. She was truly free. The choking grip of formal religion had never held her. She taught me to read cycles, to see omens, signs and portents in anything. She taught me to read secret signs in nature and life, to tap into the flow. At the time I hadn't figured out how to make the whole thing *come alive* for me, I was still draining every book I could find for knowledge. Rosemary weaned me off of other's experience, and onto my own, she taught me about flow. And she taught me about synchronicity.

She would call and say excitedly "LISTEN TO WHAT HAPPENED….so and so at work mentioned that Duran Duran song Hungry Like a Wolf".

I wondered where this was going.

"THEN on my way home, when I turned the radio on in the car, THAT SAME SONG was on X94, I couldn't believe it!"

"O.K." I said patiently, hoping this was going somewhere and having no idea what she was getting at.

"THEN just now, Jeff just pulled the Duran Duran CD out of a stack, and said 'honey, we haven't listened to this in a long time, let's play it tonight'." She took a long pause. I took this to mean that that was the end of the "story".

"Um, that is cool, Rosemary" I said, falsely trying to match her enthusiasm, "but what does it mean?"

"It doesn't mean anything Tara, except that we are in the cycle. The rhythm. There is a certain flow to life that is a mish-mash of everything natural, and unnatural. Everything manmade and … everything that was ever given thought of, created, given, and taken away in this Universe. Silly non-sensical things like pop tarts, Rolls Royce, and coloring books. They all are a part of the Universe. They were someone's idea, someone's experience. Experience has been built around those things. To tap into the flow is to get in the stream, certain signs show you."

"Yeah" I said. "I get it."

I had no idea what she was talking about. I actually thought about the Son of Sam, and how supposedly Satan told him to kill. I hoped that she wasn't seeing things that weren't there, but a part of me was curious. I realized that our perceived idea of order, and where things fit, was just that. Our idea. I also realized that there were many things I had no grasp on. I just didn't know how something as laughable as Duran Duran fit in. The Universe is orderly chaos. Things mean something to our rational mind sometimes. They mean something to the universe all the time.

Rosemary could find spirituality in everyday life. I began to notice my own cycles. Things that I hadn't thought about in weeks, months, years, popping up all of the sudden, in threes. Sometimes they *did* mean something, sometimes not. I started taking them as a sign that I was where I needed to be, I was in with the flow. Of course I never mentioned this to anyone but her, because it sounded so crazy. So what if all of the sudden pomegranates and John Travolta references started popping up everywhere. You say that stuff aloud, and you doubt your own sanity.

Most religions look for lofty ideas, and a world outside your own. In Paganism, religion is in the eggs you had for breakfast, the drive with your windows down to work, the small feather that was mysteriously by your desk.

Everything. In Christianity I looked for God outside of myself. In Witchcraft He/She was right there in front of me, maybe even inside of me. This really changed things-it meant that I had personal responsibility.

But was still trying to formalize everything. Even though I said I didn't want religion, I just didn't know what else to do. Rosemary liked to wing it. To just light a candle, and see where it took us... such was the case of our initiation.

I was chattering. I knew it. We were on the way to the Crystal Garden and I wanted to make Rosemary commit to initiating each other in a month when we went to Quebec for vacation.

Initiation into Witchcraft can be many things, but in its most stripped down definition, and in the capacity in which I am referring to it, it means a formal dedication. A consecrating of yourself to the Goddess and as a Witch. And I wanted to do it. Bad. You would think that this would scare me off, being close to an organized nature, but the reality of it is that I wanted to see if there was anything to it. In doing it I would know.

"Then there are the cords, oh yeah, and we need a blade..." I rambled. Rosemary was suspiciously quiet as we pulled into the parking lot. She stubbed out a cig and lit another one. I could tell she was getting annoyed, details like that bogged her down. She was a butterfly who just wanted to feel each moment. Watching her reaction, I chilled a bit, doubting that our initiation would ever happen. I was sulking and Rosemary smoking, when Lydia burst out of the musical Crystal Garden front door. A long time patron of the Crystal Garden, we had met her there one day while shopping for some sage wands. Lydia seemed trapped in the wrong body. On the inside she was bubbly, with an almost contagious excitement. Everything she said had a "this is the most exciting thing you will ever hear in your life" quality. On the outside you could tell that she had lived a hard life, she looked worn, or as my dad would say she looked like she'd been rode hard and hung up wet.

Rosemary perked up.

"What are ya'll talking about?" Lydia said, lighting a cigarette. Rosemary lit another one. I was irritated. I was trying to get Rosemary to talk to me, and she wanted no part of it. *Lydia's involvement isn't going to help matters*, I thought bitterly.

"We want to initiate each other a month when we go to Quebec for vacation" I half croaked out. I was pouting.

Lydia was practically erupting. "You know, you two can initiate each other, but you need a third. Tell me what day you are doing it, and I will participate from home!" Rosemary looked up from her quiet haze.

"Really?" She said, seeming to come alive. I was furious.

"That'll be great" I said, faking a smile.

It probably won't even happen. Lydia will forget and I don't care if she does. Rosemary won't be in the mood, we will never be able to ditch the boys for a night, and even if we did, what the hell would we do if we don't plan anything.

I looked down at the gravel and pretended to kick at a pebble, while they chatted on.

I was tired of Rosemary using magic to suit her moods. I felt like she was playing at something and I was serious. I had heard Kurt talk about his own experience in sacred tones. Initiation was a way to up the intensity of your commitment......this was something I wanted, and my partner just wanted to play. The subject was dropped and forgotten like a nasty diaper. Rosemary didn't want to be bothered, and I was too angry to talk about it.

It wasn't spoken of again, although I thought about it occasionally as a month passed and vacation time loomed closer. By the time we got on the plane for Canada, I had completely forgotten about it.

I hope a vacation will smooth things out between Luke and I. I deliberated the dilemma in the taxi from the Quebec airport, looking out the window as we drove. Why can't life be simple? We were both so unhappy, and I wondered just how much longer we could live like this. I hated it when people stayed together "for the kids". Those poor kids aren't stupid. I knew that if I did that, then Willow would live an unhappy life, watching us fight for fourteen years, and then finally amputating the diseased marriage when she was old enough to be on her own. I also knew that she would rather be with a happy single mom, than a miserable married one. He wasn't happy either. As we unpacked our bags in the French quarter style hotel room, I glanced over at Rosemary. I was glad she was here.

Quebec was a beautiful, classy city. The combination of being far north where even in the summer the hint of cold was never far and the European feel to the city made it an interesting vacation spot. I felt like we were too boorish to be there, like graffiti on the Sistine chapel.

We ate well, played hard, and were busy having a great time. Sticking with Rosemary most of the week kept things relatively peaceful between Luke and I. The four of us drank ourselves silly, shopped, and toured the city. I had long ago forgotten the idea of initiation, and when we decided that Wednesday would be girl's day out it didn't occur to me that that was the day that we had set up with Lydia a month before.

I was relieved. Rosemary was in a good mood, and it was a clear sunny day. We took great pains to braid our hair in little braids, and carefully did our makeup and clothes. We had gotten our noses pierced the day before, and as we took a glace in the mirror on the way out the door, I was impressed at the reflection of the sexy blond and brunette, about to paint the town red.

The day started with hazelnut coffee, and hitting up the drugstores for new makeup, neat Canadian knick knacks, and candy. As we strolled munching gummy worms, and pickle flavored potato chips I felt about 13 years old, and I'm sure we were as obnoxious as a bunch of giggly pre-teens.

"Hey, look, there is a New Age shop!" Rosemary shouted, a potato chip crumb dangling from the corner of her mouth. I looked over at the sign she was pointing at, with little moons and stars on a navy night sky were the words

NEW MOON GIFTS AND MAGICAL ITEMS

"Hell, yeah" I said, even though it was already decided that we were going in……. that place didn't know what hit 'em. We strolled in like mechanics in an auto supply store, picking up everything and commenting on it loudly to prove we knew what we were doing.

"This rose quartz is just what I need for Jeff's heart chakra." Rosemary said loudly, so that everyone for blocks knew of her intent.

"Yeah, well, I was really looking for some Shepherd's Purse for that spell on healing" I said, echoing her tone and fingering the small green packet. We were Witches, and everyone there was going to know it, whether they wanted to or not.

We ran the poor clerk to death, and bought up all the supplies of magical oils they had. Two energetic hours later we left, our arms bulging with bags. I expected that they probably put up the closed sign, and then started chugging a bottle of vodka.

When she was in a good mood, Rosemary was too much fun.

As evening approached, we made for our hotel. Girls day out had been a success. Thinking about the day I realized it was the most fun I had even come close to in a long time. We had gotten our Tarot cards read, shopped for saris and exotic clothes and jewelry, eaten at a brightly colored bistro, and sang all the way back on the metro. I was a little sad it was over. Walking into our hotel room was like being doused with cold water.

"We were wondering when you'd be back!" Luke snapped. Jeff was staring. I felt sick to my stomach. They were very clearly dressed and ready, waiting for us to go out with them. I looked at Rosemary trying to telepathically send her messages.

Please. Please. I don't want to go with them. I want to finish up the day, and keep having fun. Rosemary uncharacteristically had the same thought.

"Tara and I are going to hang out here" she announced, half believing herself. Jeff could make Rosemary do anything, so her resistance to his wishes surprised me. She further made her point by changing into white sweatpants and plopping down on the bed.

Great, here comes a fight, I thought as I settled down into a corner preparing for battle. *So much for our girl's day*. Instead of the normal three hour battle, the strangest thing began to happen. As if some unseen force were pushing the guys out the door, they got up, and got ready to go. Grabbing their wallets, and keys, saying nothing, and with looks of puzzlement on their faces, they just left. The door clicked as it closed behind them. There was a strange silence.

I looked at Rosemary. She was astonished as I was. That had *never ever* happened. Sometimes if there was a difference of opinion on what we wanted to do, there would be a quadruple fight of operatic drama and proportion, lasting late into the morning. Never had they just agreed, never had they just left. It looked like they were marionettes, limbs heavy, like they were being dragged to the door. Man, it was strange.

Much discussion of this anomaly and a few good laughs at their expense, then the realization hit me. What were we going to do now? Rosemary was lying on the opposite bed, her feet propped against the wall. We played with our braids for a moment, and I wondered what to do. I didn't want to bore her.

"Hey" I said, catching her attention. "Why don't cannibals eat clowns?"

"I don't know, why?" she said, turning to face me.

"Because they taste funny" I said, gleaming.

The laughter seemed to loosen each other up, and clear the air. We decided to look over our purchases from the day, and I pulled out a bottle of Lilith oil I had bought.

"Breathe this in" I said, lifting the bottle to her nose. I could smell the dark warmth coming from the Amber and Patchouli. The oil was a reddish brown, and smelled like sex and personal power.

"I love Lilith" I said, almost to myself.

I was starting to feel funny. Heavy. Like someone had poured thick warm water all over me. I sat under this blanketed feeling for a minute, and then turned to look at Rosemary. She was standing on the bed, moving her hands as if trying to shake something off of them. This was what she did when something intensely spiritual happened.

I tried to speak. "What is happening?" I didn't feel like I had spoken at all, but like the words had come from somewhere else.

"I don't know" she said, and by the puzzlement and panic on her face, I could see that she felt the same thing. Our words seemed to take on a thin quality. We watched the words come out as we spoke them.

And as fast as that, it was evident....... we were being initiated. I couldn't believe it.

I was all black. She was all white. We were Yin and Yang. Circling, we dove, circled, but never actually merged. I felt like I was drowning, then like I was flying. I was both experiencing this and watching it be experienced. The circling, the black and white, all of the world made sense-at the heart of it all we were all one. My conscious mind seemed far away as I became enveloped in a higher knowing. I knew. My heartbeat was the same as the heartbeat of every living thing. It wasn't just a sentence on the page of a New Age book, or a quote by a famous guru, I KNEW it. I WAS it. *We really were one!* It is impossible to describe something like this; it simply cannot be put into words. I was every beautiful poem ever written, I was the roaring ocean, the falling autumn leaf, the kill the moment the prey descends upon it. I was life, and Rosemary was life, and Luke was life, and everyone I'd ever met or seen, or ever existed. All living things, we were all the same. There was no emotion, just the stillness that comes with being. Once again, as with Lilith, the waves of the earth, and meeting God in Oklahoma, my physical body could have expired, and I would have been totally happy to merge with this oneness wholly and completely.

There was no time; it could have been years, months, seconds. Afterward, (and it ended suddenly) we sank down on the bed, spent. I felt like I'd run a marathon. We were as still as death, resting, and in awe of it all. For an hour we couldn't speak, didn't want to. When we finally did speak, the earthly quality of our words broke the spell, and landed us back to reality. The boys came back, drunk and happy from their night out. I glanced at her, and she back at me. This was our secret.

For the rest of the week, we were followed by Yin and Yang. On our seat on the metro, in a baseball stadium, in the weirdest of places, we saw the symbol. It was a confirmation; our lives would never be the same.

***

"I think Jesus is mad at me" Rosemary said over the phone.

Good lord, she has been talking to her new Christian mother. I tried to be patient.

"Rosemary, honey, the nightmares are a cleansing process. You have to face your fears. We have just been initiated; did you expect life to be the same? To feel the same?" I didn't want to admit the panicky call I'd made to Kurt after three nights of barely sleeping. The call which I was repeating verbatim.

"Well, I don't like it" she said shortly. "We've got this party tonight, and I am exhausted."

"Do you need me to come help?" I said

unconvincingly.

"No, I'll just see ya at 9. Bye." I could feel a wedge of something invisible growing between us.

It's a shame she doesn't feel good because I feel great. I felt clear. *Clearer than I've ever felt.* I thought, as I put on my mascara, getting ready for the party. My level of existence had changed, not that my problems went away, but the energy frequency with which I operated went up by a hundred degrees. It was scary, exciting, and just what I had been looking for. One couldn't go through something like that and *not* change. Although I definitely had to muster up some courage, the new level of existence required it, I wanted change so badly that I allowed myself to accept the scary parts as a price for the higher level of energy. I knew that's what it was, more light= more darkness. Gotta be a balance. Kurt was dead on.

"Tara, it is all part of the refining process." He was right, and I wasn't going to be chicken shit about it. Confidently shoving my cigarettes into my bag, I made my way to the party.

Another party. I had long ago accepted that being Rosemary's friend meant frequent parties, she was immensely social. Not that I minded a dinner party, or a party with a PURPOSE. *But not this kind*, I thought, the kind where everyone gets wasted, and passes out. I felt like I was too old for this. I made my way to the safe, sterile feel of the kitchen for a drink, instead of the more social living room, full of potential convicts. *Well, I'm here*, I thought, *better make the best of it. Oh good, somebody brought some Cabernet.*

"I didn't know you would be here!" I turned around and standing there in all her six foot glory was the silver haired Salina. Rosemary's friend from work, and a fellow

Witch, I had met Salina only a few times, but we quickly bonded. She was eccentric, beautiful, and model slim. Her white hot hair and secret smile made her very enigmatic, her smile spoke volumes. Her smile was a treat, and coupled with heavily made- up, wicked looking cat eyes, she appeared to be saying "I have a secret, and I might just let you in on it". This chick *looked* like a Witch.

We chatted for a few minutes, knowing that we'd probably be spending the rest of the party hanging out with each other. It was the unspoken rule of being Rosemary's friend, you had to share. She flitted around all night, and if you got five minutes with her, you were lucky. So we got our drinks and pushed into the living room, preparing to talk shop.

"What are you doing for Samhain?" I said, breaking the ice.

Don't know what to talk about with a Witch? Bring up Samhain, it always works. It's like talking about the weather with a regular person.

"My man and I always have a party, wanna come?" She was getting comfy in their colonial blue la-z-boy.

I was just about to reply when our attention was brought to the center of the room. Trouble. A guy with scruffy black hair, and an unkempt beard staggered by. He was walking up to people and approaching them trying to start a fight. Salina and I looked at each other. We had both been at THAT party, the one where the cops came, and we did not want that kind of trouble again. This guy was without a doubt, the worst kind of trouble.

I nodded back at her, and knew what she meant.... *let's get rid of this guy*. We both closed our eyes and concentrated. I could feel our combined power.

G*o away go away go away*. I pushed out. We felt it go

233

from ourselves, smiled at each other, then went back into the kitchen for another drink.

"So tell me about that party, I looovvvee Halloween" I said, making small talk.

"It takes us a whole month to decorate, you'd love it…wait…. did you hear that?"

"How could I have not heard that? Holy crap."

We followed the sound of the loud crash, and walking into the living room were greeted with a pretty scary picture. The trouble maker was lying on the ground covered in a red substance that looked like blood. We covered our mouths in horror, afraid to look at each other. *What had we done?* The party stopped and gathered around the scene. Jeff was panicking. He slowly walked over.

"Wait, it's o.k." he said, exhaling. "It's only red wax. He must have fallen over the speaker with the big red candle on it."

I looked at the guy. He was out cold, and a group of people gathered to carry him to the other room. My hands were shaking. Salina and I parted ways, and didn't speak to each other the rest of the evening. I couldn't get it out of my mind…..the red wax had been a warning. Power can't be abused or used sloppily; it also couldn't be used in a way that suited me whenever I wanted. He could have been really badly hurt, all because I was uncomfortable with his presence. Now I know that the smart Witch would just put protection around him, and if things got bad enough, just remove herself from the situation, not try to prove anything. I should have just left the party. But then I was amazed at how quickly it had worked, and fascinated, if not a little afraid of my new power.

***

I had a question. An infinite question, with effects that would be far-reaching. When I thought about leaving Luke it was all about timing. I was starting to understand that everything was about right timing. For most of you timing isn't a problem, because that just- jump- in mentality isn't really a part of your makeup. I had felt so many ill effects from doing just that, and in this, one of the biggest questions I needed to ask, timing was very important. *When?* I knew that I was leaving Luke, but when? When was the best time? The right time? This wasn't going to be easy, but I wanted it to be right. Right in the sense that a hurricane is right, or a forest fire. It might not be pleasant, it might be downright terrible, but it wasn't wrong. I knew that for the three of us, splitting up would be the best, but I needed help with the when. Divine help.

Enter Medusa. I saw her picture and I knew that she would be the one to ask. I don't get the same feelings that most people get when faced with the image of Medusa, I feel tingly, excited. I see her as powerful, and not someone to cross. She was all about timing, and if you opposed her at the wrong time, the results would be life altering. Medusa has a head full of snakes, instead of hair there are snakes. People through the ages have been fascinated with her, Da Vinci painted her, as well as countless others, and I have heard her described as the "single most terrifying female Goddess figure in all of time". *Whew.* That's quite a title.

You see, snakes are a phallic symbol. The snakes are on her head, aka her place of knowledge; hence, she contains both male and female wisdom. She's a really smart chick. She don't need a man. She was threatening because she didn't need a man, and her image became terrifying. Ready for my dime store psychology?

Men have certain stereotypical attributes, and women have some, so I'm not picking on anyone. My hubby and I have this little play-argument all the time.

"Men are dumb" I say.

"Well, women are crazy" he says.

"I'd rather be crazy than dumb."

"Well, I'd rather be dumb than crazy" he says back.

"That is because men are too dumb to know what's worse" I counter.

He says "you say that because you are crazy".

And on and on.

All joking aside, men are a little….um…touchy about the mental superiority of a certain X chromosome. You guys think you are smarter. Don't deny it, you do, and awesome stereotypes like Barbie and Britney don't do much to discourage you.

I easily understood why Lilith was seen as something that the male ruling body had to demonize. Here was a Goddess that took control of her own sexuality; she said it belonged to HER. She fought for it. So…..instead of a handmaiden at the temple (what she originally was in the Epic of Gilgamesh), her story mysteriously got changed to that of a succubus. Whatever, do what you gotta do. When one woman stands up for herself there are plenty of bimbos ready to step up and open their legs, then go make you a sandwich. That is probably why Lilith never made the coveted title of "single most frightening female deity". For every one Lilith, there are 100 Pussycat Dolls, wanting nothing else than to please a man….but Medusa. Here's a woman who challenges the grey matter. She is self-contained. The wisdom she possesses is limitless and more than any gender-specific identity. She's got it all……..a woman. A woman knows what men know AND what women know. Admirable.

So while Lilith became a succubus, Medusa got the worst of it. Her look could turn you to stone. She spit poison. She was butt ugly. She wrote bad checks. And she met her untimely death at the hands of Perseus when he lopped off (can you guess it?) her head. This is what we do to smart women here on planet earth.

Like I said, I liked Medusa, who better to ask when you had a question that would forever change the current of your life?

As I lay in bed I imagined Her head, squirming with snakes, writhing, twisting. What was she really like? I decided to go straight to Her. In that delicious state between sleep I pushed my heart's desire at Her, supplementing it with words. I didn't want Luke to hurt, but it was inevitable. I didn't want Willow to suffer, but I knew it would happen. *Show me the right time. I want to KNOW. Please, wise one.* Then I drifted into oblivion.

Remember the wizard in the Wizard of Oz? A large green face, larger than life spouting a knowing that was so much bigger than Dorothy with her sparkly shoes that she didn't know how to use? She came in my dream. It was fast, a little snippet that borrowed worlds of ages past. Her eyes were green. The greenest things I have ever seen, greener than Ireland, greener than the brightest emerald, a green so penetrating that you just can't imagine it.

This happened years ago, and I still remember that green.

Her energy was so overwhelmingly understanding and kind. She knew what I felt, I just knew She did. Just Her face with her bright green eyes came to me, and She said one thing.

"When you see the eye in your wine, then you will

know."

She left, and I woke up. I called Rosemary.

"The eye in my wine" I said over the phone.

"What does that mean?"

"I don't know."

"You love wine" Rosemary said, thinking for me.

"I know."

For the next couple of weeks I studied each glass of wine I drank, I expected to see an eye in it. No dice. Something in me knew that was not what She meant. I was very relieved because a good glass of red wine was and still is one of my favorite things in the world (next to nuzzling my nose in my kid's necks and the funny little songs that my husband makes up). If I saw an actual eye in it, I wasn't sure it would be the same. Still, even if I did, would that make a difference? Would some understanding come over me that would make it better when I saw the eye, or would it just be time that I would have to trust? Either way, now I was looking for an eye. When Rosemary came over, and we did our wine/Witchcraft/hang out Friday night ritual, I looked for it. I studied every eye symbol that I saw, and wondered if the secret was in the books, in the definitions. Finally, after weeks of searching, I let it go. Obviously it was going to come to me, and I would just have to trust that I would know it when I did.

"She threw it. She threw the whole thing in the yard" Jeff yelled to his buddy. The buddy that was out in the yard with a flashlight looking for the birthday present that he'd given Rosemary. *Par for the course. Those two are always fighting.*

Even though it was Rosemary's birthday party, even though the yard and house was packed to the gills with people, and even though Rosemary was wearing little gossamer fairy wings and a birthday tiara, she was mad at him for something. So she threw her present....in the yard. There had to be some kind of drama at these parties, I just never knew what it would be.

Luke was tanked, and I was getting there.

"Want me to make you a rum and coke?" Luke offered.

"No thanks" I said. I was only drinking wine these days.

I wandered the house, forgoing Luke's company, and Rosemary's and anyone else's. I felt alone as I watched various cliques do their thing. I knew that some coke was being snorted in the guest room, so I avoided them. The thugs had gotten a hold of the sofa, and last time the police had been called on them, I steered clear. Most of the decent people were outside smoking on the deck; I had quit smoking so that was out. So I made my way to the bathroom. Rosemary eventually caught up with me in there, as I sat on the blue bathroom floor rug. It was quiet in there, and I could be alone. She plopped down beside me.

"You look like a butterfly" she said, pupils looking like two ink blots.

"What did you take, honey?" I said, rubbing her back. Her tiara was askew.

"Just some shrooms.... that was Jeff's present. I threw it" she said, matter of fact.

"Oh."

"You look upset" she said, sweet as ever.

"I am just peaceful, that's all. I guess I'm not feeling social." *I don't know that I'm not feeling social, but I'm not feeling like being HERE.* I didn't connect with Luke, and Rosemary was in la la land. I just wanted to be home with a book, and away from this scene, I'd grown tired of this scene. I thought of Luke, completely comfortable with the same group of people doing the same things. I felt I'd outgrown it. I wanted a better life.

Rosemary reached up to smooth my hair, and her large Moonstone ring……blinked at me.

What the fuck?!!!!!

It was so frightening that I felt all the air and energy drain out of my body like a vacuum. Rosemary who was super-sensitive right at that moment, freaked out.

"What just happened to you? What did you do? What was that? You feel hollow. Nothing but bones. You are nothing but bones." She was clasped onto my arm, gripping it like a blood pressure cuff. She seemed afraid to let go.

"Your ring. It blinked. It blinked" I choked out.

If I'd thought that she'd freaked out before she really went nuts when I said that.

"THE EYE. TARA. IT. IS. THE. EYE. HOLY SHIT. THE EYE IN YOUR WINE. WE ARE AT A PARTY, WINE IS PARTY, FUN. THE EYE IN YOUR WINE."

She looked like she might faint. We both stared at her ring, expecting it to wink at us.

There is nothing like a shrooming friend with a blinking ring on a bathroom floor rug to make you realize that your marriage is over.

Chapter Nine

You've got to do your own growing, no matter how
tall your grandfather was.
- Irish Proverb

The cool thing about being able to pick and choose
what I wanted as my personal religious practice is that I did
just that. I scrapped the candle altar setups, and knives,
wands or anything that even though I might like the idea of,
but outside of a Harry Potter movie would make me
snicker. Every time I imagined holding up an Athame, I
knew they weren't for me. No offense to those that it works
for, but I just couldn't envision pointing a knife around, and
being theatrical, I knew that I'd just start giggling. But The
Wheel? Now there was another story.

The Wiccan Wheel or Wheel of the Year is basically a
series of eight holidays celebrating the turning of the
seasons. Most of these I already celebrated, their roots
being far older than the new Christian holidays that the
church superimposed on them. Halloween, Christmas,
Mayday, Easter, all of these started as Samhain, Yule,
Beltane, and Ostara. Back in the day, (by that I mean
around 400 A.D.) when the Christian church came to the
British Isles and tried to convert the locals, it turned out to
be harder than they thought. Just like those Pagans, they
said "sure, we will believe in Jesus, and go to your church"
but after they left Mass, went home and lit a balefire and
continued to celebrate their own holidays, plus the new
religion. Why not, they were Pagans after all-all of it was
God. Interestingly, the word Pagan comes from a Latin
word meaning "country-dweller". The people that lived

furthest from the cities were the hardest to convert, they became Pagans. The word heathen means basically the same thing "from the heath". Funny how a couple centuries can change the meaning of things.

The church officials did not know what to do. They figured the best way to get the locals to quit practicing their religion was to make new holidays to combine with the already existing Pagan ones. The church decided that Yule, which falls on the Winter Solstice, and celebrates the returning SUN, should celebrate the birth of the SON, and become Christmas. Easter or Ostara, named after the Goddess Eostre, funny enough, the Goddess of new things and re-birth, with bunnies, and eggs as her symbols, should be about the resurrection of Jesus, and so on.

I liked The Wheel. The more I read about it, the more I decided that it fell with the natural rhythms of what was already there, and so fit in with my already enthusiastic joy at the change of seasons. Focusing on the quiet of Yule with its one light took away the distraction that Christmas had robbed me of. During Beltane, the world comes together; it is the joining of people, the fertilization of the natural world. Halloween, Samhain, is the night where the veil was thinnest, the separation of spirit world and material world was paper thin. I'd been celebrating this for years and didn't even know it. Basically every holiday we celebrate has its roots in something that far pre-dates Christianity.

Yule was easy, Samhain was easy, Beltane was easy, and Ostara was easy. Even Litha, which is the summer solstice, I could easily identify with, but I had no idea about the lesser known of the holidays. Such as Imbolc, which falls February 1st, and celebrates the first hint of the awakening earth, Mabon, or Autumn Equinox, which falls around September 21st, the Witches Thanksgiving, and the first harvest, Lammas, which falls on August 1st. It seemed exciting to explore the ones I didn't know about. I looked forward to learning the finer points of the cycles of nature.

Imbolc, February 1st. I chose this holiday to single out, and really celebrate. It is kinda the underdog of The Wheel, the least celebrated. Maybe it's because around that time of year, February, I've always been sad, bored, sometimes depressed. The holidays are over, outside it is perpetually grey, and cold, and spring is a long way off. I liked the idea of the "image of Imbolc" ….the small flower shooting up through the snow, the distant promise of spring-renewal, time to shake off the winter blues, and old year, and start again. I knew that most of the holidays on The Wheel weren't going to be easy to consistently celebrate year after year, but Imbolc would be easy. Yule is basically Christmas, Samhain is Halloween, and the big ones were already spoken for. The smaller ones were just too hard to celebrate. Imaging telling your boss "but I really need this weekend off for Mabon". I figured no one would question an overworked mother taking a weekend trip for some mid-winter R & R.

At my weekly solitary Chinese dinner out, I'd decided, no matter what was happening in my life I'd go away to celebrate Imbolc every year. I wanted the repetition to teach me its meaning. It just so happened that the first year I decided that, it worked out great.

"Man, I can't believe that your parents are letting us have this place, AND they have it the week of Imbolc!" Rosemary was driving, and we were both eating Twizzlers, and checking out the scenery.

"I know" I mumbled, my mouth full of candy. I

couldn't believe it either. With a timeshare, you get one week a year, and it just so happened that their week fell right on Imbolc. In the mountains. At a ski resort. In a little Chalet with a fireplace. I could almost smell the mountain air.

We had packed up every piece of Witchery we owned- candles, sage wands, stones, incense, you name it. We'd even brought a pale pink altar cloth to set up as our communal altar. It was a hilarious sight, the two of us lugging overfull laundry baskets to the car. Chalices, and little velvet bags full of herbs threatened to topple out as we staggered. Rosemary's little blue Prelude was stuffed to the gills. We laughed the whole way there. The drive up and through the mountain was like traveling to another world, a dense fog hung at the top of the mountain, and the air was fresh, cold, and quiet. In a rare moment we were speechless as we drove to the private little cabin. It was already so magical.

The little chalet we stayed in had a stone hearth; this is where we placed our altar. It was one of the first things we did.

Rosemary walked over to the altar and rummaged through one of her massive bags of goods. She pulled out a goblet with blue and pink stones glued to it.

"I made this" she said proudly. "I thought the colors seemed very Imbolc-y."

"Look it matches the altar cloth I brought perfectly!" I held out the cloth for Rosemary to touch. It was soft pink, cashmere, embroidered with a darker pink thread.

"Let's go ahead and set it up!"

"O.k., I'll go get my other stuff." I walked over to the things I'd chosen-a few stones, a feather, and a symbol of what I wanted for my future.

244

"This book says that milk is the common offering for Imbolc" Rosemary said, grabbing the goblet and going over to the fridge.

"Yeah" I said offhandedly "that is because Imbolc, also called Olmec, actually means ewe's milk, and was named after the time of the year when the ewes give milk. Kind of a sign that the barren winter was at its end and the earth is starting to give again. Meant a lot to people back then, they lived off the land, and people died in winter because they would run out of food, they didn't have Food Lion, ya know."

"You are such a Witch nerd" she said, half irritated, half amused.

"I can't help it if I like to read."

Being in the mountains and away from my radio job, fights with my husband, and worries about my sick child, let my thoughts free. The quiet of the mountain was supporting us, the smell of snow in the air purifying. I was able to tune into the earth, and *feel* the time they call Imbolc. As Rosemary took her usual hour and a half to shower and dress I made a private ritual of silently conversing with the mountain. Sitting on the wooden deck I placed my feet firmly on the ground and listened. Just listened. The sharp air whipping around my face, I listened.

The little chalet was literally right on top of the mountain and it was perfect. As we sat eating pizza from the resort for dinner, we both talked about what we wanted from the trip. I wanted relief. My job was killing me. My marriage was killing me. My body, mind, and spirit were exhausted. We only had two days, and I needed a lifetime of super nap power to re-charge. We wanted relief, and relief we had in the best way possible. Imbolc is the promise of renewal, a break after the darkness of winter, the time as The Wheel turns yet again toward spring. A time to think about what you want to change with the waxing year.

There was a Jacuzzi, and vanity room. We took long baths, listened to Enya, and drank wine. We lit candles for the coming year, and asked for transformation. We sat by the fire, and traded stories about growing up, while doing pedicures, and manicures. We stomped on the ground to wake up Mother Earth, we went shopping at thrift stores. Magic and the Goddess was all around us. The air was almost tangible with a kind of pink fuzzy smoke, as we laughed, as we slept, everywhere. It was so peaceful, and as we saged each other before we got in the car to leave, I felt like I'd been gone for years. Like I'd been in a pillowy dream.

My inner eye was still very weak, but I'd been practicing using it. When I asked what the next year at Imbolc would bring, I saw a blazing hot pink. We both wondered what that meant as we giggled our way back down the mountain.

Being a solitary was satisfying, but when the time came for The Wheel to turn again, I really wanted to practice with someone. It was always Rosemary. Our relationship had been changing, though, and at Samhain it was all I could do to get together with her.

Grumble grumble that no good Mother P.O.S. My hands gripped the wheel as I drove to Rosemary's, thinking of the fight Luke and I had just had.
He doesn't understand how important this is to me, this is my religion! I was definitely feeling sorry for myself. He'd thrown a fit when I wanted to go to Rosemary's to have circle... *Tara, it doesn't matter what he feels. You*

have to stand up and do what you have to do, no matter what the reaction from others. You should know that by now. My reasonable voice kicked in, it was always a relief to hear it. I grabbed the cell phone.

"Hey, I'm on my way."

"Jeff wants to go out afterwards, so we only have thirty minutes."

"Rosemarrryyy" I whined. "This is Samhain for Goddess sake. The biggest night of the year for us."

"I know I know, but I promised Jeff, I'm just going to hop in the shower, come on in."

"Alright I'll be there in a minute."

Great. Just a minute for Rosemary meant an hour while she took a bath worthy of Cleopatra, I swear she got lost in there. *I'm NOT going to hang out with Jeff. I'll just go in her ritual room and wait.*

I walked to the door admiring the Halloween decorations. They pumped up the decorations to a feverish pitch, orange and purple lights were visible for blocks. A very pretty Jeff greeted me.

"Who are you supposed to be?"

"I'm Martha Stewart" he said, twirling roughly. He was defiantly drunk.

"Well, you make a beautiful woman, if I was a dude, I'd ask you out" I said, a little brusque. "Where's Rosemary?"

"She's in the shower." He looked disappointed that I was going in her ritual room, and not hanging out with him. He had too much pride to ask me to stay, and since he wasn't getting his way, he got snide.

"What is it exactly that you two are doing in there?" he said in a nursery school tone.

I couldn't resist. "Witchcraft!" I snapped. "And if you

aren't careful we'll cast a spell on you. How attached are you to your manhood?" I strode into Rosemary's sacred room, and shut the door on his stunned face.

Rosemary's prayer/meditation/ritual/just plain hangout room was comfortable and exotic. The walls were spring leaf green, and covered with various knick knacks from her travels. Scarves, "treasures", as she called the rocks, and ornate bejeweled boxes were on every available countertop, the floor was covered in an oriental rug, with some large throw pillows for sitting. No other furniture except some low to the ground end tables, and a small altar was in the room.

I paced the perimeter. *Looks like she set up the altar,* I thought in relief, as I smelled the oils she used coming via steam from her piping hot shower as they sluggishly wafted into the room. I knelt down before the tiny table. *I'll just meditate a little as I wait for her.*

Tonight felt like an ending. No matter how I looked at in, I couldn't shake that feeling. I chalked it up to my dissolving marriage. She sashayed out of the bathroom, covered in spice laden oils and trailing a ghost of steamy vapor with her.

"Let's open a window" I said, unable to breathe." Girl, how hot do you take your showers?"

She laughed and didn't answer my question, instead, she looked at me, trying to gauge something. I felt that she felt it too, that ending.

"Do you like the altar?" she said, pointing to the low table. "I have some sage to purify, some myrrh to burn, and I figured we'd pull a card for the coming year."

"I love it, let's do it" I kneeled down and wedged a ruby pillow under my legs curling my feet underneath me.

As we shuffled the deck, and lit the incense I didn't feel the connection that I usually did with her. It felt like I was standing on a dock, waving to her as she slowly sailed away.

I reached into the cauldron that held our cards.

"Death. I got the death card." I held it to my face, shocked that out of 78 cards this was the one I pulled.

"Honey, that has to be you and Luke. You decided to separate didn't you?" she said with her mouth but her eyes didn't believe it.

"I don't want to talk about it, go ahead and pull yours- we only have five more minutes."

She pulled out the Hangman. A decision.

Is she deciding to go? What does she have to make a choice between? I wondered as she studied the card.

"What do you think?" I asked, after she was unusually silent for a minute.

"I knew it, I knew it!" she mouthed. "Today I was cleaning this room, and I lit a green candle asking to be shown some light on my relationship with Jeff. He is such a jerk sometimes, and I need to make a decision. Do I stay or go?"

"Rosemary.....is that the candle you lit?" I said, pointing and suppressing a laugh. The Goddess surely has a sense of humor.

"Holy shit, look at it."

There on her coffee table was a perfectly formed erect penis shaped out of green candle wax. It had dripped out of its glass holder, making a perfectly formed phallus. I looked at it every which way, turning my head to see if I was seeing something that wasn't there. *Nope. That's a penis alright; there is no mistaking that shape.*

"Well, you know Jeff is a real dick sometimes." We

died laughing.

"Guess you got your answer." *But when do I get mine?*

When I left that night I wanted to turn around and look to see if she was still there. I knew she was leaving, I just didn't know when. The Wheel turned and turned, and the Dark of the Moon showed herself. Rosemary and I barely spoke; every time I called she was busy, or distant. When time for the rite of Imbolc came again, we were both in a very different place.

Transformation Schmansformation. I DID NOT like the way this was going. Sure Rosemary had agreed to go with me again this year, but I might as well have gone alone. She was only there physically. It had been a hell of a year for both of us. She totaled her car that she had just paid off, and lost her job in the same month. I had made the decision to leave Luke-it was a done deal. She was broke, and gripped with fear and worry. I was scared to death of losing my baby girl, and worried sick about the uncertainty of what kind of life loomed before me. We were both as broken as a forgotten Christmas toy.

The year before we had been babies, new Witches. As we prayed for transformation we had no idea what we were asking for. You know to be reborn, you must die first....well, we didn't know. We thought it was neat, doing spells, asking for help, giggle giggle, laugh laugh. You don't sign up for heart surgery and show up with a bottle of Chianti and a Sally Hanson French Manicure Kit.

Driving up the mountain we looked for signs of hope, but only leftover black snow stared back.

Maybe once we get there, set up our altar, I thought. We didn't bring as much, having not used eighty percent of what we naively brought the year before. Lugging all of the stuff in was sad. Rosemary and I tried to make it fun, but the effort was pathetic. It reminded me of the time I had gone to an amusement park and noticed a particular child that looked miserable. This went beyond "I didn't get a blue ice cream cone" misery, this went to the bone. I started a conversation with the woman that had brought him, his aunt. When he was out of earshot I learned that he'd just lost his father. Nothing could take away his pain. He couldn't ignore it; it had to run its course. No rides, no clowns, no ice cream, nothing could take pain away.

Nothing we did could make it better.

As we had our ritual first meal of resort pizza, we ate in silence. Rosemary was edgy and unfocused, and I was scared to death that when we called on the Goddess that she wouldn't come. This didn't feel comfortable, this didn't feel fun, it felt miserable.

As we laid out the hot pink altar cloth, and took our herbal soaks, and did our pedicures, I felt as if we were just going through the motions. Everything we did, from thrift store shopping to trying to find something to laugh at were acts of pain. She was there as the Crone, the death and ending Goddess, the Old Woman who does what needs to be done, so things can end, and then begin again. She had turned up the heat on our soft pink from the year before, turning it to a molten hot pink. Hot pink, my ass. All I wanted was to have some fun.

When you are in pain, clarification of the situation helps only mentally; pain has to run its course. We were at the beginning of the pain/growth cycle, and we felt helpless. As we did our goodbye sageing, I once again looked to my inner eye for next year's foreboding glimpse, and I didn't see Rosemary.

There is a certain look in the eye of a fighter. Doesn't matter what package they come in. Rosemary just happened to be in a small package, but there was no mistaking that this girl didn't put up with any crap, perceived or real. She was tiny, and stylish. It was apparent that she took great pleasure in the heaps of bracelets that she wore, and the silver that adorned her fingers, neck and ears. I was jealous of her fingernails. Mine peeled at the edges they were so weak, hereditary, from my mother. Hers were talons, carefully glossed over with Tang orange or metallic copper. Her hair changed colors with the seasons. Sometimes she was a mousey brunette; something I did not feel fit her. She was best as a blond. Not a Nordic ash blond, but a lemon juice and peroxide California blond…. I admired her when she was a blond.

She was a chameleon, and while her style didn't change as often as her hair, it changed with each new inspiration. I am a hippie at heart, and have always loved anything ethnic, cotton, or inspired by the Middle East. So when we started hanging out her style changed to hippie. It was never that she tried to copy people; it was that she simply loved style color, fashion. It was the only thing that wasn't touched by her nasty tumultuous childhood, and her enthusiasm for it was infectious. Life inspired her.

She was the girlfriend I had always wanted. The kind I envied my sisters having, but that I was too flaky for in high school. The kind that sat for hours and did each other's makeup, and discussed boys, while doing our nails and listening to Guns n Roses with milky green face masks on. She even called them "boys". Her favorite thing to say was "cute boy", as in, "I just met a cute boy", or "look at that cute boy". She was someone you could take to the mall with you.

Our friendship scared me. I was afraid it was too good to be true, that it would go away, that somehow the remnants of the dusty old fart that I was would come out and snatch up all the fun, ruin it. I was the serious one, she was the fun one. Even when I was being my funnest, I was still the serious one. It was cool to finally have someone to be a Witch with, but more than that it was great to have a friend…... a normal girly friendship, clothes, makeup, boys and all.

The way she decorated herself matched the way she decorated her surroundings. Looking at her rooms, there was the feeling of a traveler, a wanderer. Even though she had lived with Jeff for eight years, you got the idea that she had never really settled in, that she was ready to pack it all up and leave you wondering if she was ever really there at all. There was something very unattainable about her. Like she was on loan to you, like she was on loan to herself. When the wind blew her way it was time for her to go again. I waited for that wind, and one day it came.

Butterflies need to fly, it is part of their namesake. Even though my heart was completely broken when Rosemary left the country without so much as a phone call, I knew that it was what she needed. I had known it was coming. Someone like Rosemary never stayed in one place for long, never stayed with one friend for long. Once we got back from Imbolc, she was distant, and not returning my phone calls. She didn't want pain, she wanted fun.

And this wasn't fun anymore.

Chapter Ten

"Hold onto nothing, as fast as you can."
-Tori Amos, *Pretty Good Year*

For a moment, lets hop back to the Crystal Garden. My Witchy hangout.

There was a certain type of person that frequented the store, besides the New Agers, the Broken people and the undefinables like myself. There were also the Power Hungry. Those people scared me. For some reason they had power, and lots of it. Not fuzzy "yeah, I can sorta feel that" power, but real, knock your socks off holy-shit-did-that-really-happen power. They had figured out how to work the system, even cheat it. Now, I am sure that someday they will have to pay for it, because EVERYTHING and I mean EVERYTHING has a price tag. Like all those Irish fables about selling your soul to the devil for some instant gratification-eventually he will come to collect.

I had learned that to have power you had to let go of ego, little bit by little bit. It was a lifelong, self-actualized process. When you did actually gain a little power, that part of your "just wait till they see what I can do" self was long gone. The power went unused, or at least unseen. It wasn't a temporary burst of power, it was long lasting, permanent, and rock solid. The power you earned was for something greater than yourself, something greater than your own immediate self-satisfaction.

These guys were different. It was as if they had found a shortcut.

In would walk Abe, for instance. A small, white haired jokester, he was married to one of the more talented Tarot readers at the Crystal Garden. He had a pathological need for attention. It was evident in the way that he abused anyone's attention that would give it, with endless chatter, or meandering jokes. I didn't mind him, but I didn't trust him, and for good reason.

He could manipulate stones. Somehow, like the person that asks for a sip of your soda, and drinks the whole thing in one gulp, he would drain a stone of its energy. "Pull it out of the stone" he called it. It was scary, because it was raw, unnatural energy. It wasn't on par with the quiet surroundings, or the flow of the stone or store- it was the gold tooth among the row of pearly whites, the purple suit at a funeral. And he clearly got a kick out of it. He loved seeing the shocked look on people's faces when he said "give me your ring". They'd hand over the solitaire given years ago by a mate or life partner, and after turning, and twisting the ring around in the air, he'd hand it back, pulsing with power. "Oh my God" people would say, as he grinned openly.

Unfortunately, he taught this to a peculiar, dreadlocked, power obsessed young man who had started purposefully coming to the Crystal Garden. This new guy was one of those people who appeared to not notice anyone, he looked *through* you. Not in a mindless way, but more in a mindful way. He had something on his mind- some singular thing and it was power. His appearance tempered and contrasted this, making him a deadly predator. He looked like your garden variety Patchouli scented, vegan kid experimenting with an alternative path, hemp clothes and all. But if he had looked on the outside like he looked on the inside, he would have been on par with some of the more power obsessed. Singular mind, singular thought, until everything around you becomes just that, a thing.

Abe taught him this power, and it was then that the store began to change. Marnie's rocks *were* the store. They pulsed with the energy of the store, reflected it. He changed the energy. He played with all of this as if it didn't matter, as if he were playing with a new toy. He didn't realize how much that place had come to mean to me, to so many others. The air started to feel different, it became heavy, and draining, instead of light, and giving.

I found my visits becoming less and less frequent. Marnie was sick all the time, and when she was there she seemed tired, agitated. The store started closing earlier, opening later. Eventually I heard through the grapevine that since the new guy had come in and started messing with the energy of the place, the rumor was that it was going to close for good.

When I went to investigate, she had already hung up the sign. CLOSED.

I found Marnie sitting cross legged amid paperwork, rainbow colored candles, and crystal fairy sun catchers idly resting on the floor, like they too were tired and just couldn't do it anymore.

"Marnie, is everything o.k.?" I said in disbelief.

She avoided my gaze, but I could feel her energy. It felt like she was dying.

"Is there anything I can do?" I said, trying to make a connection with her.

She looked up from a box of Citrine that she was wrapping in tissue paper.

"I just can't do it, Tara, I just can't keep up" her look was pitiful, broken. Her gracefulness was gone, her patience was gone-it was a shell that remained. I saw her humanity, her reality. The angel of wisdom that I admired was gone. I felt ashamed that she had given so much to me, and all I'd ever done was ask for more. I voiced this to her with a panicky tone and a flicker of the old Marnie returned.

"The teacher is the eternal student, don't you know that, Tara? When you teach, you learn. I have enjoyed your company, your inquisitive nature, your straightforward energy. It has taught me much." She looked down, ending the conversation.

I knew it was done, that our time was done. So many things in my life were ending. Could I handle life without her quiet wisdom? As I was standing there thinking she appeared to have forgotten me, burrowing herself in all the mundane tasks that involved closing a business. I decided not to burden her further. I hugged her and left her to her sorrow…. and I never saw her again.

There was no place for me to go anymore. Rosemary was gone when I needed her the most. And the Crystal Garden was closed.

So I got help where I could find it.

Fairies, for goodness sake. I never thought I'd be trying to understand, let alone talk to the *Sidhe*. I knew they existed but thought maybe the reason I couldn't see them, wasn't consciously aware of them was similar to my opposite-of-a-green-thumb. Caring for plants didn't come naturally to me, I was too rough, and I had to work hard at not killing every bit of green I came in contact with. Maybe Fairies were the same, just not a connection that came naturally to me. I needed all the help I could get, though, and I was going to upturn every stone.

So I educated myself, read books, looked at pictures. What I learned wasn't exactly encouraging. Fairies were like the mob, air-tight, and with a definite social structure. There were the Seelie and Unseelie court- the dangerous ones and the helpful ones. You had to be careful not to approach them the wrong way, or you'd accidentally hitch yourself with the wrong kind like *Alp Luachra*, an Irish fairy who crawled down the back of your throat and ate your food until you wasted away, or the *Duende,* Spanish house fairies, that appear as middle aged women with long icicle fingers that come in to your house and destroy everything. They were extremely mischievous and the only difference between the good ones and the bad ones is that the good ones wouldn't do anything to humans if unprovoked. Still, they were a much diversified part of the spirit world, and they were supposed to be helpful to have on your side. They were fascinated with human food and drink, especially savories like butter, and sweets. Fairy social structure was highly developed, and to them humans were no more than a nuisance and sometimes a curiosity. Their world wasn't tangible like ours is, so sometimes they didn't mind a human pursuing a connection, but you always brought a gift, an offering, and your best manners just to get their attention, you know.

Even as adventurous as I am, I felt silly. The books said to tie a ribbon around some butter for an offering. *Yeah.* So there I was, 90 plus degrees outside and walking to a "fairy hill" I'd spotted carrying a rapidly melting stick of butter tied with a pink ribbon, and doubting my own sanity. But I had a reason- I needed a house. I needed all the help I could get. I wanted to be able to support myself when I moved out, and the price of the house was very important to me. I was going to be a single mother in that house, and I decided to ask the fairies for help.

How do you spot a fairy hill, you ask? Well, it is

mostly out of intuition. I had always noticed the perfectly round mound that I passed every day while jogging. I just knew fairies lived there- it seemed too perfect, too picturesque to be normal. It could have been out of a book of Ireland it was so round, so perfectly shaped, so green. The crest was an inviting orb that I pictured teeming with fairy life. I had to try.

This hill is more steep than it looks. I trudged to the top, huffing and puffing, and finally plopping down….. *crap.* Standing up quickly, I remembered that you are supposed to ask for permission to invade their space.

"Excuse me, (I learned that the best approach to the spirit world is to be frank) I am here to ask you for help, may I please sit down?" I waited a moment then sat, finally dropping my gloppy offering on the ground. The heat had made the dye from the pink ribbon streak the drippy chunk of butter. A car whizzed by.

I am a grown woman sitting in top of a hill, talking to herself, holding a pinkish hunk of butter in my hand. Woo hoo, this is livin'.

Closing my eyes, I grounded myself, and steadied my breath to a calm state. I quieted my mind, then tuned into my surroundings.

"Fairies, I've come with an offering." *Was that a laugh?* Something tinkled on the wind soft and small as a fuzzy windblown seed. *O.k. my mind is playing tricks on me.*

"Anyway, I've brought you an offering, sorry it kinda melted." I put the butter on the grass, and then smeared my hand on a tuft to clean it. *Hope that wasn't somebody's house.* I chuckled to myself.

Something almost undetectable brushed my face.

I sat up, alert. *That was cool.*

"I need a house. Something perfect for my daughter and I, some place I can heal, and I need it to be affordable. Will you help me? I will try my best to honor and respect you, and to get others to do the same."

I sat and listened. A north wind blew by, on this completely windless day. It wrapped around my face and laughed again.

"Thanks" I said, standing up. "Um, have a…good day." I felt HUGE, like a giant as I lumbered down the hill, and home to shower. All the stories, all the pictures, all the movies were true. These fairies, the ones I connected with on that day were tiny, almost undetectable tiny. Completely subtle, and smaller than a little dollhouse with all the tiny chairs and delicate little finger size blankets, and potted plants. Light. But not sweet…not like sugar and spice and Barbie's with glitter wings. They seemed more like animals to me, wild as the wild itself. I understood the caution against seeking fairies to add to your collection of experiences, like catching butterflies. My grandmother often told me of the fairies, and I never heard lightness in her voice, only respect.….they were *real*, and not to be taken lightly. They were not playthings, but valid members of the natural and spiritual world, but that didn't mean that they weren't playful. I got the feeling that fairies did whatever they wanted. It made sense why children were often more in-tune with the Little People than adults. Children's hearts are pure, and they notice the subtle things in life. Adults are so wrapped up in day to day, that we would never be able to notice something so small, heck, we don't even know where we put our keys. The whole fairy world was fascinating. I called Kurt to tell him about it.

"And then I walked back down the hill" I was talking

so fast.

"I only have a minute sweetheart, I'm going to catch a movie with a friend" he said when I was done. "Let me tell you about what happened when I had my cousin over two weeks ago. I didn't tell you but I have been working with Fairies also." He sounded pleased.

"My cousin was visiting from my hometown. He isn't into all of this, and is a bit freaked out about it, so I took down some of the more offensive symbols that I didn't feel like explaining. I moved my altar to the bedroom, and took down my pentacles. I'm not even sure that he knows that I am a practicing Witch, and you know sometimes with family, it is better to let it go."

"Yeah, I haven't told my family yet."

"He had to sleep on the sofa. When he woke up he said that he heard laughing all night, and he was a little mad that it kept him from a good sleep. He asked me what I was doing, of course I was asleep, and I wanted to reply, but my mouth dropped open when I saw him. His hair was the most knotted mess I'd ever seen, it looked like someone had been twirling it around in their fingers all night. I told him that the fairies had had fun with him. He got mad and left thinking it was me. Later when he was talking to me again he told me that it took him all day to get the knots out."

I hung up, and immediately shifted to the task at hand. I knew I had exhausted every avenue in the spirit world that I could. I asked for help, as much as I could get.....but I wasn't ready. I was moving out that weekend, while Luke was at work. When I thought about it I wanted to throw up, the emotion was so overwhelming. I was alone, and scared to death.

The Crone was showing Her face to me again.

Moving out did not give me the liberated feeling I thought it would. It was sad and so final. *Wherever you go there you are*. Ain't that the truth. Don't know what that means? It means *don't put all your hopes for change in some projected idea in the future, because as soon as that event is over, your problems will still be there*. My consolation was that I loved my new house, and knew that it was exactly where I was supposed to be.

I had picked the perfect house. It was a womb. Much careful thought and prayer went into the colors for the walls; a beautiful crimson for my bedroom, burnt orange for the living area, and soft lavender for Willow's room. I had prayed and done spells till I was blue in the face for things like good Feng Shui, a safe area, and most of all a great price, boy did I get one. I have the Fairies to thank for that. When I signed the closing papers there was definitely magic afoot.

I tried not to stare at Sterling Winston the fifth. He was the most polite, real southern gentleman I had ever met, white suit and the whole nine. All he needed was a bucket of chicken or a glass of lemonade and a rocking chair. He was obviously gay, and looked and sounded like Kevin Spacey in the movie *Midnight in the Garden of Good and Evil*. Sterling was the kind of person that was so well manicured in looks and speech that you wondered if you were sitting up straight enough, or if your shirt still had Caesar dressing on it from lunch. My Target dress, that I had complained about because it cost a whole $40, paled next to his silk Armani. He was the closing agent. He was delightful.

"Honey, this is gonna seem like a lot of papers, but I

reckon if you jus sign 'em real fast then it'll go quick enough." His voice had a musical, sing-songy quality to it.

He smiled at me then handed them over. *Is he wearing makeup? Maybe I can sneak a peek without him looking. Lord, will you just look at those perfectly manicured nails.*

"I don't mind" I said, straightening my skirt. "I'm just excited to be moving in."

"Well, honey, you sure done well for yourself. Look at this.......new homeowners discount......discount....discount." His eyes started to widen as he rattled off all the money I had saved.

"Sugar, you sure this is legal?" he said, winking. "I've never seen anyone get this many discounts."

"I'm sure" I said, breathing in his expensive cologne.

As I signed, he looked over papers and chatted with me about his ailing mother. It sure seemed like a good old southern drama, complete with family members that are sickeningly nice to each other's faces, and evil as the devil behind each other's backs. They don't call it the Ole' Dirty South for nothin'. So he was chatting, and explaining, and I was signing and stealing peeks at him. It was definitely a schizophrenic conversation.

"So then my Aunt Charlotte, you know the one with the drinkin' problem, she said to my Uncle Nelson......oh my goodness sugar, you really are savin' some money on this here house......any way then she said,'I don't care if that old coot dies right now, he owes me money'....how much did you say you talked them down from?..........I tole Ant Charlotte she ain't gettin' the house, and if she thinks she is, then she can drag herself, that bottle she carries, and her prosthetic leg over here and get it over my dead body.........looks like you saved an extra $300 here...."

My side went something like this- sign paper....nod,

smile……. sign paper……. sneak a peek at his hair….*is that a weave, or a toupee? It is definitely fake, but somehow he pulls it off, I'm not surprised. He is southern AND gay*….sign paper…..fake laugh….sneak another peek…*holy hell is he wearing lip-gloss? I think he is, either that or he has a skin condition*…….fake laugh again, sign another paper……..*I bet the suit he is wearing costs as much as the car I drive* ……….smile, and sign paper.

The crowning glory came at the end as we stood up to shake hands.

As I got up from the burgundy leather chair he said "Honey, I know you are startin' a new life, and I hope you do well. You sure got a deal on this one, I'll bet you used Witchcraft or somethin'." He winked at his own joke.

I smiled, and nodded. He didn't need one more thing to gossip about, so I let sleeping dogs lie.

"Yeah…… Witchcraft" I said, trying to sound normal.

Then he handed me the keys to my new house, and new life.

Arranging pictures, stocking the fridge, and buying staples ate up some time, and kept me preoccupied. I walked from room to room, feeling like I wanted to do something, but didn't know what. When I left I didn't take much, so I needed some random things like silverware, bed sheets and a sofa. For some reason I had taken the muffin pans, but not the sofa.

I daydreamed about what I wanted in a sofa. I know it sounds quirky, but for some reason the sofa was important to me. Life happens in the living room, and the center of that is the sofa. Following a funky retro/bohemian theme, aka, just throw together what you have and tell yourself that it is edgy, and boho, I decided that the sofa would have to be light green velvet. Never been one for forest or Kelly green, but light green, seventies pea soup green somehow doesn't bother me. I kinda like it in a nostalgic way.

I also needed it to be long, for the reason of being able to sleep on it without my feet hanging off. Good condition, but probably used. (If you know of someone who manufactures brand new lime green velvet sofa's then give me a holler). I sat on the floor where the sofa would have been if I'd had one, and pictured it, I prayed for it, then went upstairs to my new blood red in-utero bedroom, and fell asleep.

Six weeks passed. I was definitely feeling the aftershock of the divorce. Finally moving out gave me nothing to divert my attention away from my terrified thoughts. *What now? Did I really make the right decision? How was Willow doing? Would she hate me forever? Be scarred by this? Was Luke alright?* Even though I divorced him, I still cared about him. I had channeled all my angst, pain, and uncertainty into the act of moving, and once it was done, I was faced with the reality of the situation.

I did my best to mope around my house and do what I could. I picked up the phone to call Rosemary, and remembered that she was gone. I went to bed alone. I was starting to sink into the abyss.

Thrift store shopping has always cheered me up, so going to the local Salvation Army was a frequent affair. I looked forward to joking with the African-American clerk that had come to recognize me. Spending money is naughty therapy.

"Hey you" he said cheerfully.

I waved back. We didn't know each other's names.

I was about to scoop up a paisley polyester jacket for $2 when I spotted something green out of the corner of my eye. It looked big.

I walked over to the thrift furniture area and there in all its glory was my sofa. MY sofa. Light green velvet, the perfect length, used, but in good condition and with a price tag of..... dare I look.....$300 dollars? My shoulders sank. I made good money, but had to watch every penny now that I was a one income household. I could afford it, but would probably have to eat beans for a while. On a whim, I asked the clerk.

"You like that thing?" nameless Salvation Army cashier gawked.

"Yeah" I said with a maniacal grin. "I don't just like it, I love it. It costs too much, though."

"Oh, honey, it doesn't say $300, it says $30. The decimal point is in the wrong place" he said casually.

I had my money out before he could finish the sentence. My dad came to help me load it, and looked at me like I was crazy, I was bawling, sobbing like an idiot.

I had my sofa, my perfect sofa-the sofa I'd prayed for. It meant more than a place to watch *Friends* reruns and spill potato chip crumbs on. It meant that the Goddess was listening to me. Even about something as inconsequential as the color of a couch, She was listening. And to me that meant that no matter what happened to me, no matter what I felt or went through She was there. I wasn't as alone as I felt. She was there.

Chapter Eleven

Even the reverse side has a reverse side.
-Japanese proverb

I know you are probably wondering about spells. That is one of the main questions I get.

"Do you do… (quick glace around to see if anyone is listening) ….spells?" They say the word spells in a half whisper.

Then by the time it takes me to answer, they are already doubtful, and sorry they asked.

I counter with "yeah but it's not like you think it is".

They don't hear me though, their eyes betray the endless possibilities running through their heads. The fantasies everyone has about a flick of the wrist and wishes fulfilled, dark rooms with dancing candle flames and chanted words, and the homogenous genie in the bottle.

The brave ones say "can you do a spell for anything you want?"

But most people prematurely turn away from the conversation as if they have indulged too much of themselves in folly already.

I get a good hearty laugh out of all of it.

Spells. I like to say they are just a trigger point, a focal point for the conscious mind. Putting action to what you want makes it more powerful. It is not the candles themselves, or any of the spell components, it is just an energy exchange. Want a lover? You take the hole that loneliness provides and slowly transform it into a love affair where the hole once was. You don't create something out of nothing, you simply change or pull to yourself what already exists. The best spells I have ever done were simple desires that I knew were in with the flow, executed by focus, intent, and a couple of candles. Easy- peasy.

Book after book spoke of big scary words like spells, altars, and rituals. I took my time, never accepting anything because it came with the package, but testing each thing out, trying it all to see if it fit. Ritual was the main inductee, and is the meat and potatoes of my practice.

Ritual, just like *altar* is a heavy sounding word, but there are many things in our life that are rituals. The way we sleepily creep downstairs, pet the cat, then make our coffee each morning in a certain order. We use the same cup. We stand in the same place and wait for the beep of the coffee pot to sound. We sip slowly, and look out the window at the awakening dawn. That is a morning ritual, it is a series of earthly, physical things that mark a particular place in time or a feeling. We have large rituals like weddings, and throwing bouquets, decorating the Christmas tree and flowers at funerals. We have small rituals like reading to our children every night, and taking a bubble bath on Sunday afternoons. Is it the bath, or the flowers, or the coffee ITSELF that is special? No, it is *us within the ritual*. It marks time, it tells us who we are, and it re-affirms life. Most Witches realize the power of this, and create rituals to precede a feeling they wish to have. Spells and other things, along with prayer make up a large part of the practice of ritual. I needed to do a ritual. So I started with Rosemary.

Because I was alone, I closed the curtains and stripped out of my clothes. I was raw on the inside, I might as well be raw on the outside. I moved the coffee table, and made a large clearing on the floor, lighting some Rose incense and calling on the four elements to protect and guide me. Then I sprinkled salt in a circle.

Three things I took into the circle. A picture of Rosemary and I on a particular day that we'd had a lot of fun. A red candle in the shape of a rose, and a match.

As I sat naked on the floor, the shadows of my sadness surrounding me, I allowed the heavy silence drape over me as part of the ritual. I felt the emptiness, and let myself to dive into the fullness of it. I had a friend, a real one, and she left me alone. I started feeling very sorry for myself. And the ritual began.

Ritual, whether it is planned or unplanned has several cycles, it has to run its course. Why didn't I do a letting go ritual when Rosemary had first left? Because I wasn't ready. The thing you are addressing in ritual has to be faced fully. Like your early morning coffee ritual, you are staring at the promising face of a new morning. You are saying "I acknowledge that today is a new day". You aren't hiding in bed.

With this I had to face fully, and outwardly show that I hurt for her. I couldn't hide behind anger, or just choose not to talk about it. So I let it out. I sat there naked in darkness, and cried at her picture, telling her that her timing was awful. Asking her why she couldn't have waited until I had worked through the pain of divorce, asking her why she just up and vanished. I cried until there were no more tears, till I didn't want to cry any more. Then I waited in silence again, for the next step.

The darkness was slowly replaced by understanding. With a dull awakening I realized that her leaving when she did was a gift to me. It was to realize my own power fully. If she would have stayed I would have leaned on her, sucked her dry, and never known that I could make it through something like this alone. She had given me a great gift with her friendship, and with the timing of her leaving. With my sorrow all cried out, I began to feel grateful. I re-lived all of our good times, and all of the joy that I got from her presence. I thanked her for teaching me so much, and for making me laugh. I cried happy tears, until once more there was no more to cry. The best part of all was that I allowed myself to feel joy once more in our friendship, what it had meant to me.

I listened to the silence for the third and last part of the ritual, the closing. This was the part I had dreaded-letting her go. But now that I was here, it seemed natural.

Match in hand, I turned to the red rose candle.

"Rosemary I loved you, and you were my sister. When it came time for us to part ways it came as a shock to me, but I choose to accept it. I wish you peace, love, and a life that is full of learning…... I release you."

The rose candle audibly went up in a strong, unwavering flame.

I felt the peace and rightness of ending. I felt the stillness of the earth after a good rainstorm. I felt cleansed inside and out. It was done.

I cleaned up and thanked the Elements. Falling into bed exhausted, I knew that it wasn't that I'd never miss her, or feel pain over her again, it was that I had let her go. That part of me was gone, and with angel wings fluttered out of the room. Stillness licked me with her tongue and as I fell asleep I wondered what the months to come would bring.

If playing Witch with Rosemary was the honeymoon, then this was the actual marriage. The boot camp after seeing the brave, testosterone- charged Army commercials. Every commitment has the fun part, otherwise people wouldn't want to do it, but after a while you get to the bones of it. I had asked to go deeper, and deeper I went.

Alone.

***

I wonder why the black cat is part of Halloween. I can see pumpkins, various monsters, and so on, but why is the black cat considered scary? I was thinking again as I stepped around old boxes in my new attic. Pulling out the last of the Halloween decorations, I carried the heavy bin down the cream carpeted stairs.

It took two hours to deck out the new house, the end result being a kaleidoscope of orange and black, Witches hanging from the ceiling, sitting on the mantelpiece, and astride brooms. Pumpkins of every size and shape, grinning ghosts, and even a singing vampire that thoroughly spooked Willow each year. I had always prided myself on the way our house looked during October, and this year was no exception. The new house looked great!

Willow will love this, I thought as I tinkered with a burned out light in a huge Jack o' lantern.

Witches need familiars, right? *I have my Witchy house, it is a festival of Halloween colors and now I need a black cat*, I firmly decided. I grabbed my purse and headed for the car.

The SPCA was stinky and loud. In the cat room, I was placed with ten or so kittens, and expected to pick one. The one black cat in the bunch kept rubbing my leg, not in a sweet way, but in a teasing way. *This cat's got a 'tude*, I thought, and I didn't really like her but since I was a Witch, and Witches had black cats, I took her home with me.

I named her Ursula. Ursula was a terrible cat. She hid all the time, and seemed to look at me like there was something she wanted to say. Something didn't feel quite

271

right about her, so I got another cat to "keep her company". More like "keep an eye on her and make sure she doesn't slash my jugular while I'm sleeping." I named him Marduk, or Mardy for short. He was a doll, and I did feel safer with him around.

Something was wrong. I could feel it. Our new house felt foreign, occupied. Willow had been sick and cranky for two weeks, and didn't want to leave my sight. I didn't want to be in the house, and looked for every opportunity to leave, but the worst, the absolute worst thing was the smell. Under the window in the den, next to a table where I did my crafts, was the strong smell of cat shit. This was very strange, because I had searched under the table, under the window, and in every nook and cranny of the room to locate the smell. There was nothing. The carpet underneath the window didn't even smell. Just right under the window, as if hanging in mid-air was this repulsive, almost unbearable stench.

I had noticed it one day while I was gluing shiny glitter stars onto a picture frame. I had chosen to do crafts there, after having read that doing creative things rids oneself of violent tendencies. I didn't feel violent, but I sure felt sad and lonely after leaving Luke. It was hard to be all alone in the great big house on the nights he had Willow. I tried crafts to soothe my mind and spirit. It was my meditation, and dancing, and all around peaceful hangout room. The walls were sage green, and I had colorful throw pillows all over the floor. The room housed things that meant something to me, and was very disappointed that I couldn't even go in there, the smell was so strong. So I shut the door, daily checking to see if the smell was still there. After two more weeks I noticed the stench seemed to be growing in strength.

A "cat" had shown up in my bedroom. I've had many animal helpers in the spirit world, including a lion warn me about a particularly dangerous night, so I didn't think anything of it. I was dealing with divorce, and a busy career, so a spirit cat hanging out on the side of my bed at night was met with nothing more than a nod, and thirty seconds later, dead, snoring sleep.

I felt desperate. The smell was starting to pervade the entire house, Willow was still sick and crying non -stop, and I was physically and emotionally exhausted. I plopped down on a chair, holding my screaming two year old. It was a Saturday, and I tried to think of something we could do, something to get us out of the house. I didn't even have the strength for it.

As if sensing my distress Ursula walked over to us, and almost in slow motion, arched up out of herself like her shadow was coming out of her body, and hissed at me. At that moment I felt a darkness I have never felt before. At that moment I could have done any despicable deed, and it would have felt natural...... I realized Willow and I were in danger.

Goddess help us, I prayed pitifully. I felt like I was drowning, and could barely lift my arms. Helpless, I reached for the phone, which was amazingly right beside me. (*Funny, I didn't remember putting it there*). I called my sister, Vanessa, who just so happened to be in the neighborhood.

She took one step in the door, and said "something is wrong, let's get out of here".

As we drove away I flipped through my phone trying to see if I still had Marnie's number. She'd know what to do.

"I think there is something in my house" I said,

explaining the scenario to her over the phone.

"Didn't you just move in?" her quiet voice was soothing. Man, I missed her.

"Yeah" my voice was shaking.

"Did you sage the house, or put up any protection before you moved in?" she gently questioned.

"No" I ignorantly said. All I'd cared about was having the strength to get into the house, I'd never thought about protecting Willow or myself.

"Tara, you naturally put out a lot of energy, and right now you are emotional, raw, and exhausted. You and your house are energy magnets. Unprotected, anything lurking around in the neighborhood can just waltz right into your house, and it looks like something has. "

"What am I supposed to do?" I couldn't believe what I had just seen.

"I can help you get it out, but I can't come till tomorrow. Until then, sage the house, take a piece of chalk, and put pentacles or other protective symbols on all the windows and openings, that will stop anything else from coming in. Hang tight, honey, you are lucky it is just a cat."

It was nice to hear Marnie's voice, even though she sounded drained.

I hung up the phone. *How could I have been so stupid?* My sister took us back home for Willow's nap, and as I walked into the green room, the smell almost made me vomit. I would have to sage that night after Luke picked up Willow. Scooping her up, we went upstairs for her afternoon nap.

Placing her in her crib, and closing her door, I made my way to my bedroom, for a nap myself. Ever since the cat had been in the house, I seemed to be exhausted all the time. As I climbed into bed, and drifted off to sleep I was aware of the cat's presence.

My dreams were of a Halloween town. There were several very distressed people from my past pointing me to a room. I decided to follow their lead, and open the day-glow door. As I walked in, there he was. The spirit cat. He was big, about the size of a large dog, and he had this sick, clown- like grin. I instinctively knew what to do.

"Leave!" I said, my body rigid.

"Leave my home" I commanded. It didn't move. I could feel my ineffectiveness.

"Leave in Jesus name!" I shouted. I figured I'd try that. It looked at me, horrible Cheshire grin steadfast, I knew that it knew I didn't mean it.

I woke up immediately to the sound of my bedside lamp rattling by some invisible hand. It was shaking so hard, it looked like it was going to fall off the table. I grabbed it firmly.

"I know you are here!" I shouted. The lamp stopped moving.

Lying back down, it had to be done. I didn't have time to think about the fearsome supernatural occurrence that I'd just witnessed, I just had to get the thing out, or it would hurt Willow or me. I quickly fell back to the dream world. Summoning up all my power, the knowledge that this was MY house and MY turf, and all the power and determination of my father's people, I said in a powerful growl "leave my house NOW!"

I opened my eyes to the sight of the cat running out of my bedroom, down the stairs and out the door. I ran down the stairs and opened the door to the green room.

The smell was gone.

The next day I was carting Ursula back to the SPCA. She meowed the whole way, and seemed to be pleading with me not to go. I pawned her off on the lady, telling her that my daughter was allergic, and we didn't know it, which was partially true. Willow's nose had not stopped running since she'd come into our home. The lady mumbled something about some people being allergic to black cats, and not to other colors of cats. *Whatever,* I thought, *just get this thing away from me.*

Mardy found a good home with his human soul mate, my brother, and is still happily residing there. As soon as my nerves calmed, and the shock of what I had witnessed settled down, I scrubbed the house, saged it, and put up enough protection to make Fort Knox look like a sand castle.

"The Guardians, I thought they were just for ritual?" I remembered the spirits of the four elements that I asked for protection and help during circle. It seemed weird to ask them to hang out at my house, but at this point I'd try anything. Marnie said to protect my house, and dammit, it was going to be a fortress.

"Well the ceremonial magicians, mostly Enochian Witches say that only they have the right to call on them properly, which is malarkey if you ask me. The elemental spirits that dwell in the four quadrants are ageless and timeless. They are old, strong, powerful spirits that dwell in and guard the four quarters, the four elements, Earth, Air, Fire, and Water. If you call on them they will help protect your home, just make sure to be respectful, and as always you never demand, you respectfully ask. You might even see them" Marnie said.

"How do I do it?"

"Tara, you have been doing this long enough, and are in tune enough to figure it out. Just use your imagination" I heard a smile.

Use my imagination. I definitely want their help, I will never let anything nasty get in my house again. I sat for a while in meditation, focusing on the four elements.

"I know what to do" I said triumphantly and out loud to myself, as my eyes popped open and my awareness shifted to the material world.

I made a meal. Confident that this was the right thing for my ritual, I gathered representations of the four elements to honor the Guardians. Fish for the west/Water, grain bread for the north/Earth, a banana for the south/Fire, and an almond cake for the east/Air. I finished it off with some red wine. After making my sacred circle in the living room, I brought two plates and two little wine glasses, one for me, one for them. I pulled out all the stops, put on a white robe, took a ritual bath beforehand, did it up nice. *Maybe I do like formal magic sometimes.*

"Guardians of the watchtowers of the North and Earth! I invite you into my home and ask for your wisdom and your protection. Please keep the northern part of my home protected." I sat for a moment until I felt its presence. A very large bear, huge, almost to the ceiling. *Cool. Thank you for coming.*

"Guardians of the watchtowers of the East and Air! I invite you to my home and ask for your wisdom and protection. Please keep the eastern part of my home protected." A condor entered the room, once again enormous and with the wingspan of three men.

The Guardian of the South was a jaguar, and the Guardian of the West looked like a large Koi. With the entrance of each Guardian I felt warmth and a shelter that up until calling them I hadn't realized the house lacked. I ate my meal in circle, and left their portion on the porch for the animals. It was licked clean the next morning, even the wine was gone.

After a week I got worried. *Are you still here?,* I randomly said to the corners of the house. I hadn't seen them since the night I asked them into my home. My home felt wonderful, safe and cozy, yes, but I thought if they inhabited it, then I'd be seeing them often. I was disappointed and a little worried.

Another week passed and a friend came to stay from out of town. We had such a wonderful time, and even though I told her about the cat I hadn't told her about the Guardians. She was a smoker, and often went out to the front porch to light one up. One evening she came in with a puzzled look on her face.

"This is gonna sound crazy, but of all people you will understand.........did you know that you have a jaguar pacing your front porch?"

I grinned….. "Yeah, I did."

***

I loved being a Witch. Every new experience, every new thing just made me more pleased that I'd finally found something that worked for me. Even though that cat scared the crap out of me, it also made me glad (partly because it turned out well), and partly because I'd learned something *major*. I felt it, I experienced it. Now I knew firsthand what would happen if you didn't take care of your surroundings.

"The smell creeped me out the most." I was relaying the whole thing to Kurt, hoping he wouldn't think me too stupid.

"Yes, bad spirits are often accompanied by a strong

smell. You know, cat shit, rotten eggs", he sounded so blasé".

"No, dude, apparently, I don't know. You have encountered this before?" I said, astonished.

"Look, don't get paranoid. Don't hand over your power, Tara. Protect yourself, and then forget it. You invite things with your fear." I heard him take a long drag off his cigarette. I was sweating.

I WAS getting paranoid. As the weeks went on, I was amazed at my calm, and more importantly, courage, at the sight of something spontaneously moving, untouched by any human hand…….but the worst thing, the most frightening, was that smell. The smell had really gotten to me. Every day, I went in the room, and sniffed, just to make sure.

We are used to seeing all kinds of things with our eyes. TV has made sure of that, but when our other senses are engaged, it makes it all the more real. Touch, smell, taste. I could still smell that rotten stench in my memory, as if I was eating it. The kind of stuff you see in horror movies and not only had it really happened, it had happened to me! The worst was that I couldn't talk to anyone about it without them thinking me crazy, so I kept it in, and let it run circles in my psyche. At the time, the mother in me just wanted to protect, but the more I thought about it, the more it scared me. I slept in the house with that thing! Willow was alone in her crib! I had been so careless. What else was out there that I didn't know about?

Weeks passed and I digested what had happened.

The instance had shown me several things; bad energy felt *bad*, and was easily recognizable. I still felt discomfort when I could feel my spirit guides, or energy of any sort, a small voice in my head wondering if the warm heavy feeling was evil, and I just didn't know it. Now I knew. Evil energy was easily recognizable, like night and day.

Secondly, the importance of protection. If you are going to deal with energy, and actively pursue a connection with the other side, you had to prepare. If you were going scuba diving, wouldn't you use a wetsuit? Oxygen tank? You wouldn't just jump in a whole different medium, and expect it to adapt to YOU, you would drown. If you were smart, YOU had to adapt to IT. Like Marnie said, I was lucky it was only a cat. When I first started out, flipping through spell books I quickly turned past the pages with protection spells, thinking they were for people with crazy boyfriends, or people going on dangerous trips, or with dangerous jobs. But protection was for everyone. Protection is for people who don't practice Witchcraft. Protection is necessary.

Ever go into a hospital, and notice that your mood is drastically different when you leave? Or get around someone and feel icky, or go to the mall, and leave with a headache? All that is energy and you'd better protect yourself if you don't want to absorb everything you come in contact with. The more sensitive to energy you are, the more you notice it, but noticing it or not, it still affects all of us. You have to prepare yourself.

Most importantly, I learned that Witchcraft didn't run itself. Kinda like romance. There is some work to it. You have to *pay attention*. You couldn't call yourself a Witch, play around with spells, wear all black, etc. and that be it, there was some responsibility to this whole thing. This was a daily awareness. Every second I was a Witch, it wasn't a switch that I turned off. It wasn't like church on Sunday morning, and doing whatever I wanted the rest of the week. I was a Witch 24/7.

You would think I wouldn't have wanted to go back in the house, but the cleansing, and subsequent protective spells were so powerful that it literally felt like a different place. Unfortunately it was looking like the independent hippie playhouse that I had envisioned was being traded in for a lonely bed that I cried myself asleep in every night. A safe bed, but a lonely bed. Once again I reached out to the Goddess.

I had seen Mother Kali various times in my life. Hindu Gods and Goddess are part of the wonderful mish-mash of religion that we have in this country, and with thirteen percent of the world population being Hindu, you are bound to run into one of them- whether it is a statue of Ganesh in a taxicab, or a picture of Laxshmi in your favorite Indian restaurant. The Hindu cosmology reflected the vastness of what I felt was the all-encompassing nature of the Divine. I especially dug Hindu Goddesses.

I was reading THE book again, the one who had led me to Lilith. Looking again, for something to make sense of it all. Leaving Luke, although I knew it was for the best, had made me absolutely miserable. I felt so out of control. I needed a face of the Goddess to show herself to me, to help me know what I needed to know. I didn't know how to deal with all this pain that seemed to be ganging up on me. Closing my eyes, I opened the book. It fell open to the chapter on Kali. Once I read it, I knew.

Within mythology you have to find your own truth. Most mythological tales sound like an antiquated story, like a recollection from so long ago that all the components are foreign to us. How do you find inspiration in that? It used to irritate me that people would find so much meaning in something so odd, till I figured it out. You find the thing that stands out to you. The smallest part of the story, like the bravery of Hanuman the monkey god, or the details of the bloody Goddess Kali's story.

Kali's story was cool. They were in the midst of battle. Durga, the warrior Goddess and all the other Gods and Goddesses were fighting legions of demons, and the demons were winning. The problem was that every time someone had slain a demon, and his blood was spilt, that several more demons sprang up from the spilt blood. How can you win against that? Durga, in her frustration furrowed her brow, and out came Kali, like a bat outta hell. She was corpse grey, with matted black hair, a necklace of skulls, and body parts around her waist. She was a kicking, screaming, dancing maniac. Kali WAS chaos. She stuck out her long tongue and lapped up the blood of the demons like it was milk, then danced on their corpses.

Finally, the battle was won, but they couldn't get Kali to stop her frenzied dancing. Her husband, Shiva, lay down on the battle ground hoping that when She saw him She would recognize him and stop. She didn't, and danced on top of him, and it was only when he made the sound of a baby's cry, that She stopped and calmly put him to her breast to nurse.

I felt Kali as I read the story. She meant so many things to me. She was about the moment of ending. And the subsequent new beginning, a moment so new that it didn't feel like a beginning at all. She was death, the death of an old way of life, the death of a marriage, the death of the old me. She was about giving into pain with total abandonment. It was what I had asked for, but had no idea it would hurt so bad.

What was on the horizon, I didn't know, but I knew by the ending that had just happened that I was reborn. I didn't feel reborn, I felt dead. Terrified. My emotions were crazy, and I was raw. There was an air of sorrow around us all. Alone in the big new house, rehashing the mistakes I'd made, the pain was almost unbearable. Rosemary was gone, Luke was gone, and Willow spent half her time away from me. Marnie was gone, so I had no quiet wisdom, no soothing words.

I hurt so bad I thought I was dying. I fell asleep all alone, feeling stripped bare. I dreamt of Her. In the dream I was seated at a big stone clearing, calling out to the Goddess to take my pain away. I waited, and Kali approached. She was dancing and smiling at me, obviously enjoying herself. How could she be so chaotic and enjoy it? I certainly wasn't.

"Do you feel pain?" I asked. I wanted to know. She said nothing, just continued her rhythmic dance. I wanted it all to go away. I didn't want to be in my own skin. I watched Her fearsome face, with Her patient grin. She seemed to be waiting for something. I watched Her dance, and sat for what seemed like hours. She seemed so content with herself. She was at peace with her chaos, and almost seemed to be enjoying it, loving it, getting drunk off of it. How could she love the pain, confusion, and utter helplessness of feeling so out of control, of feeling like everything had been turned upside down? Then I heard her speak. She didn't move her mouth, but kept dancing, I heard Her from inside myself.

"My name means TIME. I know that pain now equals growth later. I embrace it; even desire it, because it is necessary to know. Do you want ignorance just because it is comfortable? Do you want to feel comfortable all the time?" I could feel the pace of her dance quicken. *You chose this, you chose pain, and you chose chaos. Let it be your teacher. Let it be your birth pain. EMBRACE IT.*

Dance the dance, drink the blood. As long as you fight it, fear it, you will not move on. When you accept the pain you can move past it."

Embrace pain. Wow. That was a big one. Just give in to it. Notice it, and not judge it. Did that mean I had to like it? No. Did that mean I could ignore it, or misdirect it, no. There is a difference between accepting something and embracing it. You accept a miserable mother-in-law, by embracing her, you call her up and invite her over for breakfast.

This was a whole new way of thinking for me, and for me the key to the whole of Witchcraft. No one wants pain- I don't care who you are. Especially pain you can't control, pain from an outside source. Pain you don't understand, pain that is a by-product of an action, yours or someone else's. Pain you don't expect, pain that makes you wonder who you are, pain that makes something simple like going to the grocery store a fearful event. On the flip side pain is an inevitable part of life, and as a Witch I was to seek out personal growth. Personal growth meant pain, but if you could work through it, it also meant knowledge, and then power. I *needed* Kali. She became my mascot, Matron Goddess if you will. Kali's fearlessness inspires me, and when I get to the point of helplessness, I dance with Her.

Chapter Twelve

"Sometimes being a bitch is all a woman has to hold on to."
– Vera Donovan in *Dolores Claiborne* (Stephen King)

Nice is overrated. Being nice, acting nice, putting on the smiley face. This is something we have a real problem with in the American South, because it is habit, and expected of us, not organic in any way. We are taught (especially as girls) to be smiling, robotic Stepford wives. The church fuels this monster and tells us as women that we have to be nice, that God *wants* us to be nice. Once I started following the Goddess I learned how to be a bitch. Wait, let me 'splain.

My definition of bitch is not the generally perceived idea. I don't think being a bitch lets you beat up on everyone, or berate and abuse your husband or family or kids or unfortunate co- workers. You can be a bitch and be firm and nourish yourself and your needs without being a raging monster. Women are nurturing and caring (whether it is mothering children, animals, or a career), but for every one side there has to be another. Just as all men aren't aggressive CEO-types, all women aren't casserole baking freaks of nature who always want to tickle you and paint smiley faces. We have a bitch time too, a Dark time. It is out of character for your bitchy time if you say "honneeeyyy, mommy has a tum-tum achy can you pweese give mommy some alone timesies?" Who talks like that all the time? Who feels like that all of the time? No one, unless you are walking around in a prescription drug- induced haze.

I think being a Bitch in the Divine sense of the word means that you don't have to be happy/nurturing/sweet/nice if you don't feel like it just because you are a woman. Who wakes up every morning with a genuine smile on their face 365 days a year? No one that is human (o.k., maybe Katie Couric, but is she human?). Once a month the bleeding woman takes on the Dark, the pain of the world, and she needs to know how to deal with it, and find its Divinity, instead of hiding from it. But hiding from it is all that we have ever been taught. As women and men we *must* learn to embrace our Sacred Dark.

Our society which is founded on the Christian church, says that girls must be sugar and spice, that a woman should be the old timey view of nothing more than a slave. Check out these verses in the Bible from the book of Proverbs:

31:26 She openeth her mouth with wisdom; and in her tongue is the law of kindness.

31:27 She looketh well to the ways of her household, and eateth not the bread of idleness.

31:15 She riseth also while it is yet night, and giveth meat to her household and a portion to her maidens.

31:13 She seeketh wool, and flax, and worketh willingly with her hands.

31:23 Her husband is known in the gates, when he sitteth among the elders of the land.

31:12 She will do him good and not evil all the days of her life

Can you guess what happened to this woman when she talked back, maybe she didn't want to have the law of kindness on her tongue, maybe her back hurt from rising before dawn everyday and waiting hand and foot on her husband? I'll bet her husband got up from the gates (and his seat, while she is workin' her ass off) and came over and gave her a good old smack down. Meanwhile the dudes in the Bible are all but having the law of anything on their tongues; as a matter of fact they seem to be able to do as they pleased. Men get to be mean, and women have to be nice? Really?

When bitch doesn't get to come out, then she forces her way out.

To me bitch is just another side of the female coin. When it is that time of the month (I call it my Dark Moon time), when the demands of family, and the outside world are just too much, when our body feels like it was beaten with a jackhammer, and our womb is sloshing blood that feels heavy and weights us down. When our instincts tell us to go inward, and retreat, take care of ourselves, let the dishes go to hell, pull out our big sweatpants with the drawstring; that time is when we are naturally the bitch. We are a bitch when we are in pain from a divorce, from a word spoken by a friend that wounded us, when we just feel pain and can't explain it, when we are going through the great sacred change that is menopause or just whenever.....if a woman is seen doing cartwheels, and wearing white, and plastering a big, stupid grin on her face then listen up buddy and listen close......SHE IS LYING. Even if you are one of those positive, radiant people who does feel happy and cheerful most of the time (we all hate you....just kidding), you *still* have to delve into the Sacred Dark once a month for your period. Just like periods, menopause is a journey into the Sacred Dark also, and a powerful time for women.

I'm not just spitting out rehearsed rhetoric. I live this

stuff monthly, most of us do, if we are not chickening out and stopping our periods altogether, or drugging ourselves up to the point of numbness. Maybe if we let out the natural Bitch Goddess, then we won't feel the need to call it "the curse". It's not a curse, it is a power time. It is not meant to be a miserable time, it is meant to re-connect you with your center. Our culture has taught us to masculinize a purely female time, to clean it up, to sterilize it, to make it white and God-like, not messy and bloody. It is supposed to be a time for going inward, not giving out. It is supposed to be a resting time for women, and a place where we can sit in Her/our Darkness and renew. If we continue to make excuses, and give out instead of taking some for ourselves then it will continue to be the same. A time meant to be powerful for women will be a time of shame and blindness to ourselves and *our needs*. I chalk a whole lot of this imbalance to the church, and its doctrines on women, and the influence that all of that has had on our current collective ideals.

The Bitch, or as I like to call her, the Cosmic Bitch, is another face of the Goddess, and the one I am most drawn to. Having been given a good soak in the waters of Christianity as you can see, when I discovered the Dark Mother, the angry Lilith, the death Goddesses, I thought *whoa! Hold the phone. Have these Goddess always been around and I just never knew about them?* Yeah, just check out history. Go as far back as you please, and you will find Her in some form.

How is it that this Divine part of every woman just kinda got....forgotten? And when she reared her venomous, sharp- tongued head, she was dismissed.

"She is just PMS-ing. Bitch alert."

"Oh it must be THAT time of the month."

"At first she was cool, but then she turned into a bitch."

"Why are you acting like such a bitch?"

Men get to be aggressive. The natural part of the male Divine, the conqueror, is celebrated. The war hero back then, the CEO in our time. The God of the Bible was a conquering God, just read the Old Testament; he didn't start preaching love and forgiveness until Jesus came along, before that it was all rules (Leviticus will give you a good taste of this), and conquest (try Deuteronomy and Joshua). Do you see any conquering women? Nope. There was one female judge, Deborah, who made it past the Catholic Church in the sixteenth century when they were deciding which parts of the Bible should go and which should stay. They got rid of a good hearty chunk, it's called the *Apocrypha*. Consequently, it contains a lot of parts that empower women, a lot more than in what is commonly called the Bible now.

It makes sense to me that millions of cultures over millions of years named God and Goddess figures to identify parts of themselves with. A Bitch Goddess for that natural part of our self that doesn't want to be nice when we don't *feel* nice. A Death Goddess to represent the inevitability of death, something that our culture is far removed from, but something that was an accepted part of ancient life. Ironically, a lot of the Death Deities were women, Goddesses. The Mother gives life; it makes sense for the Mother to take it away, also. Take a look online, read a book on world mythology, it is fascinating to learn about all the different names and faces of Gods and Goddesses that humanity has given name to. For instance, in the Bahamas, there was a hurricane God. Completely understandable seeing that hurricanes were a part of their lives. In the Antarctic great focus was put on the animal spirits, and a lot of their deities were animals. They needed animals to survive. I don't think they could just go munch on an asparagus out of the vegetable garden. We can easily stuff all of these Gods and Goddesses into the category of "oh they were just heathens". Really? How bout a people that eats the body and blood of God? *Ding. Ding.* Just think about it. A hurricane God makes much more sense to me and is much more simplistic than God/man walking the earth with a formula for entry into heaven, or a ticket to hell. I'll take the hurricanes, thank you very much.

If you look at all mythology throughout all time there are a few constants, throughout all cultures. Parts of humanity that are apparent in all of us, regardless of location or time in history. Death, Love, Life or Life force, Male and Female. Most cultures had a death Goddess of some kind. The Morrigan (Celtic), Kali (Indian), Sekhmet (Egyptian), Ereshkigal/Inanna (ancient Sumerian), Hecate (Greek), Hel (Skandinavian), the list is very long. Most cultures had a mischievous God, Loki, Lukumi, etc. Most cultures had a Mother Goddess figure, and there was usually a Warrior God and a Warrior Goddess. You really didn't start seeing major head-of-all God figures until the city-state thing started, and we moved away from being mainly agricultural to warring. The Goddess went bye-bye, and was told to sit in the back seat, while Zeus took the reins.

I *love love love* the Dark Goddess, and work almost exclusively with Her. That part of me, of the Divine in me wasn't known cognitively until I got out of Christianity. The closest I came was a fascination with the Crone at Halloween, with the powerful old woman who maybe was a little scary. Scary? Old, and powerful, too? I'm digging this. Where else do you see it? Old ladies are cute, or helpless, or sweet, baking biscuits, or out of their heads. But how many 80 year olds do you know that you would consider powerful? Thank Goddess for the Red Hat society, they are paving the way. When are women supposed to be powerful? When I saw Kali for the first time, I fell in love. She was crazy, and powerful, and wild as a March hare. She was also scary....scare the shit out of you scary. The Dark Goddesses are like this, powerful. You can understand why they mysteriously got fazed out of mythology.

Because they were threatening.

These faces all run together. Sometimes the Dark Sekhmet will turn into Bast, who is a playful Goddess, and sometimes bloodthirsty Kali will be seen nursing a baby. Because we all change daily, we all do. Sometimes we ARE gootchy gootchy goo, sometimes that feels natural, too. There are plenty of Goddesses that represent this Light giving energy, but I choose the Dark. It is a hole that is in me, a gap that was ignored my whole life. I have an intense desire to feed it, to uncover it, to discover it, and I ask these Goddesses for help. With the blank place before creation, the black nothingness, or the raging lost fire they appear. I fell in love with that part of myself (yes, it is possible), and She helped me see.

Everything is sacred. Every part of humanity, every part of life, *even suffering is sacred*. Our minds jump in at this statement. They fight, they struggle, and they bring up the worst possible scenario. What about the little girl who was abducted, what about the destruction and annihilation of a city, torture of woman, children, the elderly. We think of our most recent heart- breaking pain, and instantly get defensive. We didn't deserve to hurt like that. How can that be sacred?

To suffer is to be raw, stripped down, pain takes the ego away. You know WHO YOU ARE when you suffer. Pain does not allow fanciful ideas, projections, and mirages. In suffering the opportunity to know God/Goddess is greater than ever. Once you realize how temporary this existence is, you start to see pain as a lesson in the great school of life.

The less ego we have, the closer we are to the Divine in ourselves. Nothing brings us closer to this than suffering. Ask anyone who has had a brush with death, or has lost everything in a disaster, or even lost a loved one. Even though the pain can be excruciating, most people feel a renewed sense of life after it is over. Finally smelled the flowers, looked around them. Realized what is important. Woke up. Pain is a mirror whose reflection is love (or the opportunity to experience love, if we choose it).There is a silence after the storm that is sacred, and pain is just an inevitable tool.

Our white washed, pure idea of God allows no room for tearing down, only building up. Only an all powerful, white, male, pristine God who wants us to be *good* all the time and labels things as *good* or *bad*, forces us to look at suffering as wrong, and robs of the chance to really know the true nature of the divine through suffering.

Does this mean we seek out suffering? That we flog ourselves, or like the Aghoris, eat corpse flesh, hoping to bridge the gap between life, death, and God? No, well, not unless you want to, (yuck….and I'm pretty sure it is illegal). The truth is, if you are human, *suffering will find you*. All you have to do is live the life that was given to you, and pain, whether it is from a love relationship that ended, or the horrors of war, follows us. It is part of life, part of the Divine.

Nothing is one way all of the time. In Christianity, we were to be "little Christs", which meant to shun all parts of our nature, except the *good* parts. To live a *good* life, to be *good* all the time. Everything else within us was *bad*. Unfortunately essential, instinctual parts of life and nature such as sex and death also received these labels. Do you see the insanity in this? Sex in marriage: good. Sex outside of marriage: bad. What about sex in an unhappy marriage where the woman lowers and devalues herself by becoming essentially an object for her husband to relieve himself in? She takes away her Divine nature, she takes her self worth away, all because some dusty old book, and a dusty old man decides it. Is she not as valuable? An all male deity confirms that she isn't, and that her needs come second to the man in her life, who is in the image of God. Christianity took away the feminine divine, and made it only male. By default, that lowers women below men, and makes the all male qualities such as outward, expansive, aggressive, sun-energy godly, and the inward, nurturing, repressive, moon-energy of the female, well, you know what that makes it.

We sweep under the rug the things that are the opposite of the clean, light- ordered God based world. The elderly, menstruation, death, sex, dirt, earth, all feminity that is not made up of pre-pubescent innocent virgins. The angry menstruating woman, the old crone, the independently sexual woman, the "used up" woman past her childbearing years has no place, is not celebrated. The homosexual man is not celebrated, the sensitive man, the artistic man, any man perceived as "weak" read: female, is considered undesirable.

We value the light; we value things we can see. If we

can see them then we can control them. If we can see them we can identify them. If they dwell in the dark unnamable such as feelings, and emotions, all predominately female attributes, then they are not Godly. *How can we do that to mankind!!!* How can we say that it must be Spring all the time, or that we must be the age of twenty forever, or that we must take if we can and use use use up everything around us. WE TOOK AWAY THE FEMININE DIVINE. We said that giving back, and Fall and Winter, and growing old, and pain and going inward are not Divine.

What do you think is going to happen when we do that? That humanity is just going to bend over and take it? No, pastors are going to have affairs and steal money, priests are going to abuse little boys, people who preach against the sins of the flesh are going to run after the extreme corrals they are forcing their nature into. When we force things into one narrow suffocating tunnel, eventually they will bust out of the other side.

Ever "make it fit"? Cram stuff into a suitcase, and sit on it to make it close? You can't fit the Divinity of all humanity, male and female, outward and inward, dark and light into a small compartment. Eventually like the suitcase, it will break.

***

There is no proper southern housewife lurking inside my strong thirty-something body. No prim, orderly, scheduled perma-smile inside my dark soul. I am the Wild Woman. I am the primal shriek of the wind, the scent of sweat, the spin and swirl of the tornado. I am wild. I always have been.

Sitting in my third grade class at Winter's Pass, in our

proper room, with the calligraphied letters of the alphabet overlooking all we did with scorn, I longed to break free. Third grade is a transitional time. You are still enough of a kid that you act on instinct, but your other half is learning to be a cerebral part of the world. The world that has expectations that we must fulfill.

Box of crayons in hand I looked at the cheap texture of the paper, the simple black lines creating an elementary drawing of flowers. My head knew that I was to dutifully pick up the pink, and mindfully glide the wax back and forth over the petals until they were an expected pearlized pink. No going outside of the lines. Then there would be the green. Followed by my name at the top, all T's crossed and I's dotted.

I was SO bored. So un-challenged. I could visualize the finished work, and knew that it would probably hang on some forgotten wall or refrigerator, and that I would receive hollow praise on how good it looked, or how well I stayed in the lines. If it had been a grownup I would have thought *any dolt can stay in the lines, or make a petal pink, or a stupid leaf green.* I wanted to make a MARK. I wanted to *feel* something as I put it on the paper. I wanted to do something different….screw what I was supposed to do. Why did everyone else seem so content with doing just that?

Eric was coloring, his tell tale bold strokes evident in everything he ever colored. Nancy was doing a pre-outline, and not one slight mark would be outside of the lines. Jennifer liked to tickle the paper with color, so it was barely noticeable. Was this enough for them? Did they have no urge, no desire to make something else, some place for themselves, some place for the wail of humanity inside them?

I thought about it from another standpoint briefly. It was wrong to do this in some way, and I didn't know why, but if I did what I wanted to do, then I felt that something I wouldn't like might happen. It was not enough to deter me, though, and instinct won over.

The room was silent except for crayons being consciously exchanged for different colors. I picked up the black crayon. I loved the sooty way it looked. It reminded me of the new pavement in our driveway, the inky chemical smell it made after it had been baking in the sun all day. Black was my favorite color. I gripped the crayon in my fist, like a battering ram. It harnessed the blackness inside me, the wild dance I felt most when I was outside. I put the black to the yellowed paper, and joyed as the morbid streaks marred the prefabricated image. I pressed down hard, inspired by the slick look of Eric's coloring, the crayon being so thick it almost shellac'd the page, preserving it. I felt a stirring inside myself, as I knew that this picture, this art was me. This seizing of some dry thing I was supposed to do and replacing it with the black endless of nothing. The place before ideas, the place of creation. I felt a release as I pressed so hard I thought the paper would break. This was me, not the walking in lines, not the regimented facial expressions, not the forcing and strapping down of anything they could get their hands on. In this moment I was destroying it all.

I watched the factory made flowers disappear, the mass produced leaves drowning a sea of oily- slick, chthonic darkness. The crayon felt warm in my grip, and I felt the desire to walk around the room and color it, myself and everything around me black, blot our existences out, make us all the same. Replace acquired power with the equality of death. I was the opposite of the white male God, bringing light, and nice things. I was a black female Goddess bringing death and ending, restoring balance. Bringing to light the things that had been swept in the dark, for it is all a circle of light and dark, dark and light.

"Tara, what have you done!" I heard the astonishment from my teacher's voice from far, far away as she lifted my paper, heavily spread with the tarry blackness. The drones around me lifted their heads in unison to see the abomination, and then uniformly lowered them to go back to their scratch scratch scratching of coloring.

"Tara, this was bad! Go stand in the corner!" she said, larger than life, and pointing a giant fist.

Drunk with a heady release I walked to the corner, enjoying the separation that my act had caused. I wasn't like them. I was bad. And if this is what being bad meant...... then I liked it.

Chapter Thirteen

"Face it, always facing it, that's the way to get through.
Face it."

-Joseph Conrad

How much more drastic can you get? Tattooing,
scratching something permanent into your skin sure does
the trick. As I sat sweating bullets in a tattoo chair, loud
thrash metal blaring over the buzz of the needle, I thought
of the divorce. The divorce, like labor had stunned me,
made me feel like the rug had been pulled out from under
my feet.

I had prepared for giving birth when I was pregnant
with Willow by reading every book I could find on the
subject. Talking to every mom I knew about their
experience. I thought I knew. I thought I was tough enough
to handle the pain. When the first new pain of the labor
process started I was crippled. By the time we got to the
hospital, when full force labor kicked in, I was
hallucinating and dry heaving from the pain. It put me in
my place.

Divorce is a big ole slap in the face. Whether you've
been married three years or thirteen divorce is like electric
shock treatment. You just ain't right afterwards.

I've tried to pinpoint what exactly it is about divorce
that sucks so bamboo- shoots –down- the- fingernails bad,
and have come up with various theories. You remember the
googly eyed stage when you thought that you'd be together
forever, carving each other's initials into a tree. The bed is
lonely as you lie there and wonder what went wrong.
Whose fault was it? You feel like a miserable failure, and if

you have kids, *forget it.* You are the horrible mother that has screwed up their life forever. A brand that is there for life, and it is your fault. Besides loving and losing there is a whole other closet of clothes that makes the whole thing suck so bad. *Did I make the right decision?* If you are unlucky enough to have it happen when you are young you think, *have I screwed up my life for good?* Once a divorcee always a divorcee. You might start making bad decisions because you feel so bad about yourself, hanging out in seedy bars under black lights that hide the comb overs and spare tires. You might lose all that weight that you couldn't seem to get rid of in your marriage and start buying new clothes that are way too young for you. You might eat up all the attention that you get from men, and ignore your kids. Divorce is like graduation from high school. The choices you make after it will affect your life for the duration.

You don't expect it to hurt as bad as it does. You think it will be better, (*after all we didn't get along*), and it is to some extent. But all that fighting is replaced with quiet. Quiet and a sense of what really happened. A clarity after the dust settles where it becomes much clearer. You quit blaming them and see just where you screwed up, too. What do you have to show for it all? Peace. Peace after the last gun has been fired, and you start onto the war field to look for casualties. Everyone suffers. Even if you think, *they will be just fine, it is me that is having a hard time*, you are wrong. Everyone suffers. Even if it is the best thing, and you are better off being divorced, everyone still suffers.

No one really tells you all this. When the counselor says you need to try absolutely everything before you consider divorce, you don't get it. When you beg your husband to go to AA meetings, when you beg to go to counseling and he brushes you off, neither of you can see what the future will bring. A long period of brokenness and if you have the courage and character, healing.

I was getting a large tattoo of Kali on my back to have a visible sign of what would be a way of life for me now. I promised Her I would never let anyone tell me how to live again. I promised Her that I would look at pain differently now, that I would see how much it could change a person, sometimes for the much better. Even though, I was still tortuously lonely, and healing, I was feeling stronger. The pain of it all had awoken something new in me. Some new strength, some dormant power. As I consecrated myself to Kali I could feel Her smiling at me, proud. Or maybe I was smiling to myself. Maybe somehow they were connected. The truth of it all was that the Goddess was with me, and that would never change.

As a society we don't believe that one person can practice religion outside of an institution. We are vastly interested in religious institutions. Ask someone where they go to church or synagogue etc. and see what happens if they say that they don't go to church.

"Oh, so you are an atheist?"

"No, I just practice my own personal religion in private."

Somehow being an atheist is more acceptable than not belonging to a religious institution. People think we don't have the right to reach God without another man's help.

After Germany I clung to the Crystal Garden as my church, and Marnie as my pastor. The Universe took that away from me. Then I sought a friend, and Rosemary became the filter through which I experienced the Divine. When she left, and I was finally alone, it was just the

Goddess and I. After I surrendered to it, I would say that this was one of the most enriching and wonderfully spiritual times of my life. I was forced into it, as the Goddess often has to do with me, but it was worth it.

Once I got used to being alone, my days were spent doing the normal rat race succession of events. I went to work, I savored each moment with my daughter, I went to family gatherings, I cleaned the bathroom, I made myself hamburgers just the way my mom does it, and drank red wine on my new sofa. I vibrated with pain that I had now gotten used to.

But with no Rosemary, no Marnie, no church, no book telling me how to be a Witch, and who the Goddess was, I learned for myself. This was the true meaning of being a solitary eclectic Witch. I was alone, and I exercised the right to worship. I gave away or sold a lot of my books, except a cherished few, deciding not to limit myself to someone's written boundaries. I even toyed with ditching the word **Witch**, but decided to keep it because it brought me joy. I had no contact with any other Witches except Kurt, and our conversations were limited to one overseas call every three months. I deleted my name from the Pagan forums, and took *"new Witch looking to learn"* off of the listings of Pagans for our area. I gave up looking for a local store to replace the Crystal Garden, and a person to replace Rosemary. I accepted what was. I tried to shake the feeling that I was missing something, or doing something wrong because there was no one to tell me what to do.

My family are amazing people. My dad is an inspiration, my mom, out of this world self-less. My sisters and brother are strong, exciting, smart, fun people. With that kind of thing to live up to I was always trying to be something special, something amazing, always trying to define myself in some way. If I wasn't a super-Christian, I was a super-Witch. It took a lot of soul searching and letting go to realize that I didn't have to be an anything. That I could just be myself. That I didn't have anything to prove to anyone else, or better yet myself. My family loved me just the way I was, the hokey New Age question was....... did I love myself? At Winter's Pass my identity was clearly defined. We were *bad*. Uncomfortable as it was, that gave me something to latch onto. Humans really are starved for definition, something to help their life make sense. In High School, I was the bad girl that changed into the Jesus-freak. After Germany, I was nothing, and while I didn't latch onto the title of Witch as I did the title Christian, I did cling to it as a defining characteristic. When I met someone for the first time, I found myself trying to work into the conversation that I was a Witch.

One night I was woken from a deep sleep and it all became clear. I had a conversation with my spirit guides, a real one. Taken right out of a M. Night Shyamalan movie, I woke and saw them clearly, heard them clearly. Standing by my bed, they were tall and bluish-clear. There were several of them.

"Don't wear any hats" they said. The conversation was a mix of verbal and non-verbal, mental images they sent me, and thought- questions that I didn't speak. For the sake of not confusing the heck out of you, I'll write it as a verbal conversation.

"Huh?" I said.

"People wear spiritual clothing, and it limits them. Your head is the location of your crown chakra, where divine inspiration comes in. When you wear a hat it limits you to your own idea of what you should receive, who you should be. If you are a Witch, and a tidbit of spiritual information comes from Christianity, or Judaism, then you might not receive it, because you think, 'I am a Witch'. It also colors the way other people see you, and limits the way they treat and react to you." They were so friendly, so close. I could see their faces, and the conversation was effortless.

"But I like the word Witch, it makes me happy. And the conical Witch's hat is supposed to funnel power through its point." I thought about the phrase people use "I wear many hats". I thought about a fireman's hat, a nurse's hat, a police man's hat….. hats definitely defined a person.

"You can use the word Witch, just don't attach yourself too strongly to the word, and don't put a hat on, no matter what. We have many things for you, many experiences, and we want you to have them all. If you wear a hat you will miss out. For some people their path is to wear hats, and if some people took their coverings off they would fall apart. It is not your path to wear a hat in this lifetime."

The conversation went on for what seemed like hours. Parts of my brain were reacting to their presence, in awe of the peaceful connection that was happening. But mostly a sort of passed on understanding of hats was being digested in my brain. They left at dawn. I was vibrating so hard I felt ill, I couldn't eat for two days afterward.

Not wear a hat. I've always thought Witch's hats were powerful and mysterious, an antenna to the higher realms, the pointy top a radio tower picking up signals. But I could be a Witch without it, *really* do my own thing, and *really* let go of prescribed notions. I was fully aware of the freedom, the implications of that. And I fully let go.

I had nobody to distract my attention. I didn't smoke,

drink or do drugs. The forced solitude was painful, but a detox, it forced me to do some soul-searching. When I came home from Germany I was lucid for a month or two, but as soon as I chose my path, even though my guard was up, I still found myself becoming too attached to an idea. I was (fill in the blank) I did (fill in the blank). I had to be really honest with myself and see where I was lying to myself. It was a trial and error time, a school for the spiritually impaired. I was situated in a safe place that I could fall apart, wail till my throat hurt, and pour over pictures and diaries from my stint in the church, take a good look at WHY. WHY was I trying so hard to be something, anything other than what I was? Why did I have to be special, amazing, spectacular? Why did I always have to be the one who had something poignant to say? Why couldn't I just be myself? I could feel the Goddess all around, in and through me; guiding me, helping me heal and grow. I learned and learned and learned. I realized that the person I was trying so hard to prove something to was myself.

There were many memorable nights spent in the company of the Goddess. Some humorous, most, like nourishment to a starving man. I didn't feel like I was blindly groping my way through anymore, and even the times I did stupid things were learning experiences, She was there with me.

One time I mixed an Astral Travel balm, and wiped the excess on my feet and hands, thinking that since the base was made from shea butter, that it would be moisturizing. I was happily working on my Witchy product, feeling pretty good about myself, until an hour later when I noticed I felt weird. I could literally feel my spirit half- out of my body.

304

"I can't get back in my body!" I felt like I was standing outside myself making the call to Kurt. Did my voice really sound like that?

"Smoke a cigarette." He said, laughing.

"You know I quit. I have done everything I can think of to get back in. I have eaten, held a Hematite stone, and even done a full yoga routine. I am afraid to take a nap." Frustrated and fascinated, I waved my hand around making little loop –de-loops like someone on acid.

"Honey, how did you get into this predicament? How much did you put on?"

Staring into the mirror like a stoner, I looked into my eyes expecting to see someone else. I was short with Kurt.

"Well…..a lot. I didn't expect it to work. I know, I hate to admit it, but I expected to results to be a little more, …subtle."

Think, Tara. Remember that you are allowed to THINK.

It took a shower and a lot of scrubbing, and then a brisk walk to fully come back.

I'm sure She was laughing…..but not as hard as she laughed at the next one.

Reaching for the cold stone with the strange markings felt good. I had my hand in my Rune bag, and was sitting cross legged on the floor with my Rune guide open, and some Natacha Atlas playing in the background.

The whole, learn-by-asking-the universe-to-show-you thing had worked so well with The Wheel, that I decided to try it with that unique form of divination, the ancient Celtic language, Runes. I had a great time making my Runes, painting the symbols on river stones I got at the craft store. After consecrating them, I pulled one.

Hagel. I turned over Hagel. Looking down at the book, I scanned the page for its meaning.

Hagel: literally translated as Hail. Means problems that can limit growth, something that comes in fast, and furious, and then leaves just as quickly.

Greaaat. Just what I need. I thought about chucking the whole thing. It was one thing to learn a sacred holiday, but did I really want to know the meaning of Hail? Still, pulled by a sense of "finish what I started" I put the thing on my altar and waited for the day to unfold so my new friend Hagel could show me its meaning.

It had been an uneventful day, even though I looked for Hail at every turn. I took Willow to Chuck –e- Cheese, and looked for Hagel as she went down the greasy plastic slide. I looked for hail as we ate lunch at a local pizza joint, and I felt stupid as I quietly tucked her into bed, and climbed in myself. Hail was a no- show.

Hagel.....give me a break. Obviously this isn't going to work. I am definitely giving my Runes away tomorrow, the things don't work!

I snuggled into my soft sheets and grabbed the book I was reading. It focused on the life of the famous Witch, Scott Cunningham, and I had just gotten to the juicy part about Scott doing a stint with vegetarianism. It had opened his awareness, so that he started to see the spirit world with more clarity. It was kinda creepy.

I tucked the sheets under my chin, and opened the book to where I'd left off. The story was getting better. As he described seeing a large evil spirit in the corner of his room, I got chills. I remembered the cat that was in my very bedroom.

Stop it, Tara, you are spooking yourself.

As he told the story of the foul spirit, my hair stood on

end, the deathly quiet of my bedroom making the fear worse.

Then I heard a noise......a noise that came from my bedroom.

Scratch scratch.

I lay still as a pond afraid to breathe. Yep, it was definitely coming from my bedroom. I waited for the sound again, thinking that maybe I had imagined it.

You are worked up, time to put the book away, and quit imagining things.

Scratch scratch.

Nope. There is definitely something in the room. OH MY GOD. The longer I lie here the more time I give this thing to get me. What am I going to do? Maybe the cat is back, maybe I invited it back with my thinking about it, and...

Scratch scratch.

O.k. it is now or never, I have to face this thing. I looked at the door, and at the knife I kept on my bedside table. *If I grab the knife maybe I can get Willow out of here. I'm going to sit up on three. One....two....two and a half....*

Scratch scratch.

Three! I slowly sat up and looked at the foot of my bed. And there it was......the offender was sitting on my bed. I looked into the eyes of the threat. The searching brown eyes of the thing that had terrorized me for the better half of thirty minutes.

A chipmunk.

It took me a minute to digest the fact that there was a chipmunk sitting on the foot of my bed, but there he was. Three inches high, scrappy tailed, and looking at me. Not even a spirit cat, or a spirit chipmunk, a real one.

I felt like an idiot.

I had worked myself into a frenzy over nothing. I had allowed fear to come in like a hailstorm, and it had come and gone. Fear had transformed my sense of reality, how I viewed the world. How quickly I gave up my power!

Thanks Hagel, I get it.

A half an hour later and the furry offender was out of the house, thanks to an oddly peaceful call to my brother Jonathan. He figured the little guy had gotten in through some loose boards in the attic.

Maybe Runes weren't for me after all.

The next day I relayed the story to all who would hear. It wasn't so funny then, but hilarious the next day. It felt good to laugh, and I knew that too was a gift from the Goddess. Laughter, dancing, feeling my way through my own brand of spiritual practice, all of these lessons I was learning only enriched my experience.

In my new home, I had beautiful nights doing ritual dances to, of all things, Joni Mitchell. I danced till my legs starting shaking, collapsing on the floor. The ceiling fan went round and round to the song I made up to tell the Goddess how much I loved Her. I didn't care that it sounded cheesy, it came from my heart. The freedom that my new path allowed me was nothing short of intoxicating. There is a delicious, sensual, broken, swirly part of yourself that gets to dance too when you dance, and letting that part out can be scary if you've never done it before. Free dance, the kind when a small part of you thinks "I'll bet I look like an idiot" is the biggest release you can imagine. When you add in dim lights, candles, and music that sweeps you along with it, you can let your body go for a while.

This became part of my regular spiritual practice. Putting on something beautiful and playing music that matched my mood: Heart, P.J.Harvey, Tori Amos. It all worked, because I was expressing myself as a gift to the Goddess. I danced, I slithered like a snake, I softly swayed, I even sat as the music played, my awareness focused on Her. All of this brought me deep peace. I was o.k. with my life and o.k. with my pain, I had finally found my peace.

That was it. There was no big booming voice from above, taking me out of the world I was in, telling me I was special, and only I bore the truth. There was no separation, causing me to be something that others were not, there was no huge white cloaked God or Goddess who I had to reach so hard to get to, until I had reached outside of myself, and gotten lost. There was no person that I looked to for guidance, no book that I used for permission. I didn't have to try to be anything, only do what came naturally, and that was more than good enough.

The Divine is here and now, She surrounds us. As I played with my daughters brown curls, I felt HER. When I ate, when I slept, when I cried, when I shopped, I knew HER in myself. She was all things, mundane, and extraordinary. She even blurred the line, till she was all things with no divisions. No labels. The mundane became extraordinary, and the extraordinary became mundane. No BIG agenda. No Calling. No fancy stores, or costumes. No Light shows. Just what is.

***

I have always rooted for the bad guy. I used to keep this to myself, and cheer along with the rest of the crowd when they killed the vampire, or when the ghosts in *Scooby Doo* turned out to be old man Dawson dressed in a sheet. I was disappointed, but I cheered anyway.

The bad guy is so much more….interesting. I'm not talking death and torture *Saw* bad, but cool bad, like

Witches, vampires and Tony Soprano. Bad was interesting, it was personal. Good seemed impersonal. Good was this ONE THING, it was never opened to interpretation; usually we knew how it would turn out. Willy would be free, Gilligan got off the island, Julia Roberts gets the guy and so on, but bad....with bad, a plethora of endings was possible, and usually it was up to the villain's whims. You could be sexy bad, mean spirited bad, anti- moral bad, money grubbing bad, self serving bad, and evil bad. Good was just good.

Superheroes especially walk the line between good, almost heavenly good, and a touch of bad. My comic book nerd husband (sorry sweetheart, I love you) has informed me of the anti- hero. The anti-hero is someone that does questionable things for the sake of doing something for the greater good. I could really sink my teeth into that concept. Bad who does good, maybe there was hope after all.

Where did I get this fascination with the bad guy? Was it the immediate label of bad when I went to Winter's Pass, a label that I'd never even considered previously? Maybe I got it via osmosis from being forced to watch horror movies with my dad.

"Do you want to see something really scary?" The scene from The Twilight Zone movie made sure that I would shield my eyes from the TV when I walked by it. He loved those movies, gobbled them up. We idolized the Godfather, and my dad even chased us around with orange peels in his mouth. (wrong scene to re-enact, dad). Maybe it wasn't bad I liked, it was Bad Lite, Grey-Bad, Anti-hero Bad that fascinated me. Was it that good seemed boring to me? Good was rarely COOL. Cool with black suits and black cars, and low chocolate voices. Bad was dangerous, and exciting.

Just how much of this polarizing was from the church? Here was my dad sitting on a fence next to a *no sitting on the fence* sign with a cigarette dangling out of his mouth next to a *no smoking* sign, side by side with recollections of the dusty, dry, namby-pamby "good" of the church. Blah. No thanks.

Witchcraft is perceived as bad. Even though I knew it wasn't, or at least I wasn't misusing it, I liked being seen as a badass. Thanks to all the snotty nosed *D&D* players who are ruining it for us. Try to be cooler, o.k.? Seriously, though, perceptions can be used, and I can honestly say that at first I wanted to fool with the *bad* stuff, the exciting stuff. I perceived healing the earth spells as boring, and working with spirits as cool and exciting. This bothered me. I realized this in myself and tried to dislodge my brain from this association that it had taken up residence in. I needed to know that good was cool, too. So I asked for help.

It wasn't an earth shattering event, or even a memorable one. I just sat down in front of my altar with the laundry baskets of unfolded clothes kicked out of the way, and asked.

"I need to see" the right word came to me, and I said more confidently. "I need a paradigm shift."

Then I walked downstairs, and forgot about it.

Most spells and prayers are answered *slowly*. So slowly that when you finally get the answer you have changed so much that you accommodate the new reality, whatever it is, and you can't remember what it was like asking for the original prayer in the first place. Months passed, maybe even a year. It was so gradual, like pieces of a puzzle that had been split into even more pieces coming together. Sitting outside I was struck with the Oneness of nature. Another day, for a split second I felt a part of everything. Another day I realized how much we like to categorize everything as humans. Trees vibrated with life and power on a Tuesday. On a Thursday I realized that the things we gravitate to are part of our personality and are not to be ashamed of. Saturday revealed the infinity of the sky, the sky that canopied Copernicus, Ptolemy, and now me. The sky that would exist long after my presence on earth became a memory.

Here's what I came up with at the end of it all. *One day I cheered the good guy.* As I caught myself I wondered what kind of rainbow- toting granola bar I had changed into. What happened to the fascination with the bad? I realized that bad and good were the same, there was only energy and rightness for the situation. Bad and good are perceptions that we create. You wanna argue? How bout war? Who deserves to win? The bad guy, you say? Who is the bad guy? From whose perspective? Can we really know all the interworkings of that? I realize that society has rules, and that those rules keep order, because not everyone can be true enough to themselves to regulate their actions. Fine. I also realize that the rule breakers are the "bad ones". But whose rules are they? Once again, it is all perception.

I once read in a Sylvia Brown (the famous psychic) book that the spirit she channels, Francine, was asked about the other side, and what happens when we die. Francine stated that when we die, and go to the other side, we make arrangements with others. Arrangements that will help us grow and learn while we are on the earth.

"O.k., you John, you will be my husband, and leave me for another woman ten years into our marriage. The pain I experience will force me to love and trust myself, that will teach me self-love. Julie, how bout you be my daughter with Down's syndrome, and that will teach me love in patience."

John says back, "yeah and leaving you will teach me blah blah"...and it goes on. Everyone shakes hands, and gets ready to play their parts so we can all grow closer to our Divine nature. I don't know, and even though it was a hard pill to swallow, it made sense to me. The implications are crazy. Chew on it for a minute, and realize that that means that Stalin chose to be Stalin to help others learn their lesson. Perhaps his path was harder......something to think about.

Look, let me just say that I don't give two shits about the afterlife, and I certainly am not attaching myself to any one theory. Who knows what will happen to us? Nobody. That is why there are a million theories. It is called the AFTER-life; I'll deal with it after I have lived. I know that just like laws and rules, visions of a specific afterlife keep numb people in check. Some people will try to be better people on the earth if they think it will help them in the afterlife, but some won't. Maybe they won't act like an A-hole because they fear karmic retribution, but they might molest little boys because they believe that they are saved "by grace through faith and that not of themselves" which means that they can do whatever they want, and still go to heaven. Maybe they will fly a plane into the twin towers, killing thousands of people, and honestly believe that they will get rewarded in heaven for it.

I do what I can to make my life better now, to get peace, to not worry about an idea of what happens when my body is rotting in a wooden box, which is just an idea. Good and bad. *Ideas.*

To learn to drop the labels, you have to learn love. To learn love you have to learn to love yourself first. To learn to love yourself, you have to learn to be alone with yourself; *to have the courage to see who you really are*, guess what…. this takes balls. Learning to love yourself is a long process, but once you love yourself, then you learn that *we are all one*. When you truly realize that, the we – are- all- one thing becomes more than a little androgynous Calvin Klein ad- boy with bunny rabbit suspenders singing We Are the World. Loving yourself will show you that we are all one, for real. Exit all the hokey stereotypes; cue the consciousness of treating others like you would want to be treated.

Good is kick ass, powerful and cool. Good is making a good decision that may be perceived as bad….enter the Witch. I'm making the best decision for my own spirituality, AND IT IS SEEN AS BAD. I get to be bad and good. I get to have my cake and eat it too. Hurrah! Long live the Witch!

Part of the reason I always liked bad, was because I thought bad was power, and I am infinitely fascinated with power. People controlled people through various means, I thought. I noticed that no one was immune to it, that it could be in any situation, poverty or riches. It could be in any age, or gender, or family roles. Seeming opposites could be the norm. Adults could control children, and children could control adults, and those that could control large groups of people were really something. But I asked to grow, to change, to SEE myself, and in a series of really fun (sarcasm) lessons, realized that my fascination with power was because I was a control freak. Control freaks are that way mostly because they feel powerless, I grew up feeling mostly powerless, so power was a biggie for me. The cool thing is that the Goddess never takes away without giving something better. I traded in my fascination with power when I asked to grow, and She showed me that my perception was an illusion, that it wasn't real power I saw and desired- it was just controlling the actions or influencing the mindsets of another. It doesn't come from the heart. It was a bland imitation of the real thing.

So, hard as it was, I gave it up. The Dark Goddess came in, showed me that there is no real power over people because everything is temporary. I died. That part of me died. My daughter almost physically died, and I died again, wondering why She was doing this to me. I entered the holy darkness where everything I knew and valued was shown for what it really was. Nothing. Our illusion of control is nothing more than an illusion.

But how can you say that? How can you casually say that you "died"? Is this what happens when you become a Witch? You start throwing around morbid phrases intended to shock?

We all die, daily. Each person has a set of values, some their own, some borrowed, some inherited-to let go of those is to die. Our spirit can never die, it is eternal, even the Bible teaches that. The ego is the part of our self that says, "my name is Susan, I was born in Milwaukee, I love my dogs, I don't want children, I am a computer programmer, I hate bananas. My mom is my best friend. I am a Methodist. I am the loud one in the bunch, red is my signature color." Susan will act this person out, as if on auto- pilot, because she believes that is who she is. She will make decisions based on what her notion of herself is, whether or not they line up with her spirit. Like the whole wearing the hat thing. That is the hat she has created.

Our brains create these little wanted -ad descriptions for ourselves, so that if something ever came up to challenge these notions, for instance, say Susan got pregnant when she clearly stated that she didn't want kids, she has a choice. Let the old part of her ego label die, and go with what is the present moment, or hang on to her label with all she's got. It feels like a death, and sometimes it physically hurts. But when the ego dies, we grow. Goodbye to our definition, and hopefully hello to a closer relationship with the namelessness that is our spirit. The idea is that *we don't need to label ourselves eventually.*

The Universe is *constantly* handing us these opportunities to take our hats off.

Now of course, we could go the other way with this. Turn into a wishy- washy New Age eccentric with a wispy voice, and a new ego identity which is "enlightened".

"I don't knoooowwww if I like bananas, let me connect with my spirit.OMMMMMMMMMM!!!"

This ridiculousness is almost easier than to drift, to just let the old part die, and not replace it with a new one. We crave identity. I think some of it is society; some of it is just plain being human. I have to constantly check myself to see how attached to the title of Witch, or mother, or author, or wife. I don't own these things, they aren't me. They are just what I am doing right now. Get it?

The Dark Goddess is the gate through which we pass when we die, physically and spiritually. She will help you. But it still sucks while you are going through it.

I had a choice. It is one thing to ask to grow, la –de-da, but when the rubber meets the road, *whew*, it is a real challenge. When the Crone steps in and it is all hollow nothingness, and discomfort. When you want out of your own skin, and you slap yourself on the forehead and say "what was I thinking being a Witch, I want to go back to not thinking about spirituality except when I go to church." You put up with misery, and dimly knowing through your blinding pain that it is part of the lesson, feebly try to embrace it. But it is super hard to embrace your own pain.

Finally one day you see. You are stripped of your idea of control and it has left a void that at first was excruciating, but now is a part of your life. You know that you really have nothing but yourself. Really. Not your kids, not your wife/husband/partner, not your house, not anything. I would even debate your body, but we have to be housed in something so you have that to a certain extent. But as most of us know as is evident with sudden sickness of a loved one, or the discovery of cancer in ourselves, our bodies are temporary, too.

What do we have then? Where is power? With the shell gone I saw it. When I stepped out of the dark cave, it was obvious…..it was staring right at me.

Power is love.

Love for ourselves which is a humorous, scary, thoroughly enjoyable journey. Love hums, it vibrates and it LASTS. You can't kill love, and no one can take it away from you. Once it is there, or was there it leaves an eternal mark. Even if no one loves you, or has ever loved you, you can love yourself. Loving yourself leads to all kinds of amazing journeys, to real fulfillment. Loving yourself cancels out fear, and without fear, life opens up to you like a rose. There is power in it, trust me.

Power has been handed through despots, leaders, pastors, moms, dads, cops, and school teachers like a hot potato, and it is always temporary. You don't get to keep the fake, control-y kind of power. But love, life, that is the real deal, and it is there for you and I in abundance. You just have to embrace it, and be willing to go through some shit to find it.

Someone once told me "Tara, you like things to be

hard". Maybe I do. Maybe that is why I call on the Dark Goddess for help. I'm in a hurry, I want to learn and gobble up as much as I can while I'm here. Maybe it doesn't have to be that hard for you, I don't know, but if you ask for help you can get through it. There were many times I have been in the "cave" or the "abyss"- the sacred time where *we choose blindness so we can learn self trust*, and I wondered if I could make it. Seriously thought that this was possibly the worst thing that I'd ever been through and just how the heck was I going to do it. The deep knowledge of the transience of all things kept me going. Just take a look at the night sky…..eventually it will be the bright newness of day.

I don't believe the Goddess asks us to be miserable. I do believe that discomfort is there as a growing pain. Imagine what a picnic it must be for the seed pushing up through the dirt. How humorous and what a waste of precious energy it would be if the seed was thinking….PUSH……*I'm suffering for God*…..PUSH. Suffering is temporary. The Goddess is permanent. Bitterness is temporary. Love is permanent, and that is the beauty of the temporal world. The crappy things go away, but love makes an eternal mark. Love will always change a situation, maybe not visibly at first, but it will always change the heartbeat of a situation. The fool tries to get you to submit by making them fear you, the smart one by allowing them to love you.

We are all called to live the life that is presented to us with compassion, love for ourselves, after which love for others follows, and presence in each breath. It is a mystery, and I don't have all the answers. But I have peace. Even in my pain, there is peace, and that is where She lives.

O.k., now that we got all the metaphysical stuff outta the way, ready for the prince- and- princess -riding -off- into- the- sunset part of the story?

Chapter Fourteen

"Wuv, twue wuv...." – the clergyman in *The Princess Bride (movie, Rob Reiner, 1987)*

Man, am I gonna sound stupid when I ask for help with this one. I was standing in Barnes and Nobles. It was the holiday season, and the place was packed. I was there to find a book on how to be a cowboy. That's right, not a book on cowboys, the history of cowboys, or pictures of cowboys. This was a book on how to BE a cowboy. I thought of the conversation that had gotten me here.

"I have decided what I want to be when I grow up." Chris was standing over me.

I looked up hazily from my 7-11 coffee. It was four am and the host of the morning show that I co-hosted was grinning at me.

"Chris, it is too early for this, we have so much to do before we go on-air" I grunted, looking down at our prep sheet.

"No seriously, I had a revelation while I was mowing the lawn yesterday" he sounded slightly hurt. I decided I'd better indulge him.

"O.k. Go ahead." I placed our topics to the side, and sat up, ready to listen.

"I want to be a cowboy." He said after a long pause.

"You want to be a cowboy" I repeated dumbly.

"I want to be a cowboy" he repeated back.

"So....um" I started in, before he cut me off.

"Listen" he said, "It's a man's job. Real rough and tumble work. Just you and nature. None of this pansy prize wheel and givin' the weather every hour crap."

"You have really thought about this.... well ...then go be a cowboy." I had always thought that Chris would be happier doing something else. As silly as it sounded, being a cowboy was perfect for him.

"I wouldn't even know where to start" he said with a sharp change in tone. "I guess we need to go on. You ready?" he said motioning to the studio door.

So here I was trying to find this book. I must have had a helpless look on my face because a very tall, blond, attractive male clerk walked up to me.

"Can I help you?" he said in an unexpected buttery southern drawl. My god was he cute.

"I need to find a book on HOW to BE a cowboy" I made sure to emphasize the words.

"I think I know just what you need" he smiled, "follow me".

With pleasure.... ..... Lord and he smells good, too. Should I tell him? I'm gonna tell him.

"Hey, you smell really good" I said confidently.

"Thanks" he was blushing from head to toe.

Great looks, and a gentleman too? Where did this guy come from? I didn't think they made guys like this anymore.

"Well, here it is" he said, handing me the perfect book for Chris.

"Uh, is this for," he gave me a once over "you?"

"No, it's for this guy... it's a long story. But thank you so much."

I contemplated finding another reason that I needed some help just to keep talking to him.

"Mark, I need you in self-help" his walkie-talkie

blared.

"If you ever need anything…." he was blushing again.

"Thanks so much" I said, walking away. As I hit the door, I turned around, and he was still standing there, staring back at me.

***

After my divorce I started to re-think the image I had created for myself. I saw myself as the hip New Age single career mom, who used men for mental and physical company, and then discarded them at will. I WASN'T going to get married again, and I DIDN'T need anyone.

I had learned so much. Winter's Pass had taught me what I didn't want to be, and New Glory had showed me the line between passion, and illusion. Germany had introduced me to the Goddess, and started me on a path of incredible learning. Marnie had given me the confidence to make my own spiritual decisions, and Rosemary had shown me how to fly. I knew about energy, and how it worked, I knew about protection, and I finally found my inner peace. I had a way to cope with fear, and finally didn't feel like I was searching so hard anymore. I had found something that worked on a day to day basis for me.

It satisfied all parts of me, the passion, the imagination, the logic, the visceral, the responsible, the wild woman, and even the furthest reaches of my being. It satisfied the less celebrated parts of myself, and pushed them ever so slightly to make them stretch and grow. That long part of my life had been finished, or better yet, started. All that was left was the joy at the day to day life that I was now free to live. I knew where the Goddess fit. I wasn't shoving anymore. The Goddess WAS life, in a natural way.

Unfortunately that is when a re-occurring problem reared its ugly head again.

Loneliness.

Being alone in the clinging soundless house made me re- evaluate. It came to a head when one day I had done everything there was to do. The house was clean. I wouldn't see my daughter for a few more hours, and I was sitting on my bed, content, but tired of being by myself.

I had done a lot of thinking over the previous months, and realized that some part of me thought that needing, even loving someone was a weakness, a vulnerable spot. I had relied on the people in the church, I had relied on Rosemary and Marnie. And where did it get me? Alone again.

After some time, I realized the fault in this. Part of love was pain (Kali had taught me that), and to not ever take a chance again, and keep my heart closed meant that I would be alone forever. And like they say "no man is an island". I knew the difference between relying *on* someone, and walking *with* someone. It was the lesson of my life: the difference between a co-dependent relationship, and a healthy one. Seated on my bed, playing with the lace edging on my favorite comforter, I found the courage to pray.

"Mother, I know no man is an island. The flip side is that I never want to go through what I just went through again with the divorce. But I am so lonely. I need a companion. I know that it isn't a great idea to make lists, and please if there is something better for me, then scrap my list, but here it is:

I want him to be kind…….. I want to be able to have good conversations with him……. I don't care if he follows the same path as I but I want him to be spiritual, and to respect my spirituality, and my path……. I want him to have an accent, cuz I have always thought they were sexy……..I don't care what he does for work, or how much money he makes, but I want him to be a hard worker………I want him to be a man's man, but still sensitive enough to cry…….. I prefer taller than me……I really like blondes."

And the list went on.

By the time I was finished, I knew that if I ever did meet this man, then I would know. Because he probably didn't exist-he was too perfect. Still, I felt better for getting it all off my chest. I shuffled downstairs content with my prayer, and myself.

The Tarot card reader set out 10 cards. "Well, I see blah blah blah" I was tuning her out. Bored, I decided to go to my local metaphysical shop, and get a reading. I was already regretting it.

"Look, I am lonely, see anything with that?" I rudely cut her off.

Sighing, she shuffled the cards and glanced at the clock. She laid them out, apathetically, probably just trying to get through the reading.

Her eyes lit up unexpectedly. "Good news," she said, "he is right around the corner."

"Who is around the corner?" I asked, wondering what the hell she was talking about. She obviously had seen something.

"The one." She paused. "Honey, the one for you. Your soul mate. Your companion. You said you were lonely. The Universe has answered your prayers, and he is right around the corner."

"I don't believe in soul mates" I muttered, the tiniest

324

bit of hope coming into my heart.

"Well, he is here. The attraction will be mostly physical at first, from this it looks like he is a real cutie. Then it will grow into an amazing friendship, and a life's companion. Looks like you will even have kids with this guy."

"When do you see this supposed meeting?" I snapped, my arms crossed tightly.

She sighed again, then shuffled.

"Ten....I see tens. Could be the tenth month, ten hours, ten days."

"Or ten years" I said sarcastically. I handed her the money and left, feeling kind of bad for being so rude to her. A fairytale from a well meaning fortune teller made me feel worse, not better. Still, I wracked my mind for every single guy I knew. The five foot tall magician that did kid's day at the mall? Could he be my soul mate?

I seriously doubted it.

As I made my way back home, I regretted making my list. What a fool I was. Did I really want all the crap that went along with a relationship? I was very content with my life as it was *thank you very much*. I had my connection with the Goddess, and plenty of time with Willow.I had made it through the war zone that was divorce, and I was finally getting my bearings. *Another person would just ruin all that*. I thought, squenching up my forehead.

Who is pounding on my door? I groaned, laying in bed, depressed on a Saturday night. Someone was knocking on my door. I figured it was one of those kids selling magazines or something.

Pushing the covers over my head, I ignored it. *Ring*

ring. I picked up the cell phone lying on my cluttered bedside stand.

"What?" I chirped.

"I am outside knocking on your door, can you not hear that?" It was my sister, Vanessa.

"I can hear it, hang on, I'm coming." I hung up.

Opening the door, she shocked me with a torrent of words, "get dressed, we have to go somewhere, my boyfriend's mom wants to go out with me, and I told her you and I were doing something, so we have to go kill time for an hour. This is the third time I have blown her off, and I think she is starting to suspect that MAYBE I don't want to spend Saturday night with my boyfriend's MOTHER. Hey, what are you doing? You look like you just got out of bed."

She was a sight standing there with her hands on her hips.

"I'm depressed" I said, monotone.

"Well, get dressed, you owe me one."

As I started to put on my weathered sweatpants, a little voice in my head told me to try and look nice. So I grabbed my jeans and amethyst necklace, and slapped on some lipstick.

"And where are we going?" I turned the radio down. She seemed frantic, and was driving like a maniac.

"I thought we'd go to Barnes and Noble" she said, on a mission.

"Fine" I said. *All I want to do is get this over with so I can go home and go back to my pity party.*

"Hey, I don't like this Barnes and Noble, let's go to the other one" she blurted, and then did a reckless U-turn.

I could see the headlines now:

"Lonely Divorcee and Psycho Sister Die in Bizarre

Car Crash, Clutching Latte's"

"Vanessa, I don't care where we go. How long did you say we had to stay out again?" I was gripping the seat tightly.

"Another hour or so, maybe we can go get a drink afterwards." She finally found a parking space in the crowded Barnes & Noble parking lot.

"Hey I'm gonna get a frappucchino, want one?" I said, perking up a bit. *Wait, I don't think she needs any caffeine. A valium maybe, but no caffeine.*

I was starting to feel better, enjoying the sunset, and nice summer air. Maybe getting out wasn't a bad thing. We walked toward the heavy front door.

"Look, let's stay 30 minutes in here, and then go somewhere else. I don't want to run into her" she said, opening the main door to the shop.

I looked up, and standing there two feet away was the blond clerk I had met the year before. Our eyes met. He recognized, and almost seemed to be waiting for me.

"I'm going on break in a minute, will you wait for me?" he said.

"Sure." *Holy crap. I had forgotten all about him. Could this be the guy the tarot reader was talking about?* I checked my watch.

It was ten pm.

Thirty minutes passed, and we made a date for lunch that Wednesday.

The beginning of the week dragged by. I couldn't wait till Wednesday, just to find out. *Was he the one?* My mind was driving me crazy, and doubts starting surfacing. *Was I ready to get back into the game? Was this good for Willow?* It didn't matter because Wednesday came and went with no word from the mysterious blond clerk. No phone call, no nothing.

This didn't make sense or flow with how things were supposed to happen. I prayed, and then got an immediate confirmation of my prayer. The Tarot reader had said that he was right around the corner. I knew that there was a reason for it all, but it made no sense to me. I couldn't take any more rejection, failure, or pain. The pain- as- a -teacher thing was starting to wear on me. For once in a long time, I wanted to be happy, to feel good, and it looked like it wasn't going to happen. I didn't feel like I could pull any more strength or resolve out of my already depleted stores.

Bitterly, I gave up on the blond clerk, and on love.

Goddess, I QUIT!

Soon it was Friday, and I was having a male-bashing phone conversation with my sister. As I furiously popped Dove chocolates with the little messages inside the wrapper into my mouth, I let anger boil up in me.

"I wish I knew why he didn't call, he is probably just an asshole like the rest of them." I was so hurt, and couldn't believe how I'd let myself be so stupid to believe that Tarot reader.

"Yeah, they are all assholes" Vanessa said, echoing my feelings.

"I don't need a stupid man" I said, my heart hard as a rock. I popped a chocolate in my mouth and read the message written in the wrapper. *Smile at the simple things.* Whatever.

"Yeah, the other day James made me feel like a complete idiot when he...". I cut her off.

"Hang on, Ness, someone is on the other line."

I grabbed another chocolate, and clicked over.

"Hello!" I practically shouted into the phone.

"Hi, I'm looking for Tara" said a southern voice. *Oh my god it is him.*

"Yeah, can you hang on?" I said, not knowing what to do.

I clicked over. "Vanessa, it is him. It is him on the other line. What should I do?" Part of me wanted to give him a chance to explain himself, the other wanted to tell him to go screw himself.

"I don't know Tara, what you think?"

I unwrapped another chocolate. It said, *Be Kind To a Stranger.* I clicked over.

"Hi, this is Mark .I'm so sorry I didn't call, my grandma had to go to the hospital and I had to go out of state for an emergency. Please give me another chance. How bout dinner tomorrow night?"

"Sure." I said. "Pick me up at 8."

And we have been together ever since.

***

Altars are a physical view of your spiritual state. As I conversed with my new mate, the kind of man I felt like I had waited for my whole life, I explained altars to him. Just like what I had prayed for, he seemed very interested in my path.

Logically, the most visual thing in a Witches' life is her personal meditation space, her altar. I remembered the first time I heard the word. Spells, ritual, altars, all these words that were peppered through numerous books, and that make up most of the righteous army of God's nightmares, this is the jargon of Witchcraft, and I was getting used to it. Most of the words were never used in

Christianity, except maybe the word altar. What it represented at Winter's Pass was a little pressboard table at the front of the pulpit that held a hideously large arrangement of flowers. There were no altars at New Glory, just the mention of "coming before God's altar", which was a huge clearing at the front of the church, strewn with people crying, and becoming "slain in the spirit". Pastor Sam paid eighty dollars for a real bottle of anointing oil that he liked to smear on our foreheads at the "altar".

Sitting at our little table in Applebee's drinking wine, I tried to explain what an altar meant to me. He listened patiently.

"My first altar was kind of a spur of the moment thing. I had read and read about them, but couldn't figure out what they were really for-what it would mean to put pretty things on a table top. Why I should have one, what it would mean to my practice. I didn't even like the word Altar....ALTAR...wooo.....wooo. It sounded so freakin' formal, and as I've said, that is not what I wanted."

He nodded.

"Three days before my first acknowledged Yule I grabbed an empty green plastic bin that had held Willow's toys. Dumping the toys into another bin, I turned the empty container upside down. I found a red and silver velvet cloth, and some plastic Christmas candle holders with little fake, silver spray painted pinecones. I threw the cloth over the bin, situated the ugly candle holders to each side, and put a statue I had of the Goddess in the center. She was tall and wooden. Her face was so kind, and her hands were held open. *This is my altar,* I thought. When I stood back to look at it, it was an awkward feeling. It was a physical display of my spirituality.

It was all symbolism, I knew that. But what exactly did

330

it symbolize? I saw some of my uncertainty in the display, the fake greenery. I hated that. It seemed sterile, as I hadn't really put anything personal on there…..but the statue. That was the beautiful part. It really gave me joy to look at that statue."

"What did Luke say?" Mark asked.

"Great question. Most Witches are afraid to have altars because of what their family members will say. Lucky for me I am a bit of a packrat, so he just thought it was another arrangement of knickknacks. It didn't have a big blazing pentacle on it, so I guess he didn't notice it."

"I can't imagine your altar looking like that. Since I've known you I've been watching your altar, as you change it seems to change with you. It almost has a life of its own, it really is fascinating."

I stopped to order a sandwich, absolutely loving spending time with this man.

"An altar is a living breathing thing, just like what a person's spiritual practice should be. O.k., where were we? Oh yeah, like I said, an altar is really just a visual representation of my spiritual state. Sometimes I put on there what I feel, sometimes what I want to feel, sometimes I honor The Wheel, sometimes I honor change in my life. I'm kinda a complicated person, so my altar can be a bit complicated. It really took me a while to get to that point though."

I figured altars out one Ostara.

It was the Spring Equinox, celebrated March 21, and I was determined to have a holiday. We were going to paint eggs, little wooden ones I had spent $15.00 on at the craft store. I had a lemon cake mix, and I was sure that the turkey I'd bought would be a delicious addition. I popped the cake in the oven as the doorbell rang.

"Hey, thanks for coming over" I said to Laura, my baby sister. She breezed in the door and I studied her. Laura was one of those girls that pretty much out- cooled anyone in the vicinity. Her expressions were hard to read (a Capricorn trait), and they in no way mirrored her merry, insightful insides, but intimidated others. She was not afraid of much. Her razor sharp sarcastic sense of humor, and kind, open heart made her a blast to be with.

"So what is it we are celebrating again?" she asked, casually lying on my sofa, sipping a beer.

"It's called Ostara…" and with that I spilled the history, story, and every minor detail I could think of. My hands were practically shaking. I was worked up, wound up, in my head.

She looked at me like only someone that has grown up with you can do, knowing exactly what it is that you are up to. With that look, I felt a small ping in my head. For a second, this was just anything else I had gotten excited about…God….the church…etc. I was back to the old habit of externalizing it, and not enjoying the Divine that was already present.

DING. The kitchen timer broke my thoughts and I ran to take the cake out of the oven, and check the turkey. I was quiet as Laura watched me turn the cake out of its pan. In an almost boring, non- dramatic way the cake broke into three big pieces. I promptly freaked out.

"SHIT…look at my cake, this sucks. I guess we'd better paint the stupid eggs." Laura eyeballed me and innocently followed me to the table where I had artfully arrayed the eggs, and pastel paints. We seated ourselves, and proceeded to paint. I enjoyed her company, but as we painted, I felt like I was doing just that…painting. No magic, nothing special, just a broken cake, and wooden eggs. I was so stuck in my head and my ideals, I was missing the point.

Laura said nothing and just kept watching me panic as nothing went as I had planned in my perfect Ostara. When I took out the turkey, it was raw on the inside. Seriously. It might as well have been raining outside.

Laura gave me a big hug, sensing I was about to cry. She grabbed a handful of cake, and shoved it in her mouth, forcing a laugh from me.

"Listen, Tara, I have to go. Thanks for inviting me. I know you had things planned a certain way, but maybe the magic is in the day itself, and not what you planned. I love you."

She shut the door, and I stood there stunned, letting her words sink in.

I ran back into the bedroom and stared at my perfect Ostara altar. That is another thing altars are good for. A place to think.

A sunshine yellow cloth cupped the fake forsythia branches strewn on top. A statue of the spring Goddess Eostre sat in the center next to some of the wooden eggs, her golden hair mimicking the emerging Spring sun. I stared, and let my thoughts free. They wandered, rested, then came to the point of wisdom that I needed.

I stood up, furious with myself, ripping the plastic branches off and throwing them in the nearby wastebasket.

WHAT AM I DOING? THIS ISN'T ME!

I thought about the holidays I already celebrated like Christmas. I didn't hope that decorating the tree would show me it's meaning…..the meaning was in the moment, the people, the same time every year, the smells, the repetition. I couldn't force meaning, I had to be present.

I cleared the altar, and sat staring at its smooth wooden finish, thinking for the first time what I felt. What I wanted, regardless of what I thought I should put on it. I grabbed the moon cloth I had longingly looked at, but then put away, thinking it wasn't "Ostara-y" enough. I placed beautiful, radiant Eostre to the side and picked up my snake Goddess, knowing in my heart that She was what I really wanted. I couldn't mentally explain why I wanted these things on the altar, I just did. Why I chose the colors, the stones, the statues, the pictures, whatever I chose. I felt them before I thought them. I grabbed them before I thought them.

Making myself a little plate of broken cake, I went and sat before my real Ostara altar. I closed my eyes, and tried to get past the riffraff chatter in my head, to the pulse of life outside the house walls-the smell in the air, the way my skin felt, the cadence of my breathing. I *tuned into* Ostara, and if I could have visualized that particular Ostara it would have been what I placed on the altar in front of me. I tapped into the rythym and was able to manifest it. It was a moment of great change. From that moment on nothing went on because I thought I should put it there. If I chose something it was because it inspired me, or because it was beautiful, or simply because.

O.k. so, did I figure it all out, no. Am I going to write another *Witchcraft for Beginners* book to place in the already numerous pile, of course not, Goddess knows we don't need any more of those. I'm just hangin' out tellin' you my story. The reason I said I haven't figured it all out is because, *hello*, you can't. What do you think mankind has been trying to do since we walked upright? Figuring happens in the brain. In Witchcraft as in any other religion, sometimes you have to feel something first, and then check it out with your brain later. Your intuition will never lie, your brain will. Your brain is a mini-computer that has been fed facts, some facts will accommodate realities, some facts will oppose them. It all depends on what facts you have been fed, whether you are ready to realize that they are just that, and whether you are ready to let your spirit, soul, heart or whatever you want to call it dictate your reality instead of your brain, which wants to limit you.

But do we ditch our brains entirely....honey, have you read any of this book? Ditching your brain will land you in the middle of a cult, or a drone like quasi-religious existence. Our brains are there for a reason. God told you that if you jump off a building you will fly? Cool. If your brain isn't screaming *no*, then there is a problem.

Here's the thing. Since we so quietly decided to accept as a society an all male god, a thinking God, and subtly ignore the mother Goddess, an emotional, intuitive Goddess, then that is how we have gotten so far away from learning how to feel. How to sense, how to value our intuitive self. How to know that that part of us is extremely valid and a plumb line. I let my brain rule, then after much fanfare, uncovered my intuition. I hope you all can do the same. I hope you can do it more easily. I wish you the best of luck.

And so comes the end of the book. The last part that predictably ties it all together. The happy ending to the story, the princess walks off with the prince AND learns her lesson. I have to tell you that even though I don't *love* the idea of Christianity, and yeah, I still get angry with it from time to time, I did forgive, I did realize, I did let go. This is how it happened.

***

I wondered if the image in my head was how She really looked. Danu was one of the newer Goddesses I had prayed to for help, a Celtic Goddess with a vast history. I was fascinated when a late night computer search turned up her name. I knew that I was ready to move to the next level, but was fully aware that to move on, I had to unload some old, outdated ways of life. Dusty mindsets, long ago forgotten, but still pulled out occasionally. I was keen to the idea, loving the pain/growth/realization cycle I had been through many times before.

You jumped in Danu's river (something I had visualized in meditation), completely submerged yourself, until you awoke on the other side of the riverbank. The problem was, every time I envisioned myself going under, I could only go in up to my neck. I knew something was holding me back. Something I needed to be rid of, but after driving myself nuts, turning it over and over in my mind, I couldn't think of anything.

Brrrrrgh. Brrrrrrrrrrrgh. Mark was futily trying to get the engine to start. We had just eaten at a restaurant in a local strip mall, and were looking forward to a Saturday afternoon nap with a belly full of Chinese food. But the truck wouldn't turn over. *Wonderful,* I thought sarcastically. It was starting to drizzle.

With an irritated drawl, Mark dismissed me. "Honey, you are going to have to go somewhere else, this is going to take a while" he said, popping the hood.

"But where am I going to go?" I whined. I surveyed the shops in the mall. Grocery store? No way was I going to walk around a grocery store for god knows how long. I was too stuffed to think about food. Hardware store, double no way. I was so full I wanted to sit, but I certainly wasn't going back into the Chinese restaurant we'd just left, it was too packed.

The only option I had was a Christian coffeehouse. Yeah, I said Christian coffeehouse. Spotting it months earlier as they were moving in to the storefront, I rolled my eyes at the combination of God and latte's, and imagined what it must be like in there. *Unbearable*, I thought as I twisted the Carnelian and Moonstone pendant that hung around my neck. Some vacant eyed teen wearing a Jesus T-shirt and strumming a guitar, gushing about "what the Lord has done for me". Overpriced trinkets bearing lambs, lions, doves, and John 3:16....and probably bad coffee to boot. All the Christians I knew were notoriously cheap.

"Baby, I can't go in there" I said, trying to think of where else I would go. It was pouring rain.

"Why? Do you think you will melt?" my new boyfriend sneered. *The poor thing*, I thought. His hair was already plastered to his head, and I knew I'd just be getting in the way. Hot coffee was starting to sound really good.

"I guess I'll be in there, come get me when you are done" I said miserably, making my way to the Jesus-fest.

I opened the door, putting my best don't –mess- with-me face on. The blast of cold air felt great, a contrast to the muggy rainy day outside.

"Praise Jesus, how are you today, ma'am" the barista said.

"Fine" I growled, not wanting to make eye contact. I couldn't believe I was in here, I did not belong here. Already the fake smile of the counter boy and the sound of the youth group practicing in the back were making me feel like I had bugs crawling all over me. Oblivious to my disdain, the barista fired off another question.

"Would you like to order something?" he said, pressing.

I felt guilty. I figured that if I was going to be here a while, I'd at least better be doing something, or else I'd invite some recent starry eyed convert over with my "I accidentally wandered in, and am too embarrassed to leave" look. So I ordered a coffee, grabbed my mocha, and hurriedly paid, scanning the café for a lonely corner table to hide at. As soon as I could I was getting out of there.

I made sure to sip slowly, only stealing glances at the décor when I was sure no one was looking. It basically looked like a Christian bookstore with a counter selling coffee and a back room where I was sure they held mini-services, and "youth fellowship". The walls were covered with pictures of Jesus, and Bible verses. Christian Knick-knacks such as etched glass lambs, expensive framed pictures of Jesus on the Sea of Galilee, and numerous T-shirts with Christian motifs were for sale. I sheepishly looked around me. I was lucky enough to be seated next to a spinner rack crammed with Christian bumper stickers. "Jesus Freak" and "In case of rapture this car will be unmanned" blasted me with shiny, slick, bold- faced color every time I turned my head.

I hated all of this-hated it to my very core. Despised the people who kept looking my way and smiling a brainwashed smile at me. Abhorred the crappy contemporary Christian music that played over the loudspeakers, even more disgusted because if I wanted to I could sing along. Mentally I dared people to come up to me and start preaching, I knew the drill. The stuff they teach you when "witnessing to an unbeliever" was firmly etched in my memory. The rote answers they give you for any question or statement the "sinner" might come up with. *Try me, bitches. I'll make you go crying back to momma.*

Tara, what are you so afraid of? I heard Her voice clearly, I knew it was Danu. I raised my head, and looked around. Christianity as I knew it was such a vortex. The smiles, lessons,constant church, and close group of people with no contact to the outside world- I hated it so bad. But why? Was it Wolfgang and Hilde? I searched myself. No, even though I thought them seriously faulty people, I had long ago forgiven them.

What about the people at the church, who forgot me as soon as I had "failed"? My feeling toward them was the same as it had been with Wolfgang and Hilde. Once I had realized that they were fake, I had let go. It had all made sense, it was easy to let it go. Once I knew who they were, I had zero expectations from them. They were just playing a game-trying to earn a living and protecting themselves from anyone who might break their streak.

But why did I cringe every time I saw a Jesus fish on the back of a car? A "real men love Jesus" T-shirt? It wasn't because of Jesus, I still prayed to Him from time to time, thinking Him the most wonderful example of the purest love…..he hung out with prostitutes for god's sake. Treated them as equals. Invited them to dinner. It isn't His fault that some of His followers went all bonkers and control-y, completely taking His message of love and acceptance, and turning it into the opposite.

Mother, I really don't know what the deal is here. How is it that I can forgive regular people for doing stupid things, even see it as part of their spiritual development, but when it comes to Christians I have no tolerance? I felt Her listening, but knew I must find the answer for myself. I knew that only then would I be able to go under the river fully.

All of the sudden it hit me like a ton of bricks. THIS WAS THE THING I WAS HOLDING ON TO. This of course was no coincidence, being led here, forced to sit in the middle of what I had left in a blaze of glory. I stared down at my cold coffee.

Please help me find the answer, I asked honestly.

My ego wrestled with the concept of letting it all go. *But these people hurt you, ruined your life.* I heard my ego say. I laughed it off. Not all Christians hurt me, just a handful, and they certainly didn't ruin my life. I was happier and more at peace than I had ever been, if anything, by ousting me from the church, they set me free. They enabled me to find my own way, a way that had brought me incredible satisfaction. My pride had been hurt, that was all. I had expected perfection and infallibility, instead I got human nature corrupted with power and unreal expectations, and it was a blow.

I had wanted an answer that would make the world make sense; I had wanted to be a part of something bigger than myself. The people at New Glory had seemed confident. Real. They had an answer for everything. It was a very intoxicating notion to sell that we had "the truth". Once I realized that it was a prideful man's folly, and had nothing to do with Jesus, once the façade was cracked I had to learn to look at the world all over again. The Goddess taught me that She was in everything. Not the way the Christians said, which meant, "yeah, God is in everything.....beautiful". Then their eyes would glaze over as they talked of autumn leaves, and rolling hills, it was easy to find God in those things. But what about human suffering? What about mediocrity? What about human nature? They never addressed human nature, it was neatly categorized for them. Bad and good. Sinner, and saved. It had all appealed to me, sucked me in, until I had forgotten what I thought.

Basically I had let myself get brainwashed. I had given up my power, the reins of my life. But it was ME not THEM that had made that choice. It was ME. How could I blame them for their path? In doing so I was no better than them saying that I was wrong. I was saying that they were wrong-it was all the same thing.

I felt my heart change, and the veil of my own illusion lifted.

I looked around the room with new eyes, I no longer saw with hate. I saw humanity. Some people were going through the motions of religion, I suspected because they didn't know what else to do. Some people, like me, were looking for something. Some people had been born into the religion, and would probably always follow it. For some people, this was their path, and it was just as valid as mine. The truth was, I was no better than these people and they were no different than me, we were all just trying to live in some way or another. We were all just trying to make a connection. I felt like one does when they realize their truth, when the light bulb goes off- I felt incredibly relieved.

With this realization, it was easy to let go of my anger and hatred, and say a silent prayer to the Goddess that everyone would find what they were looking for, no matter what it was. My heart swelled with love. Love for everyone around me. Love for myself, Love for God and the Goddess, love for Kurt, Rosemary, Luke, and even Wolfgang and Hilde. I felt like bursting. We were all one, and I was a part of that oneness. Everything that I had experienced had a purpose, and not just for me, it held a purpose for each person that I'd encountered, too. We were all sisters and brothers on this earth; we were all just trying to make it. It was an amazing revelation. I felt like flying.

I get it Danu! I get it!

So that day I thanked Christianity, thanked all the people in the now half-deserted café'. I thanked Wolfgang and Hilde, thanked Pastor Sam, thanked Winter's Pass, New Glory and Baptist Christian. I even thanked all the nutty teachers at the Institute of Biblical studies, they had helped get me where I was today. And as I walked to the door in response to Mark's honking, I became fully submerged.

I went under Danu's River.

Epilogue

"Let's light the candles" said the redhead, the one called Fire. The autumn night blew past, swirling the incense around them. The black haired one, the one called Air, stared at the altar. It was a combination of three, Maiden, Mother, and Crone. The sight of the finished altar always gave her chills. Then the red haired one spoke.

"Shit, I think I forgot the matches, well, I ain't goin' inside, I went last time for more chips" she said defiantly, hands on her hips.

"Awww, I don't wanna go" the dark haired one whined, trying to look busy. They turned to the third Witch.

"Do you know what I like about our religion?" said the blond, the one called Water. The other two looked at her. She smiled, and then paused for effect. "You can say shit, and it is perfectly o.k......... you can say shit in our religion."

The three Witches laughed.

And the coven meeting began.

So You Wanna Be a Witch:

This little collection is not for the people who build a bonfire in their living room after reading this book and toss it in. If you are happy with your spiritual path, good for you, I wish you the best. But if you read this book and said to yourself… "oooooh. I wanna be a Witch, too!" then I'm offering a mish-mash of websites, books, and a little information (read: opinions) of my own. It's a place to start.

Where? When? What?

Paganism, just like any other belief system has a variety of ways that it can be practiced. It is very, very broad. My first suggestion to anyone seeking, or just curious, is to read, read, read. Read everything you can get your hands on, and discard the stuff that doesn't seem to stick with you. Usually the stuff that you remember, that stands out to you, is already in your consciousness anyway. The flip side to this is that if you find a tenet being repeated over and over in everything you read, it is probably something you should listen to and at least consider. Information that tends to keep coming up again and again is usually there for a reason.

Secondly, put your personality into play. Are you one that would much rather stay at home with the cats than go out on a Friday night? If so, maybe a solitary path is best for you. Do you have Irish roots, Italian roots, Indian roots, Jewish roots, African roots? Look up the Pagan practices of your forefathers, and you might find a perfect fit. Really into ritual? Check out ceremonial magic, or magick (as they spell it). Want to stick to a strictly Goddess/female oriented path? Dianic covens, and female-centric Goddess worshippers are everywhere. Always been fascinated with Hoodoo, but never thought that a white kid from the suburbs could practice it? Go for it! The point is, find something that suits who you already are, and aligns with your natural interests.

Remember, we are all going to our destination somehow, you might as well enjoy it. Religion doesn't have to be a punishment.

Ethics:

Ethics in Witchcraft can be tricky. Of course the Wiccans would want me to say "an ye harm none do as ye will". So there, I said it. I'm not saying that I don't adhere to that, I'm not saying that I do. When it comes to ethics, you have to learn by trial and error. Most Witches I know can be described in this excerpt from one of my favorite books, Terry Pratchett's *Witches Abroad*:

"Your average witch is not, by nature, a social animal as far as other witches are concerned. There's a conflict of dominant personalities. There's a group of ringleaders without the ring. There's the basic unwritten rule of witchcraft which is, "don't do what you will, do what I say." The natural size of a coven is one."

Witches aren't followers; the Craft just doesn't attract the sheep kind of person. So if I were to tell you p*lease be careful when messing with another's will, seriously you will get burnt bad*! Most of you would nod in righteous agreement. Say "well of course, we'd never do that." Imagine only using your powers for good. That is all fine and dandy, but just wait till someone pisses you off, really wrongs you. Can you be the bigger person? Probably not.

I'll tell ya how it will go down. You might wrestle with the concept of sending negative energy, then one night in a fit of self pitying anger will do something nasty. *Because your cause is different.* That person will get the flu, or break a leg, or lose their job, or have nightmares. I'm not saying not to do it, I'm just saying BE PREPARED TO ACCEPT THE CONSEQUENCES. Know that it will come back to you. Maybe not now, maybe not for a while, but you need to know that what you send out will come back times three. It's not just a Wiccan thing, it's a Law of Entropy thing. If you don't mind taking a punch to get back at the intended person, then go for it. Do an actual hex. *Most of the time* it won't actually solve anything, but go ahead and do it. You might feel better….for a while….until they retaliate, and then you retaliate to their retaliation. And it goes on and on and on….the cycle continues until someone stops it. It's like picking up a ping pong paddle to play. When someone puts down the paddle, then the game is over. Hexing is something that most people will never get a grasp of. Trying to explain its place (and it does have one) is waaaay too much to go into now. The important thing to think about is, what kind of energy do you want to keep batting around?

Speaking of energy, take a look around and see what kind of energy is in your life. It is a direct result of what you are sending out, consciously and unconsciously. Do you yell all the time, at your kids, husband, co-workers? Can you not understand why everyone speaks harshly with you? Are you the Drama Queen (my favorite) who supposedly *hates* drama, and can't understand why her life is so full of it, but the second it comes around gobbles it up? Sending out energy involves more than what you do in front of your altar and with some candles. It is in what you say, what you think, who you hang out with, what you fantasize about. Your will to make it happen. That is the heart of Witchcraft- Witchcraft is a lifestyle. Most of the morals I practice are common sense, and trial and error rather than a deep seated conviction.

I've seen Witches firsthand that try to control everyone and everything around them. On the outside their lives are great, they have good jobs, they excel at what they want to excel at, but inside they are the same wormy apple. Miserable. They keep doing spells to make their lives better, and with each manipulation they feel worse. They can't get enough, and will never be satisfied. The more they do the more they want.

That is my little speech on ethics. I probably will get crucified for not telling you all those wonderful things about not harming anyone, or only sending love energy, but you will probably ignore it anyway. Have fun getting burned. You want to be a Witch, after all.

Spells:

Spells are one of the fun parts of Witchcraft. The way I do it really depends on the situation. Sometimes an idea for a spell pops in my head, sometimes I adapt it from something out of a book, sometimes I just start gathering materials and tapping into my intuition to figure out what I need what I need in the moment.

Spells are like days. Each spell will feel completely different. Some spells you will do and think "damn, that was powerful. I really felt that working! I'm the shiz- nit!" Some spells you will feel absolutely nothing. Some spells you will feel working, but the energy feels different than what you intended. Find something that feels right and do it, then observe. Watch the way it works. Sometimes it works the way you expect, sometimes not- either way you have to trust that it is for the best. Remember that we aren't looking for too many quick fixes. We want to grow. More power, remember?

I'm a big fan of sympathetic magic. Use water if you want something to happen smoothly and slowly. Use fire if you want it to happen quickly, and if you don't care if it burns a bit. For instance, I wouldn't use fire for a weight loss spell, unless you want to puke up or crap out five pounds in 24 hours due to food poisoning. Get it? Earth is lovely for job spells, and spells for solid type things. Use air to understand the nature of things. Air is always great for understanding.

Books are great, don't get me wrong. I have listed some great references in that section. There are many capable, wonderful authors out there. Just make sure that you realize that books are *someone else's* ideas. If you are burning a green candle because Joe-schmoe said to do it, and what you really want is a red candle, then it won't be as effective.

Spell work is intensely personal, and if you don't feel a spell don't do it. If you pick up the candle, and think "I'm just not feelin' this", it might not be time. I don't usually adhere to the cast-spells-in-accordance-with-planetary-movements mentality. Moon charts are extremely useful, but most of the time you don't *feel* like doing a banishing spell at the full moon. A lot of the planetary stuff comes naturally. Make sure to tune into the Flow, the Divine before each spell, and you will be set.

As far as materials go, get what you like. If you have money to blow and you want to get high end reiki charged candles that are all soy with free-trade bamboo wicks, then go for it. If that will add to your practice aka, you will be more into it, then by all means do it. Everyone is different. I buy my candles at Target. Every year for my birthday I go

348

altar candle shopping, and stock up on all the colors. A friend gets hers at the dollar store. Do whatever floats your boat.

As far as all the other tools go, I recommend getting something that is quality. I never wanted an Athame, but I own a Boline (Druid in origin, used for cutting herbs), so I got one that will last. If it is something that you will use a lot, it needs to be sturdy. *Azuregreen.com* has some great stuff.

Oh yeah, I almost forgot, don't share what you did with too many people. If hubby makes fun of you or your sister says "do you really think that will work?" then you will dilute your power. Keep it sacred.

Altars:

I have to say that I have definite opinions on altars, or if you don't like that word, meditation spaces. To me they are like decorating your home, only in this case you are decorating your spirituality. Make it pretty if you like pretty things. Make it utilitarian if that speaks to you. Keep it away from other people and pets. If your kids smear chocolate handprints on it, then give them their own altar, and tell them to keep their paws off of yours. *It won't be sacred if you don't make it sacred.* At first it might just feel like you are staring at a tabletop or shelf, but if you make it sacred in time it will vibrate with your energy. The great thing about this is that most people will stay away naturally, it will become as personal as your underwear (and who wants to mess with someone else's underwear?) Use the thing. Do spell work there. Sit before it and pray- make it a living, breathing part of your practice.

It doesn't have to be huge, covered in black pentacles with blades and chalices. It can be simple with an oracle deck, a candle or a seashell. My favorite trick is to go to the fabric store, and buy a quarter yard of fabric for an altar cloth. There is a huge selection, and I have piles that I change with the seasons and my mood. But I'm high maintenance like that.

Covens:

I have been in a coven (teaser: my next book) and listen up, cuz this is important. *If you choose that path, make sure that you choose your coven wisely.* You will be joining in an eternal bond with these people not unlike a spiritual marriage. You will always be a part of them, whether or not the coven dissolves. Just keep that in mind. Also remember when the inevitable power play comes up, that Witches are by nature solitary creatures. We may gather in groups to combine our power, but in the end, *we are all our own Witch.* No matter how compatible the members are, there will ALWAYS be a difference of opinion. So think it through thoroughly before you join. Covens are like Hotel California, you can check out anytime you like but you can never leave.

Gaia:

I just LOOOOVVEEE to see a Witch who is a second degree Wazoo in the Great and Powerful Order of the Super De Dooper Cauldron Hoppers throw a cigarette butt on Mother Earth. Or put a plastic bottle in the trashcan because they are too lazy to recycle. Not all of us can afford hybrids, but as a Witch the earth is our mother, hell, as a *person* the earth is our mother. Do what you can, but do something. Please.

Your Local New Age/ Witchcraft Bookstore:

There is probably at least one in your area or within a twenty mile radius. If not then the internet will have to do. Girls and boys, can I tell you some stories about New Age bookstores! Each one is different, and each one takes on the spirit and personality of its owner. If you walk in and it doesn't feel right, then leave. You think "well I'm just going in there to buy a book, what harm can that do?" A LOT of Witchcraft store owners use magic to get you to buy stuff. A weak minded person, or someone with no training will wonder why they can't seem to leave the store, or why they feel compelled to buy something they don't really want. I have been in this situation several times, and it is a terrible feeling. I actually had a shop owner follow me to my vehicle and place her hands on it, trying to use magic to get me to stay. It felt like trying to dislodge myself from sticky taffy. So just watch it, there are plenty of crooked people out there!

Herbs, Stones and other natural stuff:

This is really a matter of taste. I am definitely an herb Witch, I just am drawn to them. Stones it took me a while to warm up to. Some of you will like or be attracted to neither. Don't feel bad if your magical partner is rambling on and on about harvesting some sacred Woodruff for the Maie Bowle, and you could care less. Everyone has a different spiritual gifting; it is just a matter of finding it. But definitely give working with stones, and herbs a try. They don't bite. Usually.

Divination/ fortune telling via Tarot, Runes, pendulums etc.:

Aren't you tired of me already? No. Well good, because I have a lot to say on this subject, too. I have been working as a trance channel psychic for years so I have definitely learned by trial and error on this one.

This is for those of you who have never done divination, or are messing around with your first Tarot deck, and don't feel like you are getting anywhere. Talking to spirits if you use a medium such as Tarot, is like learning a language or playing an instrument. It takes *a lot of time* to learn. The Tarot, especially, is complicated. Just know that it will take years to learn, and be patient. When I first started out I practiced on my friends, I don't recommend that now. People want to know something, and even if you say "hey, I'm really new at this", they will probably take your advice. People's lives aren't something to play around with.

You can use a book for guidance, but I don't recommend reading the meanings out cold. After time, and pulling a card daily, and really getting to know your deck, or runes, or pendulums, or I Ching, you will get the feel for it. Maybe after a year or two you will be ready to do some readings for friends and family.

For god's sake ask for help and guidance from Spirit Guides "of the highest vibration". You don't want any low level entities giving you faulty or erroneous information. Spirits like that are very controlling. Most of us have sort of a morbid fascination with the spirit world, and at first are very impressed by it. Get used to working with your Spirit Guides, and then believe it or not it will become almost commonplace to you. The *wow* factor will go away which is good, because that reaction in yourself can be very distracting.

Anything worth having is worth working for, so if you are new to the Craft and you are really attracted to a certain form of divination, then form a relationship with it.

Relationships take time. Put aside your desire to show people what you can do, and put in the time and effort to be a good reader. Eventually it will pay off.

General Ickiness:

Ouija boards: why don't you just throw open your front door and invite whoever shows up first to come in? That is what an Ouija board is. Asking for trouble. Look, I realize that a lot of Witches use them, but to me it is waaay too much work to try to make sure that you aren't getting the wrong kind of spirit giving you advice. If you are an extremely practiced Witch, then why not just ask for help directly from the spirit world anyway? What do you need a ouija board for? If you are a newbie, you are essentially opening yourself to a very diverse spirit world and getting what you get. I knew a girl who had something hang out in her bedroom for a month after messing with one. It overturned her bed sheets, gave her nightmares, and sat on her chest so she couldn't breathe. If you want to play, just go play a Harry Potter video game instead.

Witch Wars: beef with another Witch that results in smacking each other in the face with spells, back to the ping pong mentality. Let it go. Remember that wars have casualties. These things can go on forever.

My name is Demand- Etta: Please be respectful when calling on the Goddess or spirit helpers. They aren't here to serve your ass. You have to ask nicely.

Being a Witch Nazi:

If someone else tells me not to blow out a ritual candle because I'm going to "insult the element of fire" again, I'm going to puke. I also kill bugs. I don't go around stomping ants for fun, but if they are crawling on me, or in my house, in the paper towel and toilet they go. So sue me.

Everyone has their own way of doing things, and after time you will form your own opinions about what is right and wrong for you. Don't kill people, steal or break any laws. There. Leave everyone else alone. I'll never forget the time I went for a walk in the woods with a new Witch. I bent down to pick up a branch that had fallen off of a tree....she gasped and expressed her disdain at my not thanking the tree for its sacrifice. The whole way home I heard her self-righteous speech. How could she know how I express my thanks? A lot of us who follow earth based religions at least have a little bit of the lovey dovey hippie type in us, and most of us have a background in organized religion. Be careful not to trade in your former religious self righteousness for the same thing in your new religion. Not only is it irritating, it is obnoxious, and it makes you sound like a moron. Just don't, o.k.?

Pentacles:
If you are wearing giant clock sized pentacles reminiscent of Flava Flav, please hop down in front of the computer, make yourself a little cocktail, and do some research of the meaning and history of the pentacle. Unfortunately pentacles are like tattoos and piercings, society mostly rejects them. I would say that to most of society, pentacles are one of the most offensive and misunderstood symbols around. If you are going to wear one, you'd better know your stuff, and you'd better be prepared to face whatever looks, ostracization, and nastiness that you are going to have to deal with from the general public. Don't be one of those dolts that make us look bad by not being able to answer questions about the power symbol you are wearing around your neck.

I am begging you not to wear one because you want to

stand out, or you want to be different. It is a symbol, and like all symbols it stands for something. You are going to look like an insecure identity seeker if you wear one just to offend. If you are walking into your aunt's Baptist church wearing a pentacle the size of a milk saucer then you need to go into therapy. You have issues. Leave well enough alone, and think for a moment just what you are trying to prove.

It takes a while to warm up to the pentacle. Most of us have been taught that it is Satanist, or an evil symbol. If you take the time to learn about it you will see that it is a very powerful symbol that holds the entire cosmos, and workings of the Universe in its five points. Wear it carefully and with respect.

But there are some who just can't do it. If you just can't seem to put one on, your mother will disown you, or your husband will leave you, don't worry! There are plenty of protective power symbols out there. The Rune Eloh, the eye, the ankh, the spiral. Once again, do some research, and find one that speaks to you. So what if you are the wacky soccer mom who wears an eye around her neck. If they notice they won't say anything to your face. They probably don't say most things they think to your face anyway.

The Wheel/Witch Holidays:

If you want to make The Wheel a part of your life, give it *time*. Imagine explaining Christmas to someone who has never celebrated it: it would take a couple of years for them to start to get it. I didn't really appreciate The Wheel until I had celebrated it for about four years, then I really started to understand. Light a candle at Yule, take a walk on the sleepy earth at Imbolc, plant a seed at Ostara, make love at Beltane, eat sun shaped pizza at Litha, review the year at the first harvest, Lammas, have a party at Mabon, pull a Tarot card at Samhain. If you keep it simple at first, it will go better. So be patient, and give it a try.

In conclusion:

Whether you are a third degree Dianic High Priestess calling down the moon in front of a hundred people, or Suzy Cream Cheese casting spells in her bathroom so her mommy won't find out, you need to know this. We never arrive. We are never superior. This is a path that is in constant movement, constant growth. We don't go by the linear societal timelines; we go by The Wheel, the energy cycles. A wheel always turns, sometimes it turns slowly, sometimes it turns fast, but you want it to turn, that is what a wheel is for.

Always seek; always connect with the Divine, with the Divine in yourself. Try not to judge, to think you are better. Once you get going on a path, watch out for being an elitist- thinking that because you are Gardenarian or initiated into the Fellowship of Isis that you are better. At the end of the day you have to swig Pepto Bismol for indigestion, and mow the lawn just like everyone else.

The Universe is so vast, so expansive; there will always be something to learn. If you get stuck up your own rear end then you are stuck. Your personal wheel won't turn; you will stagnate and get frustrated. Be bigger, be better. Grow, baby, grow!

For fun I have included some of my favorite Witchy books, websites, movies and whatever the heck else I felt like putting in there. Remember that these are just places to start. There are many resources out there; this is just to get you going.

Websites and General Witchcraft Supplies:

Azuregreen.com – they have everything you could ever want, at good prices.

MountainRoseHerbs.com –their herbs are organic, harvested in a way that is earth friendly, and superbly fresh. I'm in love with them.

Sunseyeoils.com – these oils smell good, and are effective. Collect 'em all.

Sacredsource.com - for us statue freaks, they have a ton of Goddess and even God statues. (We don't wanna leave Him out).

Amazon.com- Just type in W*itch,* W*itchcraft*, or *Paganism* and look at all the books that come up. You can really check out a book before you buy it, get a free sample if you own a Kindle, and even get a paperback secondhand if you are short on dough (or if you just want to lessen your footprint on Mother Earth). It is especially fun to read the book reviews from pompous know- it -all practitioners.

Essentialoil.com- if you want to use pure oils in charms, and bags. This is the real stuff, and well worth the money, they will last for years. My wish list is a mile long.

Conjureoils.com-Absolutely fabulous, and just reading her descriptions is an adventure. Plenty to whet your Witchy palate.

Snakeandsnake.com- moon calendars and other stuff. Can't live without my yearly moon calendar.

Witchvox.com- Pagans in your area, articles, and local stores. Witchvox is kind of a big deal. Ask any Witch, and she/he will know just what you are talking about.

Inanna.virtualave.net- my absolute favorite! Has detailed info on Goddesses all around the world, you can spend a lot of time on this site. It is a free site, so make a donation, if you can.

Herb Ladies:

Susunweed.com- she's fun and a little wacky, but she knows her stuff. I while away the hours on her very interesting forum.

Sagemountain.com - (Rosemary Gladstar's website) - Super Maven of Herbs, not only are her books great, but her website is too.

Blogs:

All you have to do is Google *Witchcraft blogs* and a zillion will come up. Every Witch practices differently,so reading several of these blogs will give you an idea of the many different ways to practice. I am not lying when I say that there are a ZILLION practicing Witches writing blogs. For the sake of not typing till my fingers fall off I will list just a small, diverse handful just to give you an idea of the variety of Witches out there.

Confessions of a Pagan Soccer Mom- *Confessionsofapagansoccermom.com*

An Inner Journey: The Moon,Mythology and You - *reclaimingthedarkgoddess.blogspot.com*

Sex, Magick,& the City- *carolinadean.blogspot.com*

I Heart the Goddess-*iheartthegoddess.com*

Spellbound By Moonlight- *dancingsoraya.blogspot.com*

Rue and Hyssop-*rueandhyssop.blogspot.com*

Mother Moon-*mothermoonsmessage.blogspot.com*

A Witch's Daily-*sobeit- whatthedaybrings.blogspot.com*

General Fun Stuff:

Bachflowertherapy.com- these things work. Seriously. Essence drops to combat everything from apathy to shock.

Shira.net- shake your power center, feel like a goddess. (Bellydance website)

Halloween.com - the best time of year.

Alabe.com- Free astral charts! No spam!

Books:

Anything by *Scott Cunningham*. This guy paved the way when there were few books written on the subject. He passed away in 1993. He was remarkably UN-opinionated.

Book of Shadows, Phyllis Currott- This is a story about one woman's journey into Witchcraft, and one of the first books I read on the subject. A great place to start.

Trust Your Vibes, Soul Lessons and Soul purpose, True Balance, Sonia Choquette – I love Sonia, she is honest, and a good writer. Her books, (especially if you are *new* to working with guides, or learning about intuition) are a good introduction, and easy to read.

A Still Small Voice, Echo Bodine- no nonsense, straightforward book about learning to listen to and trust your intuition. Also a quick read.

The Witch's Guide to Fairy Folk, Edain Mc Coy- great place to start if you want to work with the Fey.

The Path of the Priestess, Sharron Rose- This book touched me deeply. Sharron chronicles her journey to the Goddess. Absolutely beautiful and inspiring.

The Mists of Avalon- Marion Zimmer Bradley -I didn't put this in with the fiction because this is such a powerful book. Leads you through the life and times of King Arthur's court viewed from the eyes of a woman. Great emphasis on the Goddess.

Celebrating The Great Mother; A handbook of earth honoring activities for parents and children, Cait Johnson and Maura D Shaw- if you have kids, great resource book. Buncha ideas for Witchy things to do with your kids.

Mysteries of the Dark Moon, Demetra George- Book that led me to Lilith, Kali and Medusa.

Animal Speak, Animal Wise, Ted Andrews- Handbooks I use for animals that show up in my life, and why. He has written a ton of books, I recommend them all.

Diary of a Witch, Sybil Leek- It's out of print, but you can usually get a copy on eBay. She goes for the shock factor 1960's style, but this woman was a true Witch.

The Power of Now, A New Earth, Eckhart Tolle-This guy's books changed my life.

Protection and Reversal Magic: A Witch's Defense Manual (beyond 101), Jason Miller- If you don't mind ceremonial magic, this is THE BEST book on protection I have ever read.

Books on Herbs/Stones/Tarot/The Wheel/Hoodoo:

Anything by *Susun Weed* -all of her herb books are informative and passionate.

Anything by *Rosemary Gladstar*- you can't go wrong with her. I especially love her books on using herbs in beauty treatments!

Herbal Rituals, Judith Berger- this book reads like a well crafted poem, and takes you through the months of the year with herbs. Magical book!

The Green Witch Herbal, Barbara Griggs-not intended to be a "magical" book per say, but has a lot of great advice on herbs.

Love is in the Earth: A Kaleidoscope of Crystals, Melody- if you own no other book on stones, own this one.

It tends to be pricey, but you can usually get a reasonably priced one secondhand.

Hoodoo Herb and Root Magic: A Materia magica of African-American Conjure, Catherine Yronwode- Hoodoo is not for the faint of heart, but if you are interested, this woman knows her stuff.

If you are interested in Tarot, read anything by *Rachel Pollack.*

Llewellyn's series on The Wheel-*Candlemas, Feast of Flames*, Amber K-*Yule: A Celebration of Light and Warmth*, Dorothy Morrison-*Halloween: Customs, Recipes, and Spells*, Silver Ravenwolf-*Autumn Equinox: the Enchantment of Mabon*, Ellen Dugan-*Ostara: Customs, Spells,& Rituals for the Rites of Spring,*Edain Mc Coy-*Beltane: Springtime Rituals, Lore and Celebrations*, Raven Grimassi-*Midsummer: Magical Celebrations of the Summer Solstice*, Anna Franklin-*Lammas: Celebrating the Fruits of the First Harvest*, Anna Franklin

If you want general Witchcraft books on everything under the sun these guys have written them: Patricia Telesco, Edain Mc Coy, Patricia Monahan, Christopher Penzack, Ellen Dougan, D.J. Conway, Doreen Virtue, Raymond Buckland- I could go on forever, there are tons of good ones out there. Borrow or buy and enjoy!

Fun Witchy Fiction:

Wyrd Sisters, Lords and Ladies, Witches Abroad, Masquerade, Carpe Jugulum, Terry Pratchett - Humorous tales about three very colorful Witches. Addicting books. Even though these were written to be amusing, and not seriously, I think he "gets" Witchcraft.

Juniper, Wise Child,Colman, Monica Furlong -What

can I say about these books- they get to the true heart of Witchcraft. Written originally for young adults, these are loved by all ages.

Mistress of Spices, Chitra Divakaruni - Enchanting book about an Indian herb Witch.

Harry Potter series, J.K. Rowling- The famous boy wizard.

The Witching Hour, Anne Rice- Why not? Loooong book, but a fascinating story.

Witch Child, Celia Rees -Written for teens, this is an engaging read about a young Witch during the Witch trial-era in colonial American history.

Movies: These are just for fun. As you know, Hollywood rarely gets something in their hands that they don't royally screw up.

Practical Magic- great movie, based on a book by Alice Hoffman. About a family of Witches in Massachusetts.

The Craft- About a group of teen Witches. Faruza Balk's a real badass in this movie.

Harry Potter- either you love him or hate him. I'm an admitted Harry Potter nerd.

The Mists of Avalon- movie based on the life-changing book. Don't expect the same effect from the movie, it is a little hokey, but still enjoyable.

Bibliography:

Chapter Two -"Slain in the Spirit", wikipedia.com
    Chapter Seven- Cunningham, Scott <u>Wicca: A Guide</u>
<u>for the Solitary Practitioner</u>
    Llewellyn Publications, 1993
    Chapter Twelve -Browne, Sylvia May, Antionette
<u>Adventures of a Psychic</u> Hay House 1998
    So you Wanna...Pratchett, Terry <u>Witches Abroad</u>
HarperTorch, 2002

Acknowledgements:

A huge thanks to everyone who had to listen to me blather on and on about this fab new book I was writing. To Kris and Ness- my sweet friends, to M- I still think about you a lot, to E, for being there at the beginning, to Greta for my first edit, to C. Dean for showing me how much still needed to be done, to Jaidis Shaw for the final edits, to Judy for supporting me alongside the quesadillas, to my loving husband for pretending to be interested in something that wasn't a comic book, to D- you really were a great influence, to M.M.- I miss you, thank you for everything, to my dad for never bullshitting me, and being a constant mentor, and to everyone that I have called friend over the years. If you were a part of this story, you had a place in my heart.

and to Kali. There is nothing I can ever say that will show You how much I adore You.

Contact the author:

email TaraBlack@live.com
Facebook Page http://www.facebook.com/#!/pages/On-the-Right-PathWalking-Through-God-to-Get-to-the-Goddess/283917794974583
Website-www.Tara-Black.com

Edits: Jaidis Shaw www.junipergrove.net

www.ingramcontent.com/pod-product-compliance
Lightning Source LLC
LaVergne TN
LVHW091247080426
835510LV00007B/146